Praise f  D0907626

'A cracking account . . . If only more wine books
were as much fun to read as this one.'
Sunday Age

'A very colourful and fast-paced journey into wine history.'
Daily Telegraph

'A wild, boys-own adventure . . . It's quite the ripping yarn.'
Herald Sun

'It's a bit of a thriller, a tale of layered intrigue, a journey through
history and an intriguing insight into the verifying of
label-less bottles of apparently priceless wine.'
The Age/Sydney Morning Herald

'I loved *Stalin's Wine Cellar*, a ripping romp about Sydney wine
aficionado John Baker's adventures in trying to acquire a
priceless collection of booze in post-Soviet Georgia.'
Canberra Times

'James Bond was famously au fait with the finest vintages,
and it's not hard to imagine him front and centre in this
twisting, true tale of vinous espionage that brings more than
a splash of Fleming or Forsythe to the wine-book realm . . .
a tale heady with fear, frustration, envy, exasperation and,
at one point on the streets of Paris, disaster.'
The Australian

'The words "wine book" and "ripping yarn" aren't normally seen
in the same sentence, but *Stalin's Wine Cellar* is just that.'
Max Allen, *Sun-Herald*'s *Good Food* magazine

'A wonderful yarn.'
Geraldine Doogue, *Saturday Extra*

'Simply the most riveting wine book I've read for years. If a
book about wine could ever be a page-turner, this one is.'
Huon Hooke, *The Real Review*

'A wild, sometimes rough, ride in the glam world of high-end wine.'
Better Homes & Gardens

'The ultimate wine-meets-history tale . . . Read paired
with a glass of your favourite wine.'
Gourmet Traveller

'A seriously rollicking read.'
GQ

'The wine book of the year for all sorts of reasons.'
winepilot.com

'A corker of a yarn.'
Mosman Daily

'A scintillating ride into the glamorous world of high-end wine.'
Toowoomba Chronicle

'It's part travel memoir, part mystery and part wine almanac.
It's a deliciously unique read, too.'
Who Weekly

'*Stalin's Wine Cellar* is a pretty ripping read with
a swaggering narrative voice.'
Kitchen Arts & Letters bookstore, New York

PENGUIN BOOKS

STALIN'S WINE CELLAR

John Baker was a hotelier and rock 'n' roll promoter in the eighties era of Midnight Oil, INXS and Cold Chisel. He became a wine merchant creating a number of fine wine stores, including Quaffers Double Bay Cellars and the Newport Bottler, as well as the importing business Bordeaux Shippers. He likes wine from anywhere (as long as it's very good) and is now more involved with a mixture of projects including the business of olive oil, as he says it's good for his health and less punishing the next day.

Nick Place is the author of five published novels and several non-fiction books, as well as comedy and screenwriting, occasional poetry and even an original stage pantomime. He has also enjoyed a long and diverse journalistic career across all media, mostly covering sport. He lives in Melbourne, where he is an enthusiastic supporter of the single malt whisky, wine and coffee industries.

STALIN'S
WINE CELLAR

JOHN BAKER
AND
NICK PLACE

PENGUIN BOOKS

To my mother, Norma Grace,
who gave me a sense of adventure.

PENGUIN BOOKS

UK | USA | Canada | Ireland | Australia
India | New Zealand | South Africa | China

Penguin Books is part of the Penguin Random House group of companies
whose addresses can be found at global.penguinrandomhouse.com.

Penguin
Random House
Australia

First published by Viking, 2020
This edition first published by Penguin Books, 2021

Text copyright © John Baker and Nick Place, 2020
Maps by Alicia Freile, Tango Media Pty Ltd, 2020

The moral right of the authors has been asserted.

Based on a true story; some names and distinguishing details have been changed throughout.

Cover images © Alamy (people & flags, Stalin) and Shutterstock (hand, wine bottle)
Cover design by Adam Laszczuk © Penguin Random House Australia
Text design by Midland Typesetters, Australia
Typeset in Adobe Garamond Pro by Midland Typesetters, Australia

Printed and bound in Australia by Griffin Press, an accredited
ISO ANZ/NZS 14001 Environmental Management Systems printer

NATIONAL
LIBRARY
OF AUSTRALIA

A catalogue record for this
book is available from the
National Library of Australia

ISBN 978 1 76104 366 6

penguin.com.au

CONTENTS

PART III: AFTER GEORGIA

PROLOGUE

Airport
Tbilisi, Georgia
July 1999

The airport looked like pretty much every other small city airport in any part of the world. Not particularly modern, not particularly ancient. Just bland.

Kevin Hopko and I walked through the doors and saw two men, one in a T-shirt and black leather jacket, unshaven, with bleary eyes. The other one in a business shirt, no tie, and a blazer. Looking sharper and more alert. He had to be Giorgi Aramhishvili, mid-thirties perhaps, so maybe a decade younger than me. Not as old as I'd imagined. He had a mop of black hair that looked as though it didn't like being tamed, especially at 1.30 am in a too brightly lit airport arrivals lounge. Giorgi was of average height and had a bit of a girth on him that spoke of a love of good food and wine. He was smiling broadly as he walked towards us, holding out his hand and saying, 'Mr John Baker! To meet you is such a pleasure at last.'

His accent thick but understandable.

'Hello, George,' I said. 'Thank you for meeting us at this time of the night.'

'Do you joke?' he laughed. 'You are our most honoured guests.'

The other guy, in the jacket, was introduced as Nino and I guess he didn't speak much English because he only nodded at us and sort of grunted. He handed me a business card:

AGENCY FIRM "GOODWILL"
"BACK WIND" LTD
"ORBI" LTD

NINO MESKHISHVILI
Chief Consultant in Special Issues

---

72 Abashidze Str., Tbilisi, Georgia; Tel./Fax: (995 32) 232 958
75 Kostava Str., Tbilisi, Georgia; Tel: (995 32) 388 416
4 April 9 Str., Poti, Georgia; Tel./Fax: (995 393) 26 155; (995 393) 23 878
Mobile: (995 77) 303 665; (995 99) 501 501

I took in the names of his three companies: 'Agency firm "Goodwill", "Back Wind" Ltd, and "Orbi" Ltd'.

I said, 'Chief consultant in special issues! It's nice to meet you, Nino.'

He had coarse dark hair that might have been wavy if it weren't cut short in a military style: a hairstyle that matched the hard, almost brutal, features of his face. He grunted again and shook hands rather formally.

As Nino also gave a card to Kevin, and shook hands, I watched Kevin's face, already a polite mask as calculations and appraisals took place behind those eyes of his that see everything, never missing a trick.

I smiled, and said to George, 'We should get our bags.'

'John,' he said, 'You do not need to worry about that. I will take care of customs. Come, come.'

We were led out of the arrivals hall through a side door and from there up a flight of stairs to a small room that had a sign saying 'VIP Welcome Area'. There were two other men inside, in suits, smiling professionally, and we were introduced. One was from the Georgian Ministry of Industry and Commerce, and the other was Mr Revaz, who George told us was a very senior executive from the winery. Neither appeared to speak English, so there was a lot of nodding and smiling as Nino poured us all a glass of what turned out to be a sweet sparkling wine and handed around a large plate of chocolates. Just what you need after flying from Sydney to London, then another seven hours back east, arriving in the middle of the night and jetlagged half to oblivion.

It was almost 2 am. Toasts were made to our arrival, and to our success, and to the business we would do together, and to me, and to Kevin, and to Australia, and to wine.

Finally, George said again that he would take care of customs, and I wondered what that meant given we only had three suitcases of regular checked-in luggage with nothing to declare. It crossed my mind that I didn't know the rules in this place. I was a long way from home.

As George shook hands with me one more time, our gaze met and we regarded one another for a moment, before he hustled out of the room to leave us with three men who spoke no English and looked like they had better places to be, such as bed. I remember wondering to myself whether this unlikely venture was actually going to work, or if I was going to regret ever setting foot on Georgian soil.

Or maybe something in between.

Kevin's face remained a polite mask. I knew that he wouldn't give me any sign of his opinion until we were alone, and I respected that.

Instead, Nino poured another glass of the sweet wine and offered it to me. In my experience, sometimes the only thing to do in life is embark on an adventure and see where it ends up, and this was very definitely one of those times. I took the glass from Nino, raised it in his direction and drank.

Whichever way this went, it was not going to be boring, I thought. And on that front, looking back now, I was completely correct.

But I should tell you how we got here in the first place. It started months before, on the other side of the world.

Far Eastern Europe and Russia

FINLAND
Helsinki
St Petersburg
Tallinn
ESTONIA

LATVIA
Riga

LITHUANIA
Vilnius

BELARUS
Minsk

Moscow

Nizhny

RUSSIA

Voronezh
Saratov

Kyiv
UKRAINE
Kharkiv

Volgograd

MOLDOVA
Chisinau
Odesa

Rostov-on-Don

ROMANIA
Bucharest

Crimean
peninsula
Massandra
winery

Krasnodar

BULGARIA
Sofia

Black Sea

Makhachkala

GEORGIA
Tbilisi

TURKEY

AZERBAIJAN
ARMENIA

N

KM 0   100   200

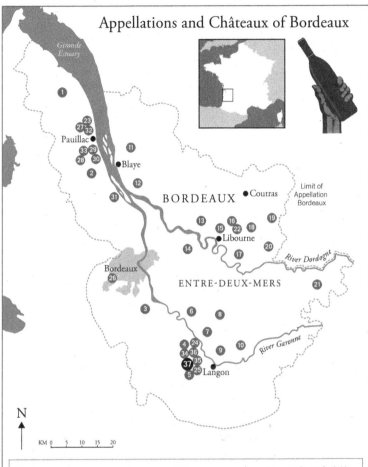

Appellations and Châteaux of Bordeaux

Gironde Estuary

Pauillac

Blaye

BORDEAUX • Coutras

Limit of Appellation Bordeaux

Libourne

River Dordogne

Bordeaux

ENTRE-DEUX-MERS

River Garonne

Langon

N

KM 0   5   10   15   20

1 Médoc	14 Graves de Vayres	27 Château Lafite Rothschild
2 Haut-Médoc	15 Pomerol	28 Château Larose
3 Graves	16 Lalande-de-Pomerol	29 Château Latour
4 Cérons	17 St-Émilion	30 Château Léoville Las Cases
5 Sauternes & Barsac	18 St-Émilion Satellites	31 Château Margaux
6 Cadillac-Côtes de Bordeaux	19 Francs-Côtes de Bordeaux	32 Château Mouton Rothschild
7 Loupiac	20 Castillon-Côtes de Bordeaux	33 Château Pichon Baron
8 Bordeaux et Entre-Deux-Mers	21 Ste-Foy-Bordeaux	34 Château Raymond-Lafon
9 Ste-Croix-du-Mont	22 Château Cheval Blanc	35 Château Rieussec
10 Côtes de Bordeaux-St-Macaire	23 Château Cos d'Estournel	36 Château Suduiraut
11 Blaye	24 Château Coutet	**37 Château d'Yquem**
12 Côtes de Bourg	25 Château Guiraud	
13 Fronsac and Canon-Fronsac	26 Château Haut-Brion	

PART I

BEFORE GEORGIA

1

A MYSTERIOUS LIST

Sydney, Australia
September 1998

I graduated from university with a degree in economics but no idea of what I wanted to do or where I belonged and so I began exploring. It meant that I have had quite a varied career, looking for opportunities in everything from running hotels and music venues to wine retail and wine importing businesses to olive oil production. Mostly, heading into the events of this book, I had spent my recent career developing up-market wine stores in the wealthier areas of Sydney, transforming your basic takeaway wine and beer outlet into a more sophisticated and richer experience. Think of a really inviting bookshop, like the ones in the Darlinghurst part of Oxford Street, if you're from Sydney, but really, any bookshop with books laid out for you to browse, with knowledgeable, friendly staff who can point you to authors you might like, even offer a comfortable armchair for you to sample a book before you buy. I wanted to create that same intimate, warm vibe for buying good wines.

These days, such boutique wine retailers are standard but, back then, they were not so common and I had done well out of the concept, starting with The Newport Bottler on Sydney's Northern Beaches in the 1980s, where I refined the concept.

By the time I bought the Double Bay Cellars in the heart of the city's prestigious eastern suburbs, I had developed a taste and also a business sense for rare and museum wines, the types of aged and potentially valuable wine that are often sold at auction. My delving into this segment of the wine world was fortunately timed because Double Bay was the perfect market for such expensive treasures.

Kevin Hopko was and is even more of a natural entrepreneur than I am. He joined me at Double Bay as the store's general manager but I never really relinquished control of that role, and he didn't seem to mind as he was happy to work collaboratively and occasionally follow his own path when it suited. A quiet Canadian, Kevin is a master of old and rare wines, with an incredible nose for value and profit, and also a masterful eye for potential holes in a deal or anything untoward. I had come to rely on his antenna for such moments. As Double Bay Cellars' reputation grew, we would be alerted to entire cellars that might be for sale, usually promised to hold dazzling French wines and other liquid jewels worth notable sums of money. Sometimes they actually did, and we would buy the contents of the cellar and sell the lot as a special event in the store at Double Bay.

With our eye for what was valuable in a cellar and many discerning and enthusiastic eastern suburbs customers, I had a lucrative and pleasurable business.

It was one of these cellars of untold promise that saw me picking up Kevin in my Citroën on a spring morning, the car still new enough that I savoured the idea of the longish cruise out to Terrey Hills on the city's Northern Beaches. Two of my staff, Frank and Jillian, were in the larger van, our estimate being that this cellar would be too big to fit in the small van and the boot of my car.

Sydney was in the grip of pre-Olympics roadworks and an infrastructure frenzy, so it was slow across the bridge but then we got moving as we headed out to the Northern Beaches. The sun was shining, we had the windows down.

Kevin said to me, 'How are you going with the list?'

'For today?' I asked. Every time we bought a cellar, we had a list of the wines that were supposed to be in there and that we had agreed to buy, on inspection. Experience told us the reality could vary a little from the list, with some wines present that hadn't been mentioned and other stated bottles missing entirely – most likely was that the number of some wines would vary.

But Kevin shook his head. 'Not today's list. You know what I mean. The List.'

I smiled but shook my head. 'To be honest, badly,' I said. 'In fact, it's in the glove box. Let's go through it one more time while we drive.'

He dug into the glove box and pulled out photocopied sheets of the fax that had arrived from an occasional client/associate of ours, Harry Zukor, a few days before. Harry was what we'll charitably call a wine entrepreneur, a man with an eye for a deal and the rat cunning to take an angle off everybody involved. I always liked him even though I wouldn't say faith and trust were high on my list of reasons why. Business was never boring when this smiling rogue walked through the door with a proposition, and in fact we were heading to one right now.

A friend of a friend of a friend of Harry's had apparently moved back to the UK, leaving his property in Terrey Hills with a large cellar full of historic and valuable wines, cultivated over decades.

The price tag was $150,000 for the lot, which in 1998 was not a small amount of money. Plus, it had to be paid in cash. Everybody always wanted cash. Surveying the Terrey Hills list of reported cellar contents, Kevin had calculated we would be able to sell the wines for a lot more than that and, in fact, this could be a very decent jackpot. And so we drove north.

Now Kevin was squinting again at the sheets of the other list, the one we called The List with verbal capital letters. Harry had faxed them to me with a one-word note on the front: 'Interested?'

They were bizarre, to say the least.

At the top of the first page, in small fax-font letters, was written 'Mineral Exploration'. Underneath was a column of what seemed to be names or just words. Oprien, Palmer Madeira, Ikem and Latur.

Broin, Porto, Marsala and Gilsher.

In the next vertical column, adjacent to the names, were what appeared to be dates. 1891, 1847, 1888, 1899, 1725, 1834.

Then another column with more numbers: 0.75, 0.8, 0.75, the occasional 0.4. The final column had a whole new set of random numbers: 5, 11, 3, 2, 6, 1, 12. Kevin was now examining the page, frowning.

'What's with Mineral Exploration?' I finally pondered.

'I reckon it's a furphy,' Kevin said. 'I mean, Harry only ever deals in wine with us, right? And look at that second column. It looks like dates, maybe of vintages.'

'And the column with the 0.75s could be the size of bottles,' I said.

'So, the 0.4s would be half bottles?' Kevin nodded. 'Yeah, I suppose that could work. But 0.8? What's that?'

'I'm not sure. Even so, none of these names mean anything. Have you heard of them?'

'No,' Kevin said, and that was significant. Kevin was thirty-three years old at the time, sixteen years younger than me, but he had been in the industry for years and had paid attention to wines and vintages that fetched the big prices. If he didn't know a wine, then something was seriously amiss.

'We're going to see Harry in a few minutes,' he said now. 'Let's just ask.'

'Where's the fun in that?' I replied. 'I reckon he's dangling it so mysteriously for a reason. Let's see if we can solve it; just think on it for a bit.'

We arrived at the property, where Harry was already waiting, today in his dove grey Daimler, which was carefully parked away from where we'd be loading boxes.

The first thing he said to me was 'How'd you like the fax?'

'It definitely caught my attention,' I said, smiling. 'Give me a few days.'

Harry almost laughed, but instead nodded. I could tell he was enjoying this little game. We'd either mention the list when we were beaten by the code, or when we'd solved it, or he would call a meeting when he got tired of waiting and wanted to cut to the deal, whatever the hell that was.

But now we had work to do. Frank and Jillian arrived in the van, Harry unlocked the empty house and led us all into the cellar. It was pitch-black.

'Harry,' Kevin's voice said out of the darkness. 'Is this sale because of a divorce?'

Harry's reply sounded slightly shocked. 'No,' he said. 'They've just headed home to England. Why?'

'No reason,' Kevin said pleasantly. 'Just curious.'

Frank had found the light switch and we all blinked, our eyes adjusting. The cellar suddenly shone, with many bottles in long racks, a covering of dust on the collection. Kevin walked the rows and pointed out the highlights, confirming the bottles were present which had convinced him this would be a good deal for us. There were two full sets of Penfolds Grange, for starters, plus other vintages of Grange. Kevin raised his eyebrow as he pointed to several bottles of Château d'Yquem on one row. That made my spirits soar. Possibly the greatest winery in the world: any time older vintages of Château d'Yquem are on a sales list, you know you're going to attract a crowd.

There were five cases of 1966 Château Lafite Rothschild and a few Château Margaux among the wider collection.

Jillian was impressed. 'John!' she said. 'The cellar is a good one. I see Lafite, I see Grange. *Est voilà*, Yquem!' I loved Jillian for her general excitement about life, her style and her calm influence in the store. She didn't really have much of a French accent, having lived in Australia for a long time, but she was well-mannered, always immaculately dressed and extremely knowledgeable about wine. Many customers, especially men, only ever wanted to be served by Jillian.

'*Temp à travail!*' I said, smiling.

'Are you trying to say it's time to work?' she asked.

'I was. Close?'

She wobbled her hand. 'So-so. Keep working on it.'

She and Frank headed up to the van to get some boxes and packing materials, leaving Kevin and me alone for a moment.

'Why did you ask that question about divorce?' I asked Kevin quietly.

'You can guarantee, if a cellar is being appraised in a divorce, the good bottles won't be in here,' Kevin said equally softly. 'The poor wife usually opens the door to let you in and has no idea that the cellar has already been gutted and she's not getting even close to the promised 50 per cent. If Harry had said yes, I would have tried to disappear and search the whole house.'

Frank, Jillian and Kevin began packing the wider collection into boxes, taking particular care with the older bottles, including the section of the cellar where the two full sets of Grange, and other Grange, were to be found. There were two cases of the legendary 1955, which is reputedly the best vintage of Grange from the 1950s. As I examined them, two other bottles caught my attention, sitting just off to the side, with different length necks. I crouched and pulled them out of the rack. Both had home-made labels, almost like a clothing name tag, literally stuck on with tape. They read 'Lady Grange'.

My heart started beating. Well, what is this?

I had only ever heard rumours of a white Grange. In the late 1950s, pioneering winemaker Max Schubert was ordered by his bosses at Penfolds to quit his attempts to make an iconic red wine based on his passion for European wines. Legend has it that at this time he was planning an iconic white wine too, but owing to the heat from his employers, he secretly kept working only on the red wine that became the famous Penfolds Grange Hermitage. So the white Grange project died as quickly as it started and plenty of wine experts don't believe Schubert ever even made it to the stage of bottling.

Yet I appeared to now be staring at what might be the proof that he did. Could they be real? I quietly carried these incredibly rare bottles out to my car and stored them in the boot.

As I walked back into the house, I was able to relax. The event I had planned off the back of this collection was going to be good. In fact, I was predicting a stampede for these wines.

Frank, Jillian and Kevin were all obviously convinced about this cellar as well. I could tell that they were excited by the Terrey Hills collection and so I knew we had the quality of wine required to more than cover the purchase price.

Over the course of the morning, we packed up the entire cellar: Frank, Jillian and Kevin methodically and carefully nursing the bottles into strong boxes, verbally checking them against the list as they went. The commentary went: 'Not six bottles after all, only five . . . it says four bottles but there are six.'

We called this 'overs and unders' and it was standard when packing up a cellar. The team was a well-oiled machine. In fact, the only weak link appeared to be me. A few hours in, midway through packing one of the full sets of Grange, I unthinkingly picked up a bottle of 1954 Penfold's Grange by the neck – a rookie error – and watched the ageing neck snap in my hand, a weakness in the glass of the old bottle giving way.

Oh shit, I thought. This is a real problem. Now we have two complete sets of Grange except for a '54. What am I going to do? The team were somewhere between horror and amusement. They knew how difficult it would be to find another bottle of that vintage to make up the complete set.

Frank asked, with a kind of half-smile, 'How exactly are you going to fix this one, my boy?'

And then Harry wandered in and found out what had happened. He was particularly unhappy.

'John, you're too casual with important bottles,' he raged at me. 'It's happened before and it's not on. You've got to be more careful.'

I was still cranky at myself, but I wasn't about to let Harry know that. Instead, I shrugged. 'Harry, it's broken,' I said. 'It's gone. Bottles break. It happens.'

This has actually been my attitude forever. Treat rare wine with due care and respect, sure, but remember it is only an object, not life or death. And occasionally a bottle gets broken and yes, it's very disappointing. But that's it. It's done. It would be fair to say Harry, with a cut in this overall deal, didn't share that philosophical view.

'What are you going to do now?' he wanted to know, arms waving, always the dramatic Hungarian. 'You've got two complete sets of Grange, but now one doesn't have the '54.'

I thought for a few moments. The 1954 Grange is actually not a great vintage but it's pretty rare, coming only three years after the original 1951 Grange. I knew we had no way of finding another bottle of the wine available for immediate purchase.

'I guess I'll have to sell one of the sets without the '54,' I said. 'I'll just advertise it as two sets of Grange anyway and deal with the missing bottle when a buyer appears. Sometimes you just have to work it out as you go along.'

Harry shook his head, exasperated, and muttered as he walked away. But it was okay. I knew how he ticked and was confident he'd recover when he saw the sales figures in a few weeks' time.

And I was right. Because the sale, back at the Double Bay Cellars, was indeed a very good one.

In fact, it's amazing how an invitation to taste and buy some of the best wines on the planet can open the most carefully guarded diaries. Captains of industry who you'd struggle to schedule a face-to-face meeting with if you pleaded for a year suddenly somehow found windows in their calendars to wander into my bottle shop at 6 pm on that particular Thursday.

The Thursday night tasting of the Terrey Hills cellar was presented as an invitation-only 'rare and museum wine' sale, strictly non-transferable, and the customers who mattered paid attention to that detail. It's not every day that you can taste a 1990 Dom Pérignon, a 1966 Château Lafite Rothschild – it actually turned out to be slightly disappointing – and a 1955 Penfolds Grange. Of course, the 1983 Château d'Yquem was a highlight, even for a relatively recent vintage. It's not like we were pouring out the famed 1847 Yquem – potentially the world's rarest and most expensive white wine – but any Yquem creates a stir.

Our first guests arrived early, almost right on 6 pm, because the keen collectors knew that some wines would be in limited quantities. They were offered a glass of the 1990 Dom Pérignon on arrival and a list of all the wines available, including the two sets of Grange.

By 6.30 pm, everybody had arrived and guests were already picking wines from the lists and the timber display boxes around the shop. Frank and Jillian were fairly cooking behind the counter with boxes already labelled with customers' names on hold, while they collected other wines.

As all this was going on, I noticed a silver-haired gentleman arrive, wearing glasses and casting a very professional eye across the wines.

I wandered over to him, shook his hand and said, 'I'm assuming the '55 Grange I'm presenting tonight meets with your approval?'

Don Ditter warmly greeted me as the gentleman he was, chuckled and said, 'Well, John, it's okay but it's no Koonunga Hill.'

We both laughed.

Don had been Chief Winemaker at Penfolds for more than a decade from the mid-70s, and created the Koonunga Hill label among others, having taken over from the legendary Max Schubert. I'd invited him along, hoping he'd come as one rarely tastes wines of the calibre that we were pouring that night, and also because he somewhat represented the Grange that was a huge feature of this collection. Don had made a number of the vintages that were in the sets and I thought my buyers might enjoy meeting such an esteemed winemaker.

But I also hoped that I might be able to take advantage of his presence to ask him a question. Frank, Jillian and Kevin seemed to have everything in hand, so I took Don upstairs to my office, where we sat down and caught up.

Finally, I said, 'Don, I have a query that I think you could answer better than anybody else in the world.'

'This is going to be good,' he laughed, eyes twinkling. 'No, I don't want to buy into your shop.'

'Don, you couldn't afford it,' I said. 'Business is off the charts. No, I wanted to ask you about the mythical white Grange. There was some talk that Max Schubert wanted to create a white Grange. There have been rumours that he did, but was shut down, as for the red, although he obviously and famously kept going with the red. Is it true? Was there a white Grange?'

Don took off his glasses and cleaned them with a cloth from his pocket. 'Ah, the Loch Ness monster of wine. It was a crazy decision by the bosses. Imagine if there was a white wine to go with the red, now that Grange is the famous Grange.'

I laughed. 'It's like that great quote by George Harrison, who said, looking back, if they'd known they were going to be The Beatles, they would have tried harder.'

Don chuckled. 'Exactly. I would have bought a few more bottles of the good vintages for my own collection too, if I'd known Grange was going to be Grange.'

I persisted, 'But did Max actually make it?'

Don shrugged. 'Max didn't talk much about it when I knew him, which was years after that all happened. It was only those three years, from when they shut down the project in 1957, that he worked in secret. Maybe he had a crack at a white. There's probably no way of knowing for sure.'

'Except perhaps for these,' I said, reaching into the cupboard next to my desk and producing the two bottles of Lady Grange from Terrey Hills.

Don leaned forward, squinting, mouth slightly open. He finally said, 'Where on earth did you get these, you crafty bugger?'

'They were part of the recent cellar we bought,' I said. 'The one walking out the door downstairs. According to the owners, Max and his wife were friends with Frank Matich, the racing car driver, and his wife. Max apparently gave them to Frank's wife as a present. I'm not sure how they got from Frank's wife to this cellar.'

Don was still peering at the bottles.

'Those handmade labels look about right for a Max experiment,' Don said. 'They just might be the real thing, Johnny. They just might be. To be honest, I am dumbfounded.'

'Dumbfounded!' I said.

'Yes,' he said. 'Just to see and handle these bottles. They look right, and seem to fit the rumour that has persisted all these years.'

'Well, they're not the only interesting bottles in the building tonight, Don. Let's go and make sure you don't miss out on a glass of the Yquem.'

We went back downstairs to where the event was still in full swing. Don tasted the 1966 Lafite, then the 1955 Grange. With his approval, I introduced Don to the room, explaining his chief winemaker role at Penfolds and his involvement with Grange. Don spoke eloquently about his happy times at Penfolds and a little about Max Schubert, and declared the 1955 he had in his glass to be superb and in pristine condition. He even took a moment to acknowledge what an extraordinary collection of wines we had in the store that evening, which no doubt swung any buyers still on the fence, although I don't think there were any by then.

To finish the evening, Don moved on to the sixteen-year-old 1983 Yquem, taking his time to truly appreciate this masterpiece of winemaking.

CHÂTEAU D'YQUEM

There is wine. And then there is Château d'Yquem.

I am not the only one who places the world's greatest Sauternes on such a lofty pedestal.

Consider the events of 1855 when French Emperor Napoléon III decided to classify the greatest wines being made in Bordeaux. Among the Médocs (red wines grown on Bordeaux's Médoc peninsula, and specifically along the left bank of the Gironde estuary, one of the most magnificent viticultural strips on the planet), sixty-one châteaux (vineyards) were classified as premier crus, from first growth to fifth growth, by merit. Only four labels were deemed worthy of being designated first growths – the best of the best. I'm not sure exactly how many chateaux existed in 1855, but there are some 12,000 châteaux (vineyards) in the region today, so to be classified at all is highly prestigious.

Meanwhile, among the Gironde region's Sauternes there are twenty-six designated premiers crus. And yet, beyond those fine wines, there was one more. A single château's wine label was awarded the even grander title: Premier Cru Supérieur.

That's right, Château d'Yquem was officially and exclusively recognised as superior even to the best of the best.

The Russian fascination with Yquem, as it is known in wine circles, is said to date back to 1859, when a Russian Grand Duke, Konstantin, the brother of Tsar Alexander II (grandfather of Tsar Nicholas II) visited Bordeaux and fell in love with the Yquem Sauternes.

Back then, the Russian aristocracy didn't do things by half, so when Constantine decided Yquem was a wine he should carry home to St Petersburg to share with his brother, he breezily bought one tonneau – or 1200 bottles, equalling 900 litres.

He paid 20,000 francs. *Fine Wine* magazine estimates that the rest of Yquem's highly rated 1858 vintage sold for an average of 3500 francs per tonneau. It's no wonder that the Yquem winemakers bottled the Duke's purchase in gold-engraved crystal decanters. In future years, Nicholas II's love of Yquem would see special bottles also made for him, featuring his royal seal.

Some of these – an 1865 vintage – turned up in an auction of wines from the Massandra Winery – the official Imperial Russian winery, still based in the Crimea. Five of those bottles of Yquem sold for £6200 each, a huge sum at the time.

Future American President Thomas Jefferson was another who fell in love with Yquem, increasing the château's global fame. In the 1780s, Jefferson spent time as the US Ambassador to France, and clearly saw sampling the local wine as an important part of that brief. Jefferson bought 250 bottles of Yquem's 1784 vintage for his own collection and then returned to buy more bottles, of the 1787 vintage, for another American politician, George Washington. (These activities also paved the way for the infamous Jefferson wine forgeries that were to come – of which more is written elsewhere in this book.)

The magnificent 1847 vintage is often regarded as the Rolls-Royce of all the magnificent Yquems – probably followed by the legendary 1921 vintage. The 1847 Yquem has variously held the record for the most expensive single bottle of wine ever sold in the United States and the most expensive white wine ever sold, full stop.

Partly it's the renowned quality of that year's produce, but the 1847 has also developed its own mystique. For example, *Fine Wine* magazine tells of a dinner on 7 June 1867 at Café Anglais in the 13th arrondissement in Paris. In town for the 1867 Exposition Universelle and in attendance for this dinner were

Russian Tsar Alexander II, his son, the future tsar Alexander III, and Prussian monarch King Wilhelm – soon to become German emperor at a ceremony at Versailles. At Café Anglais, the Alexanders and Wilhelm enjoyed the 1847 Yquem with their fish main course, before also drinking a Château Margaux 1846, a Château Latour 1847 and a Château Lafite 1848.

History like that cannot be manufactured and the 1847 Yquem remains the most romantic, treasured and now extremely scarce of the world's great wines. Today, buying a bottle of 1847 Yquem would probably cost US$200,000+. But good luck trying to find one in good condition and of outstanding provenance.

The two sets of Grange had been set aside for a standalone auction on the Saturday but otherwise we moved pretty much the entire cellar at the Thursday night tasting and then over the weekend, for maybe $300,000 – an enormous taking at the time for a single weekend. A cellar like that with certified provenance, collected and stored correctly, creates genuine excitement in the wine community. In fact, some got a little too enthusiastic. At one point, as two customers literally started a polite but firm tug of war over the last case of Château Rieussec, I had to step in and suggest half a case each might be a nice solution. 'Of course, of course,' the buyers agreed, remembering themselves.

Even Harry was satisfied with his cut. And especially after one of my regular customers, young Chinese collector Tony Huang, walked in on the Friday morning after the tasting and cheerfully said he'd like to buy both sets of Grange.

'That's excellent, Tony,' I said. 'Here they are in special presentation boxes containing each set. They're going to be auctioned tomorrow.'

'What if I just buy them all now?' he asked.

'Well, if you're sure,' I said. 'I could cancel the auction.'

I told him the top end of what I expected them to sell for at auction and he smiled happily. 'No problem,' he said. 'I'll take them all.'

'Great,' I said. 'Look, there is one small hiccup. I'm afraid one of the sets doesn't have the 1954.'

Tony thought for a fraction of a second and then shrugged. 'Oh, well. I'll take them anyway.'

Just like that, I didn't have to worry anymore about how I was going to auction an incomplete set the next day. And in fact, I also no longer had to worry about how I was going to auction the wines when I hadn't been able to find an auctioneer available to work the next day. And I had no idea how to be an auctioneer myself.

I helped Tony load the boxes into his car and cheerfully waved goodbye.

Life works out.

2

CRACKING THE CODE

Everybody had worked hard across this special event, including over the weekend, and so I manned the shop on Monday, which was traditionally a quiet day and gave me a chance to stare one more time at Harry's nagging list, the unfathomable names refusing to unlock their mystery.

Frank had the day off and Jillian was coming in for the afternoon and evening shift.

Kevin was busy fielding some of the other unlikely wine adventures that came across our desks on a surprisingly regular basis, including some from Harry. For example, an investment banker that Harry had known his entire life knew somebody who apparently had a collection of the original artwork labels done by the artists for each vintage of Château Mouton Rothschild. Given this was exclusive artwork done on commission for the château and now entirely housed in a gallery at the château, such a claim was impossible. Meanwhile, another tip to the store revealed that somebody was allegedly digging tunnels under Woolloomooloo to store or hide a huge collection of wine and also, inexplicably, Fabergé eggs. Or we could have a shot at thousands of bottles of rare Château Margaux wine, reportedly housed in Jakarta, which would need to be bought unseen. Kevin waded through them all, sniffing for an opportunity that might even be real.

I was content to quietly man the store along with a casual staff member after such a big weekend. I think I was on my third coffee of the day when a middle-aged man in an expensive suit wandered in, explained he had been away for the weekend and asked if we still had any of the rare and museum wines from our advertised event.

Hardly any, I told him. 'Sorry, it was a very popular event.'

He said, 'Can I ask: do you still have any *Chat-oh de Eye-key-em*?' Pronouncing it like 'Ikea'.

'The *Château Ee-qu-emm*,' I translated. 'No. It went quickly, as you can imagine. I'm sorry.'

'Oh, well,' he said, peering at other labels before drifting off.

And then it hit me.

I stood there, frozen to the spot. My heart was pounding. I picked up the phone and called Kevin. 'I've got it!' I told him. 'I've cracked the code.'

'The code?' he asked.

'On the list! Harry's crazy list.'

'I'm on my way,' he said, and hung up.

⤦

By the time Kevin arrived, I'd called Harry to check he was at his office and told the uni student behind the counter that they were in charge until Jillian arrived.

Kevin walked in, took one look at me and said, 'You're pacing. It always means something when you pace. What's up?'

'I've cracked the code,' I said. 'The List. I've got it. Come on, Harry is waiting for us.'

I explained my theory to Kevin on the way and he laughed out loud.

'Even crazier than I could have dreamed up,' he said. 'You think you're right?'

'Yeah, I do. It just seems like it would work.'

Harry's office overlooked Darling Harbour. Lots of glass partitioning. Mostly his business was property development, where he would invite others into his property deals so they would provide the capital. Wine was more of a hobby, but of course one that he looked to profit from at every opportunity. For Harry, that's what the game was all about: the scoreboard.

We joined him in his private office and he opened a bottle of white wine, hiding the label so we couldn't see if it was a reputable producer, poured us a glass and then sat there, hands clasped on his stomach, waiting.

I tasted the wine. It was actually very drinkable.

I announced, 'The list is phonetic.'

And knew I was right by Harry's sly smile.

I turned to Kevin and took from him the now battered list. 'Wherever this list was created, it was made by somebody who didn't speak French but had to read the French labels to somebody else. So, they've said them as they've read them, as best they could, and then the person compiling the list has written them down as they heard them, again, as best they could in their own language, which was obviously also not French. Then when the list was recently translated back, again as best they could, we end up with phonetic names. Therefore, Château d'Yquem became Ikem, like Ikea. Château Margaux became Margot.'

Kevin ran down the column, reading them out. '1877 Château Lafite, an 1891 Yquem . . .' He looked up. 'It all lines up. Harry, if John is correct, it's a list of some of the greatest wines in the world.'

Harry's eyes were gleaming with the pure enjoyment of future profit.

'See, I knew you'd have fun with it,' he said. 'And it's true. In fact, it gets better, believe it or not.'

'How could it get better?'

He poured himself another glass and offered us one. We shook our heads.

'The cellar is real,' Harry said. 'It's in Georgia, formerly a member state of the Soviet Union, now enjoying the budding shoots of capitalism since the Iron Curtain came down a decade ago. They're big fans of international investment. A friend of mine, Neville, recently bought into a Georgian goldmine. There's a winery nearby which is owned by one of Neville's new mining buddies and he told Neville about the collection, including having the Georgian cellar book translated from Georgian, as best they could, and hence this list.'

Harry sipped his wine and leaned forward for emphasis. 'John, Kevin, there are tens of thousands of bottles under there, and they're all real. You've read it, some go back to the early 1700s.'

I asked, 'How well do you know this Neville guy?'

Harry shrugged in his expansive way. 'We've done some minor pieces of business together and we both owned wineries in the Hunter Valley. He came to me with this.'

'He's in mining?' I asked.

'Yes, gold, nickel,' Harry said. 'Is doing some major exploring in South Africa at the moment, as well. He's looking beyond Australia's resources boom.'

'So where do we come into this?' Kevin asked.

Harry shrugged. 'The price tag from the Georgians to buy the lot is one million dollars, US.'

'Cash?' I asked, eyebrows raised.

'No,' Harry chuckled. 'Unfortunately, this is one time that international law demands the whole deal is done correctly and above board. Well, maybe.'

'Why'd you come to us?' I asked again. 'I don't have that kind of money sitting around, Harry.'

'I know, but we need your skills,' Harry said. 'You and Kevin know great French wines and how to manage cellars, and I knew you would appreciate the scale of this. Somebody needs to authenticate the wines, and pack them – not by the fucking neck, John – and get them to an auction house in London or New York. This needs to be done correctly and well. Our idea is to form a partnership and do it together.'

Kevin was scanning the list again. 'There's well over a million dollars' worth of wine if this list is true,' he said. 'Well over. Maybe three or four million at a decent sale, and that's only at first glance.' He looked at me. 'How do we find out if it's real?'

I grinned. 'Do you speak any Georgian?'

'Well, probably we visit this Neville bloke before we dig out our passports,' Kevin said. 'Is he around, Harry?'

'Of course. He's got an office in the city, at Circular Quay. We'll need to cut him in on the deal if we do it, and you need him anyway, to hook you up with the locals. My understanding is that they're colourful.'

'What does that mean?' I asked.

'You've always told me you like adventures, John.'

Kevin and I looked at one another and Kevin just shook his head.

'A goldmine,' Kevin said.

'A wine goldmine,' I replied. 'If this list is even vaguely accurate, this may be one of the great wine treasures on the planet.'

'Going to Georgia is a lot different from heading out to Terrey Hills,' he said.

Harry sipped his wine, letting us digest it all.

But then he sat back in his chair, sipped again, and said, 'Fellas, there's one more thing. I still haven't told you the best bit.'

We were silent. He had our full attention.

'Okay,' I said. 'I know you're enjoying yourself, Harry, so I'll play along. How could it possibly get better?'

Harry said, 'Wait until you hear who the wine belonged to.'

'Who?' Kevin asked.

Harry smiled an infuriatingly smug smile. 'I couldn't possibly tell you. You have to hear it from Neville.'

'Harry,' I said. 'You're a lot of fun to do business with but you can also be a major pain in the arse.'

He laughed happily. 'I'll take that as a compliment, John,' he said. 'But trust me, you'll thank me later.'

3

STORY TIME WITH NEVILLE

It took a week to set up a meeting, but we finally found ourselves in one of the glittering silver towers near Circular Quay where the mining magnates have their harbour views and their leather couches.

I'd come from another meeting on the Northern Beaches and so Kevin had hitched a ride with Harry. As we waited for the elevator, Harry taking a phone call on his mobile, I asked how the ride had been. Kevin smiled slightly.

'We were slumming it in the Daimler today. We got here and he went around the block three bloody times looking for a street park. When we were going to be late, he finally headed for an underground car park, and asked if I would go fifty-fifty on the parking fee,' he said. 'A supposedly multi-million-dollar deal in the offing, and the guy in the high-six-figure car is unhappy about paying twenty bucks for parking.'

'Well, we can't say we don't know what we're getting into,' I said.

Harry rejoined us and we sailed to the top of the building, where the foyer was all thick carpet and no doubt original paintings of Australian landscapes. I thought I might have spotted a McCubbin down the corridor but couldn't be sure from a distance. A television was playing silent footage of what appeared to be promotional videos for various mining companies. Kevin nudged me and lifted his chin as a short video spruiked Alaniya Mining with some touristy-looking shots of an old-looking city, a river surging through it, which a caption at the bottom of the screen identified as Tbilisi, the Republic of Georgia, followed by the usual images of bulldozers and giant trucks. A suited man with serious eyes and a darkish beard was shaking hands with a younger man with carefully combed hair, also in a dark suit. Then the video faded and became a new one for Siyabona Mines. A world map highlighted South Africa.

Neville's PA stood, said Neville was ready, came around his desk and ushered us into a huge office with floor-to-ceiling windows showcasing sweeping, sun-drenched views of the harbour bridge, the opera house and all the way to the Heads.

Many business meetings are power plays in one way or another, but I didn't feel like we needed to play any games as we met. Neville apparently had the connection to this mysterious wine collection in Georgia, but we obviously had knowledge and expertise that he needed. 'Nice view, gentlemen' is all I said as I sat down at the table.

Kevin, being Kevin, just glanced at the multi-million-dollar view, shrugged and turned his back to one of the great postcard scenes of the world.

Harry did the introductions to Neville, the man from the video with the serious eyes, but now in shirtsleeves and a tie. Slightly more grey in his hair and beard than the video had highlighted. We all shook hands.

Standing next to him was a tall woman with vividly red hair and wearing a very expensive deep-blue suit. She looked to be around forty years of age, with thin metal-rimmed glasses. Neville introduced her as Paula Stanford, a senior member of his personal legal team. As I shook her hand, I tried not to be distracted by the question of how many people he must have on his personal legal team, as opposed to his corporate legal team? My entire legal team usually meant, in practice, me.

We all sat down and got straight into it.

'The short story is this, gentlemen,' Neville said. 'You may or may not know that, like many former Soviet states, the Republic of Georgia has been enthusiastically looking to join the wider economic world since the dissolution of the Soviet Union in the early nineties. From a mining point of view, this presented a strong economic opportunity because the region around Tbilisi, the capital of Georgia, is known to be rich in gold deposits and other minerals. Previously, state-run mines operated there but in the vacuum of Georgia becoming a republic, we saw an opening.'

Neville explained that he had now formed Alaniya Mining with a local Georgian businessman called George.

'George from Georgia' was Kevin's first comment after the initial hellos.

'I know,' Neville said. 'It seems unlikely, but actually it's a very common name over there, as is his surname, Aramhishvili, which is a mouthful but turns up everywhere you go, from government ministers to businesspeople to shopfronts. His real name is Giorgi, but when dealing with westerners like us, he goes with George. Anyway, it turns out George also owns the Georgia Number One Winery in Tbilisi.'

I had to work hard not to look at Kevin, who I could tell, out of the corner of my eye, was gazing straight at me. Giorgi, the owner of the Georgia Winery, in Georgia. I was pretty sure that if Neville told us this man had a dog, its name would be George.

'So, while I was over there, signing the mining deal,' Neville continued, 'George told me he was also the owner of this winery and they were looking for a buyer for the cellar of wine, told me the whole story and said he thought it would be attractive to a buyer from the west.'

'Why the west?' Harry asked.

'I think nobody over there can come up with that kind of money, or wants to,' Neville said. 'I mean, some might be able to – people are starting to get rich over there after ten years of non-socialist enterprise – but why not go after American dollars, if you can? That's their attitude. Also, the key to this whole sale is being able to sell the wines outside of Georgia, and that's where they lack the necessary knowledge.'

'That makes sense,' Harry said.

Neville leaned forward. 'So, I'll get to the point, gentlemen: to have access to a cellar with up to 50,000 bottles of wine, with this kind of remarkable provenance, strikes me as a really great opportunity to—'

'I'm sorry to cut you off, Neville. But what provenance?' I asked.

He looked at me in surprise, I thought because I had dared to interrupt him, but then he looked at Kevin, Paula and finally Harry. 'You haven't told them the provenance of the wine?' he said.

'I didn't want to spoil your surprise,' Harry replied.

'You don't know where it comes from?' Neville asked us, genuinely taken aback. 'Its history?'

'Believe me,' Kevin said. 'We're more than ready for somebody to finally tell us.'

'Wow, okay. I assumed you knew,' he said. 'Well, here's where I would expect the deal becomes amazing from the point of view of wine merchants such as yourselves. Because if it wasn't good enough to have tens of thousands of bottles of incredible wine from pre-1900 to sell, what does it add to the sale price if it turns out they once belonged to a man called Emperor Nicholas Alexandrovich?'

We digested this.

'Nicholas the Second. The last tsar of Russia,' I said.

'Exactly,' Neville said. 'And then after him, to Josef Stalin.'

'Neville,' Kevin said pleasantly. 'Maybe you could be so kind as to walk us through it from the start.'

Paula quietly handed Neville a couple of pieces of paper, which he glanced at as he spoke.

'Sure,' he said. 'Look, I'm not an expert on Russian history, but I have done some reading and I had my staff do some research since I was over there and here's how I think it plays out. Nicholas the Second was a huge fan of drinking. He wasn't much of a tsar, depending on who you read, to the point that a peasant wizard you might have heard of called Rasputin captivated Nicholas's wife and then the Tsar himself, and all but took over the decision-making for the entire country – which the wider Russian population wasn't thrilled about. While this happened, Nicholas seems to have enjoyed hanging out with soldiers, and he really enjoyed getting drunk. There are diary entries where he talks about nursing hangovers after a night of imbibing with officers and there are records of official lunches and dinners where the magnificent wines just kept on coming out.

'At his palaces, he amassed a serious collection of wine, including some of the greatest French labels. I'm hoping you guys can understand just how great, better than I can with my limited knowledge of your industry. Russians – well, at least the tsars in St Petersburg – seem to have had a fascination with France back then, through the mid- to late-1800s and then into the early twentieth century, and Nicholas was buying wine at an astonishing rate from all the great wine houses, while he and his aristocrat mates were also buying art and other French treasures, often before the rest of the world had cottoned on to the fact these were even treasures.'

Harry stirred in his seat. 'One Russian aristocrat, Shchukin, for example, collected more than 270 paintings, including pieces by Monet, Cézanne, Gauguin, Picasso and Van Gogh.'

'The problem was,' Neville continued, 'Nick the Second was better at judging wine than he was at reading the political winds in Russia, and so was enjoying all the extravagances of his station when World War One ended, Rasputin got brutally murdered and then the Russian Revolution came marching to the Tsar's door in October 1917. You probably know the story of how he and his family were led down to the basement and executed; Anastasia and all that. There are question marks over parts of what happened, but nobody doubts that Nicholas was murdered by Bolsheviks, and high among those forces, ploughing literally into the aristocracy, was Josef Stalin, fresh from Tbilisi, Georgia, where he had already gained a reputation for being quite the hard man.

'After the revolution, all of the estates and possessions of the Tsar and other banished or murdered aristocrats became the property of the state and in time, after Lenin's death, the state was ruled by none other than Stalin, who it would seem personally enjoyed the Tsar's old wine cellar and added extensively to it. But then, World War Two started in earnest and Stalin apparently became worried that the advancing Nazis might actually invade Russia, and so he sent many of the treasures away from St Petersburg, stashing art and riches and, yes, wine in all corners of the country.

'According to George, my business partner who told me a lot of this bit, Stalin split the wine collection into three, with a huge chunk sent to the Massandra Winery at Yalta in Crimea, the official national winery. I don't know where the second chunk went, but some he sent to his home town, Tbilisi, to this little-known winery where it would not be found, and it's still sitting there today, half a century later.'

Harry had his hands on his belly, enjoying our reaction. Kevin took a sip of water. I took a deep breath.

'That is a fantastic story, in every sense,' I said, choosing my words carefully. 'How many bottles are there supposed to be?'

'Most of it is Nicholas the Second's collection but some is apparently Stalin's personal collection,' Neville said. 'Apparently there's another section of the list that we haven't got yet which itemises the wines that were Stalin's personally chosen ones. George told me it was originally 200,000 bottles but racks have collapsed, some have disappeared and now it is estimated that 30,000 to 50,000 bottles remain.'

'Really,' I said, struggling to keep the scepticism out of my voice. 'Up to 50,000 bottles of some of the greatest wines in the world, sitting underground and forgotten at an obscure winery? Having passed through the hands of the Tsar or personally selected by Stalin? It's just too outlandish. Surely, to take this seriously, we need some hard evidence that they exist.'

Neville smiled at me. 'I have photos,' he said. 'Did I forget to mention that George took me down there for a look?'

I laughed out loud. This guy was a true boardroom player, having fun with our ignorance and the fact he had hidden cards. On cue, Paula, the lawyer, handed him an envelope. She had barely said a word for the entire meeting, but I was certain she had a good reason for being here. Neville took the envelope and fished out a handful of photos, scattering them across the table so Kevin and I could see them. Harry only took a passing interest, which suggested he had already seen them.

The photos were terrible quality, shot with a basic camera flash flaring too brightly in a deep, cavernous, dark space, but you could make out what appeared to be endless bottle necks lined up until they disappeared into the gloom. A lot of cobwebs. He showed us some other pictures of smashed racks, with broken glass on the floor, which made me shudder to consider what must have been lost if this was all real.

'George says he doesn't know much about wine but he believes some of the wines are quite valuable,' Neville said. 'You can see where the racks have collapsed. The racks are mostly rusted. I should have mentioned that: the cellar is really damp, too. Like, wet. The majority of the bottles I saw didn't have labels anymore.'

'Excellent. Hundred-year-old wines without labels,' Kevin said.

'Man, that makes it tough,' I said.

'Is that a deal-breaker?' Neville asked.

'Well, no, but it's not great,' I said. 'There are ways of telling whether a wine is what it claims to be without the label. It's not the be-all and end-all but you'd need to be able to really prove it in other ways to be able to sell the wines. Château-stamped corks and capsules can be just as important.'

'Is there anything else we need to know?' Kevin asked. 'Are they all French wines?'

'My understanding is that of the bottles that are left, 20,000 bottles or so are old Georgian wines,' Neville said. 'I didn't know the names, but you might. It all looked genuine to me. What do you think?'

4

THE FELLOWSHIP OF THE WINE

What did I think? Wow! While I tried to be poker-faced in the discussion, my head was exploding with fantasy and possibility.

The romantic in me wanted to race home and pack a suitcase. The prospect of hunting out some of the greatest French wines, from the 1800s, in a foreign cellar had already sparked my sense for adventure. Even if they apparently didn't have their labels.

Now that I knew the supposed provenance of the bottles, with their connection to Nicholas II, Stalin and the potential Nazi invasion, it all seemed too incredible to be true. I *had* to find out. Such wines, from this era, with such a provenance are so far and away beyond even the thought of a humble wine lover and wine store merchant from Australia – in fact anywhere – that to even be able to ponder their existence was blowing my mind. If true, raising and then selling this cellar would be a pinnacle of the global wine industry and, somehow, I had found myself in the middle of the opportunity.

The adventurer in me was in full flight, but unfortunately, life rarely allows you to behave in such reckless ways.

First, we all had to talk business.

I kicked things off. 'Neville, it is a fascinating story and an absolutely intriguing proposition,' I said. 'I think Kevin would agree with me that to really know if this is serious we need to establish what is actually there, if the wines are what the list purports them to be, and answer the big question of whether or not the wine is in a saleable condition.'

'Absolutely,' said Kevin.

'And I guess there is no other way than Kevin and I travelling there to do that work. If we were to go, we'd need to be there for a number of days, to inspect the stock and particularly the most valuable bottles. We should try to use the list we have, or obtain an extended one in advance, to identify, roughly, say, approximately 6000 of the oldest and rarest and mainly French wines. If we can do that, we could do an accurate stocktake of these and as many of the others that we have time for. I see it as an essential first step. The question is whether you'd like to come with us?'

Neville smiled at me, with a businessman's warmth. 'I have a little too much other work going on to go and crawl around a dusty cellar for two days, John. That's why I was hoping you would be interested.'

Was there an insult buried in there? His time was more valuable than mine? I wouldn't think so. Maybe he was just stating a fact about being busy? I let it slide and said, 'Well, your assistance may not be essential as long as we can get access to the wines, and you obviously know people there who can assist us.'

'I believe so,' he said. 'With respect, do both of you need to go?'

He looked at Kevin. 'What do you bring to the table, Mr Hopko?'

'Nothing but boyish good looks and a winning smile,' Kevin said, deadpan.

Paula shifted in her seat. Harry's face had a deeply amused look that I suspect was standard in this situation, when people were butting heads over deals.

'Neville,' I said, 'we can't do this without Kevin. He is probably the foremost expert in Australia in assessing and selling aged rare wine. He has connections in the UK and Europe, which could be vital, if the wine is good enough to sell. Most importantly, he is a bit of a ferret when it comes to rare wine and knowing when a cellar or sale smells off, or not.'

Neville smiled, nodded, and said, 'Okay, fair enough, which leaves only one question. What do we need you for, John?'

'Neville.' I smiled pleasantly. 'I didn't come here to play games. I presume I'm here because Harry knows that I'm the only wine merchant in the country crazy enough to consider flying halfway around the world to chase a mythical cellar that may or may not have belonged to two of the most famous men in Russian history. This stash of wine sounds literally incredible and you've got to decide whether you want to find out if it's real or not. Kevin and I can do that for you. I get the romance of the provenance and the adventure of it, but we're both here for the business side of it. If you want to work with us, then great, let's consider this proposition. If not, it was nice to meet and I'll go back to my cellars in Double Bay and get back to business.'

Neville looked at me, and Kevin, and finally Harry.

'Yeah, okay,' he said to Harry. 'It could work.'

I'd read Neville correctly. He was one of those people who has to push you in the chest to see if you push back or curl up into a ball. Now that we were through that moment, you could feel the warmth return to the room.

Except where Kevin was sitting. His face was a blank mask. I almost laughed.

Neville was saying, 'Look, I'm sorry for being a bit unpleasant, but I needed to see how you'd react to being pushed around, before I could trust that you could potentially handle negotiations with the Georgians.'

'They sound like they're characters,' I said.

'Actually, they are,' Neville said. 'Well, George is, and some of his offsiders. They're fun and you'll probably like them a lot, but you need to be on your game. If I can't be there, I wanted to know you two are up to it.'

'So, if we've passed the audition, what happens next?' Kevin's voice was amiable and polite.

But of course, Harry was way ahead of us already.

'What I'm proposing is this,' he said. 'Neville has the local connections to make it happen. You two have the skills and knowledge to establish whether the cellar exists, whether the wines are genuine and what the potential sales price might be. I put the whole thing together and remain as the Australian point of contact while you're over there.'

'We form a partnership?' Kevin asked.

Finally, Paula spoke up. 'What Neville and Harry are suggesting is a straightforward 25 per cent share for all four partners,' she said. 'If you deem the cellar is valuable enough to buy, all four partners agree to come up with a share of the one million American dollars and any other potential costs of shipping the wine out of Georgia, or ancillary expenditure. Then any profits are split equally.'

Kevin and I raised eyebrows at one another. It sounded reasonable, and between us we'd have 50 per cent of the partnership.

'What about the expenses of going to Georgia, to try and authenticate the wine?' I asked.

Paula said, 'Neville's thinking is that in forming this initial partnership, it should be done properly. I'll draw up the papers to form a partnership of the four parties, and the partners then will each invest enough money to pay your airfares and accommodation and anything else you might need to complete this research phase.'

Neville and Harry were sitting quietly, letting the lawyer lead the business chat.

'It really all does come down to that, doesn't it?' I said. 'Finding out whether the wines are genuine.'

I tend to be pretty direct when dealing with people in business, so I turned my attention from Paula the lawyer, looked Neville in the eye and asked straight out, 'Okay, Neville, if we are to entertain this proposition, I have a question for you. How serious are you about this endeavour?'

He smiled at me. 'Serious enough that I'm putting my money in,' he said.

From a businessman at his level, that was all I needed to hear.

'Kevin?' I asked.

'Let me get back to you,' he said mildly. 'I want to have a think about it.'

Okay, so Kevin was still cranky about Neville asking us to justify our existence.

I nodded and said, 'Yes, I agree. We'll need a few days to think about it. It's quite a task and commitment, so we need to decide whether it's worth it.'

Harry lost his look of smug amusement for the first time in the whole meeting.

'Worth it?' he said. 'It's Stalin's personal wine collection!'

'Allegedly,' Kevin said.

'It's been sitting there since the Second World War,' I said. 'Another couple of days can't hurt, for us to decide if we're in.'

ST PETERSBURG IN ITS POMP

If I could time travel, there's one city I would have loved to visit, and that's St Petersburg circa 1895.

Maybe even earlier, fifty years or so after the city was founded in the early 1700s by Tsar Peter the Great, who established the city as a gateway to Europe.

Peter won the swamp that would become St Petersburg after victory in a protracted war against Sweden. Having decided this would be the place for a new Russian capital city, he drove thousands upon thousands of conscripted builders so hard that many died, while he employed German and Dutch architects to direct the shape of the new city's buildings. Peter even ordered future residents, such as administrators, from across Russia to move there to give the city an instant population.

Impressed by Venice, Peter directed St Petersburg to be a city of canals, necessitating major alteration of the Neva River delta, with transport by boat around the city, even if the northern climate wasn't quite as accommodating to drifting around by gondola. He was a fan of Versailles and had several palaces built around the city in grand fashion, including the waterfront palace and the Grand Peterhof Palace. St Petersburg was very quickly a different beast to Moscow.

By the 1740s, Empress Elizabeth had replaced the fanatical Peter and St Petersburg was taking shape, with many Russians now choosing to live there and Europeans flooding into the city as well. Italian architects built astonishing palaces and the cream of European musicians, artists and other artisans flooded into the Empress's court.

Peter's dream had been that the city would be enlightened, cultural and a deliberate window to the west, bridging the gap to Europe, and remarkably that's what happened. For almost two centuries.

Actually, I would definitely set my time machine for the mid-nineteenth century, in the period after the Napoleonic Wars, when there was a cultural revolution across Europe and St Petersburg came into its own as one of the great cultural, wealthy and diverse cities of the world. At that time, St Petersburg was home to scientists, writers, intellectuals and creative types and bubbled with culture.

You were as likely to hear French being spoken in the street as Russian during the city's heyday, and the emperors were not shy about indulging their love of fine European things. Actually, the Russian aristocrats were enthusiastic patrons of some of the great French painters, before the rest of Europe caught up, and Tsar Nicholas II was famous for his love of French wine. Only the best of the best would do.

I think a lot of people would pinpoint the Russian Revolution of 1917 as the end of St Petersburg's greatness. Revolutionary forces had been operating in the city for decades, including the assassination of a tsar, Alexander II, in 1881, and once Lenin's Communist Party took over, the city's excesses and its love affair with the fine things from Europe were doomed.

Millions of people fled St Petersburg in the wake of the revolution, and after the outbreak of World War One it was renamed Petrograd, because the name St Petersburg was considered too Germanic. Three days after Lenin died, the city was renamed again, becoming Leningrad, and Stalin's Great Purge swept any last sensibilities of European culture and lifestyle from the city's streets.

5

SHOULD I STAY OR SHOULD I GO NOW?

The decision of whether or not to proceed was left there, to Harry's chagrin. Kevin and I were the two who were going to have to cross the world, chasing this potential Lasseter's Reef of Stalin's wine. We had to decide if the return was worth the potential effort. And Kevin had to decide if he could forgive Neville for what he called 'my first tryout since a coach put me through a skating and puck-control test at junior ice hockey'.

'Look, it wasn't that bad,' I said. 'He seems like a nice guy. This is potentially a big deal. He just wanted to know that we wouldn't crumble at the negotiating table.'

It was agreed that while we mulled over our decision, Paula would start doing paperwork and Neville and Harry would get us contact details for the relevant people in Tbilisi, so that things could move quickly if we did accept.

'I hope you will join us,' Neville had said as he walked us to the door at the end of our meeting. 'As you may have gathered by now, ten years after the Iron Curtain fell, Georgia is the Wild West. It's definitely not boring. In fact, it's a pretty crazy place to try and do business. If you do go, my advice is just be low-key when you're there. There are a lot of people with dollar signs in their eyes, guns on their hips and a taste for western luxuries.'

That didn't sound so different to some customers I'd dealt with over the years so I relaxed, decided to do some research, waited for the Tbilisi contact information, and got on with things. I was busy preparing for one of my regular feature evenings, when I would clear out the shop and turn it into a series of tasting stations, where customers could come for the chance to try some really spectacular wines of the world as well as learn a bit about them. Of course, the night ended with strong sales of the magnificent wines being offered. I held these events every few months, when I had a good enough selection to justify a feature evening.

The first customers started arriving at 7 pm but some were bound for disappointment. The way I structured the event was that they would turn left through the door and try a mid-level wine, then go to the next station to try a slightly better or more complex wine and so on, working their way through ten or so stations until they finished with the most outstanding wine. Often this was Château d'Yquem, because it might be the only chance Sydney wine lovers would have to taste it, short of spending hundreds of dollars on a half-bottle. But smarter customers, who had been to the events before, now knew the system and would walk in the door and turn right, going straight to the feature table for whatever were the very best wines at the tasting. This was where disappointment awaited them in the form of Kevin, who was pouring those wines. These queue-jumpers would be invited, with Canadian politeness, to start at table number one and work their way up, along with everybody else.

Once the evening was over and we'd packed up, Kevin and I shared what was left of a bottle of the Yquem that had been that night's feature wine. In the time since we'd seen Neville, Kevin had seemingly gone to live in a Sydney library because he had magically become a world-leading authority on Russian history. I knew a little on the subject myself, having taken an interest in my youth because of developments in my life.

My family had lived in Italy for a year when I was eleven years old – well, I'd actually spent part of the time in an English boarding school with my brother and sisters, but I saw enough of European life to change my opinion that the Aussie boy's lot of sport, surf and mates was all there was in this world. Even for a headstrong pre-teen, living in Alassio for a year and enjoying family travels in Italy and around Europe, it was hard not to absorb the culture, if only by osmosis, just by being domiciled. Then, when I was sixteen, my mother remarried to a man called Jerry Kucera, a Czechoslovakian who had escaped certain death at the hands of the Nazis in World War Two by managing to ski across the border. That was a pretty dramatic and exciting story for an Australian teenager, and then two years later we actually went to Czechoslovakia, to see Jerry's brother and wider family. It just so happened that we arrived almost immediately after the Dubček uprising, or what is now known as the Prague Spring, where the Soviet Union crushed Czech attempts to give citizens wider rights than those allowed under Communist rule. The eight-month civil unrest had been quashed by the time we arrived but there were still Russian tanks in Wenceslas Square during our visit.

I'd been fascinated by that part of the world ever since and so had an interested and working knowledge of Stalin's rule, although Nicholas II not so much.

Luckily Kevin had been doing his homework.

'I'm almost suspicious because it checks out too well,' he said, with that Canadian lilt of his. 'Everything Neville mentioned anecdotally was right, as far as I can tell. Like, Josef Stalin did come from Georgia originally. He apparently didn't like to talk about it because he was all about how citizens should identify with their nation, not home towns, which kind of works perfectly into the idea that if he was watching the start of World War Two and worrying about the Nazi advance and decided to start stashing treasures, like the wine, he'd send it to some-where he personally knew well but wasn't an immediately obvious place for looters or officialdom to go looking.'

I sipped my wine. 'So, nothing in this history lesson answers the big question: do we do this?'

'I've been going through Harry's list of what is supposed to be in the cellar,' Kevin said. 'If the wine turns out to be real – and that remains a big if – it's worth a bloody lot of money.'

'If Stalin's personal collection is in there, as well as the Tsar's wider collection, that is a major selling point,' I said. 'Neville said there was another separate list that outlines Stalin's personal collection. That on its own would be huge, before you even get to the really old, rare classics. I mean, what is Stalin "provenance" worth? Surely a fortune, even to people not interested in wine, and particularly Russians.'

'If we can get the bottles out of Georgia, and to a major auction house,' Kevin said.

'And if we can prove beyond doubt its provenance, and that it's genuine,' I said. 'Especially given we'd be arriving at Sotheby's or wherever with maybe 30,000 wet bottles of wines without labels.'

We sipped for a while.

'And assuming we're happy to be partners with Harry and Neville with his bullshit hardman tactics,' Kevin said.

'Ah, let it go.' I waved a hand. 'He's all right. The guy is in mining. Maybe that's just how it rolls in that industry. You've been bounced around more than that in your time, usually by me.'

'Yeah, but then you pour me good wine, like now, and we make money together.'

'Well, that's the plan with Georgia too, isn't it?'

We sipped for a while, thinking.

'This is nuts,' Kevin finally said. 'You know that, right? Totally nuts.'

'But imagine if they're real!' I said. 'You know how I feel about wine, Kevin. It's an organic, living, breathing thing. It evolves and grows and changes as it matures and particularly when you pull the cork.'

I got up from my seat and started walking up and down the room.

'He's pacing,' Kevin said. 'It always means trouble when Johnny's pacing.'

'Imagine if these wines are legit,' I said. 'They must have been in the actual cellar when Nicholas the Second and his family were executed. They would have seen the rise of Stalin and the fall of the Iron Curtain. They have lived so much history! They have witnessed the whole of twentieth-century Europe and more, lying there, alive in their comfortable cellar. How could we not go and see if they exist?'

'Look, you know me,' Kevin said. 'I can enjoy turning all of that around in my head, I really can. Intellectually, I can really enjoy all that history talk. But ultimately a bottle of wine, for me, is a commodity. I'm more interested in what those historic bottles you're all excited about would fetch at auction. And I believe it's a lot.'

'What's a bottle of 1847 Yquem worth?' I asked, waving my almost empty glass of a much younger Yquem vaguely in his direction. 'One of the greatest wines ever, and one of the rarest. The list says there are three in that cellar. *Three!* What are they worth on their own? But if you add the history; if you add the fact that the bottle might have been held in the hands of Stalin, or Nicholas the Second . . . what is it worth then?'

Kevin said, 'In 1985, Christie's sold that Lafite, claimed to have been owned by Thomas Jefferson, for what?'

'One hundred and fifty-seven thousand dollars, US,' I said automatically. We'd all marvelled at that sale price. It remained one of the most expensive bottles of wine ever sold.

'And the provenance of those bottles was sketchy, if I remember correctly,' Kevin said.

I nodded. 'Found bricked up inside a wall in Paris, allegedly. The owner, some flamboyant guy claiming to be a Dutch duke or something, wouldn't say exactly where so nobody could check.' (In fact, the alleged Thomas Jefferson bottles were the subject of several investigations, especially by the American industrialist Bill Koch. They were proven to be fake more than twenty years later.)

'So, we could be walking into something like that,' he said.

'That kind of price tag?'

'Yeah, but also a high level of examination from start to finish.'

I said, 'We don't know much about this local guy that Neville is in business with either. Giorgi or George. He owns a goldmine and the winery? Is it his decision to sell or are there other partners we'd have to deal with? I was a bit concerned by Neville's comment that George said he didn't know much about wine but thought some of the bottles might be valuable. That sounds disingenuous to me, or like he's bluffing. If he had really just told Neville the entire backstory of the Tsar's and Stalin's ownership of the wine, then he has to know the wine is valuable.'

'I guess that's all part of the dance,' Kevin said. 'Maybe he was fishing to see if Neville personally knew anything about wine? Or maybe the Georgians genuinely don't know what it would be worth on the open market?'

'Perhaps. Or this could be the biggest wine con in history,' I said.

'Well, we've got phones and we've got email, right?' Kevin said. 'We can start talking to George and ask some of these questions, get a read on things before we commit to getting on a plane.'

'Or,' I said, the adventurer in me rising, 'we could just go and see for ourselves.'

Kevin raised his glass and said, 'It does sound like quite the escapade.'

The next day, I rang Neville and Harry and said we were in.

NICHOLAS II, THE LAST TSAR OF RUSSIA

Now we'd decided we were going to go, I put some time into educating myself about Nicholas II, the last, doomed tsar of Russia.

It was hard not to want to know more about the man who had apparently bought tens of thousands of bottles of the very best French wine. Especially as his people were on the brink of rising against him and the aristocracy, for what Lenin and his supporters considered a life of excess. Had Nicholas really been so unaware that he'd called for more wine, instead of sensing the Bolsheviks' bloody revolution in the air?

It would seem so.

Nicholas was the eldest son of Alexander III, born near St Petersburg in 1868. He became the Tsar in 1894, despite reportedly confiding to a friend, 'I am not prepared to be a tsar. I never wanted to become one. I know nothing of the business of ruling.'

Hardly a strong start to his reign, and it got worse at his coronation. Not only did he get a bit carried away, organising 85,000 military personnel to be in attendance and a choir of 1200 to sing for his wife, about-to-be Empress Alexandra, in the lead-up to the event. Unfortunately on the day itself, scores of people were reportedly stampeded to death in the crowd, as Nicholas and Alexandra smiled happily and waved, unaware of the tragedy unfolding. Likewise, deeper into his reign, came the disastrous Bloody Sunday, when his troops fired into a crowd of peaceful protesters who were seeking to establish a people's assembly and improve working conditions. More than one thousand people were killed, leading to strikes across Russia, suppressed by Nicholas's troops. The tension remained and, what with the brutal suppression of the strikes, anti-Semitic pogroms, a violent quashing of the 1905 attempted revolution and the execution of potential opponents, he attracted the nickname 'Nicholas the Bloody'.

Even marrying Alexandra wasn't the smartest of moves, although it would appear that Nicholas wed for love. Alexandra was from a German aristocratic dynasty, which wasn't ideal as the world lurched towards World War One, when she would be treated with suspicion by the Russian people as a potential German saboteur. She spoke mostly German whereas he spoke Russian, so often they communicated best by speaking English to one another. The pair had five children, including Anastasia, who would become a legend in her own right as the princess who may have survived the family's execution.

But they definitely knew how to live well. Accounts report that the Emperor's kitchen had a staff of more than fifty and offered three levels of meal: 'simple' (only four main courses at breakfast, lunch and dinner), as well as 'holiday' and 'parade'. The Tsar's obsession with all things French extended beyond wine to his employment of one of the great French chefs, Pierre Cubat, who was supported by a local crew trained in the very best culinary schools in Paris. The menu was largely French. Some accounts have the Emperor and his family eating off golden plates, but others say they ate using silver cutlery off Romanov-monogrammed china, which was smashed as soon as it was not in perfect condition. As well as Cubat's creations, endless exotic delicacies were imported from Europe, and there were so many leftovers that they often made their way into St Petersburg's best restaurants. Kitchen staff also made extra cash selling leftovers to a crowd that would gather outside after meals, including, some said, members of the aristocracy.

By all accounts, Nicholas was timid and indecisive yet tried to maintain a veneer of control. Alexandra dominated him and he leaned on advisers who may or may not have had the country's best interests at heart. While Nicholas reigned, he believed strongly that God had ordained him to be emperor and therefore his rule was absolute and could not be questioned. As the public grumbled, he continued to live very large in his 1500-room Winter Palace, and part of that lifestyle was buying copious amounts of the best French wine, with the first growth Bordeaux wines flowing into St Petersburg.

One article named Nicholas's personal favourite wine as the 1847 Château d'Yquem while another suggested he also favoured Château Léoville's 1874, 1881 and 1887 vintages, along with Château Lafite, the 1887 Mouton Rothschild and Larose. From the early 1880s, he had a dedicated wine merchant, Diktay, who sourced his wines. An estimated value of his wine cellar at the time came in at $75 million in today's currency. Another account detailed the royal court consuming more than 1100 bottles of wine, almost 400 bottles of Madeira, fourteen dozen bottles of sherry, almost twenty bottles of port, and 150 bottles of vodka, on top of champagne and cognac. That was over two months.

When not drinking, Nicholas loved his family and apparently filled his official diary with news about his wife and children, instead of reporting a log of official state duties. But things started to slide out of control when their son, Alexei, was diagnosed with haemophilia, and Alexandra turned to a charismatic former peasant turned failed monk, Rasputin, to try to cure the boy.

Rasputin, who had become known within court circles for his alleged prophetic and healing powers, appeared to help the boy's condition and soon came to be seen as a central, if completely illegitimate, figure in the family and also the running of the country, which not everybody was thrilled about. With Rasputin spending an increasing amount of time with Alexandra, all kinds of rumours about his lifestyle and lusty appetites bounced around St Petersburg. As World War One raged, Nicholas went off to war, appointing himself commander-in-chief of the Russian army. He managed to oversee a humiliating defeat to Japan while pushing to expand Russia's territory into Asia, but heavy drinking with the troops continued, as did momentous hangovers. One diary entry read: 'Nicholasha treated us to a great dinner in his tent. I tasted six types of port and got a little juiced, which helped me sleep well.'

Even at war, his love of wine was not put aside.

Rasputin's legend was made when the people who brazenly murdered him told unlikely stories of how cyanide poisoning and repeated shootings had failed to kill him on the night; his body was eventually wrapped in a rug and dropped into the icy Neva River.

Rasputin's final prophecy to Nicholas – that if he was to be assassinated, the royal family would also be killed by the people – turned out to be correct. Despite peacefully abdicating as the revolution took hold, Nicholas was assassinated in a Siberian basement along with Alexandra and their children, ending 300 years of Romanov rule. In 2007, the romantic idea that a couple of the children had escaped and survived was quashed when researchers DNA tested bones found away from the rest of the family's remains.

There are accounts that the revolutionary soldiers who took over the Winter Palace looted the cellar and led a military and public drinking binge that lasted weeks, yet there are other stories of Lenin controlling the cellars, art and everything else formerly belonging to the aristocracy, with Stalin taking over upon Lenin's death, thus preserving countless cultural and viticultural treasures.

It leads to the question: was the Emperor's cellar raided and drained, or did it survive for Stalin to shift years later, in the face of the Nazi invasion? This is what Kevin and I hoped to find out.

6

FLYING TO TBILISI

If this all happened today, you could google the life out of every angle of what you were potentially getting into. But this was in 1999. Dial-up modems still went *bing-bing-bing* as they connected, then took forever to load a single web page, and you only had access to early browsers like Netscape and Internet Explorer. At the time, Kevin was even involved as a consultant in a crazy plan that one winery had to sell bottles of wine online through some kind of web-based shop. They spent hundreds of thousands trying to develop a virtual cash register. For the most part, websites were basic and vast worlds of knowledge had not yet made their way online.

But some had. I spent midnight hours as the departure day loomed trying to find out anything I could about where I was about to land. The best site I managed to dig out was from the United Kingdom, a government-created trade industry site that had basic information on modern Georgia.

'Georgia lies in the area of land known as the Transcaucasia which stretches between the Black and Caspian Seas, an important junction between eastern Europe and Asia,' I read. Georgia was apparently roughly the same size as the Republic of Ireland and had a population of about 5.4 million people. President Shevardnadze, a former USSR finance minister, had been voted into office in 1995 and four years later was very much in charge.

I was most interested in the comment that economic reforms in 1996 had seen inflation controlled, exchange rates stabilise, GDP growth of 10 per cent and privatisation of around 50 per cent of the economy. Presumably including wineries and goldmines. Neville had really not let any grass grow under his feet before sweeping in there to try to do business. I had to give him that.

The site told me that people spoke a specific Georgian language and that the capital, Tbilisi, where we were headed, was a city of 1.2 million people.

Encouraged by the information, I kept up my online research, looking for more info about this part of the world. I discovered that Georgia had been one of the most affluent states behind the Iron Curtain, with productive farming land and industry, but had suffered badly since the collapse of the Soviet Union. The state had become independent in 1991 but that only led to a vacuum of power, leading to civil unrest, a breakdown in law and order and finally a full-blown civil war. It was only the return of Shevardnadze as president that turned things around, I guessed because he brought some old-school Soviet ideas about how best to deal with pesky civilian uprisings. The uprisings duly stopped, although as I browsed more websites, it became clear the United Nations was still involved in trying to negotiate a solution to the ongoing separatist conflict in Abkhazia on the Black Sea coast.

Georgia had a new currency, as of five years before: the lari, which is divided into 100 tetri. I wrote a note to myself to check whether I'd also need US dollars while we were there, if not for everyday transactions then maybe for potential 'negotiations' at the winery. I checked the trade website again and it told me that all official transactions had to be in the Georgian lari.

When I asked Kevin about what type of currency and how much he thought we should take, he had a considered opinion on the reality we'd shortly be facing. 'John, I was reading that 70 per cent of Georgians apparently live below the poverty line,' he said. 'You offer them genuine US dollars, and it's going to open a lot of doors. Also, we don't know if that 70 per cent figure includes some of the people we're trying to do a million-dollar deal with, so I think we definitely want to have some greenbacks to help things along if needed.'

'I agree, but the whole place also sounds a bit frontier town, from what Neville's told us and what I've read,' I said. 'We have to be careful how much money we walk around with.'

'Well, that's true of most places,' Kevin said. 'You ever visited Detroit?'

'I haven't,' I smiled. 'But let's definitely take some US dollars.'

As we packed our bags, an astonished Frank and Jillian found themselves in charge of the Double Bay Cellars for a week or so. It wasn't unusual for me to be overseas – I sometimes headed to the UK or Europe on wine-buying exercises, but they were unsubtle in their surprise about and suspicion of the mission Kevin and I were about to embark on.

'So, basically we tell customers that you're off drinking with Mikhail Gorbachev, if anybody asks,' Frank said.

'I think you'll find you are behind the times,' Jillian said. 'Boris Yeltsin is the boss over there now.'

'Well, you realise that's Russia, not Georgia,' Kevin said. 'But yes, we're off to buy wine bought by the Soviet motherland.'

'Just another day in Double Bay,' said Jillian, shaking her head.

Early on the morning of 14 June 1999, Harry picked us up in the dove-grey Daimler and drove us to Sydney Airport's international terminal. Kevin sat up front and I sat in the back.

'Would you like some music?' Harry asked, and then turned the radio on loudly without waiting for an answer. The chorus of Britney Spears' debut hit ricocheted around the car. She was number one on the charts and on high rotation that winter.

I asked Kevin, 'Where do you stand on the Princess of Pop?'

Kevin was looking out the window at the gymea lilies that lined the freeway to the airport.

After some thought, he answered, 'She's no Aretha Franklin.'

We stopped in the drop-and-go section at the front of international departures. Harry took a photo of us and our boxes of equipment, with a look on his face that was torn between genuinely wishing us luck and trying not to think about the fact that he had been forced to pay for a quarter of the $7699, before tax, that it had cost for each of our flights. We were taking the kangaroo route to Singapore and on to London, before a third flight back east to Tbilisi, where a nasty dose of jet lag, sweet Georgian sparkling wine and rich chocolates would be waiting after thirty-plus hours of travel.

As promised, once we'd committed to the venture, we'd formed a partnership between Neville, Harry, Kevin and me, and each deposited $10,000 to fund the partnership and pay for our flights, accommodation and even potential excess baggage costs for any wine we hoped to bring home to Australia.

Kevin and I carefully kept a checklist of everything we would need and to be sure we had packed them as we made all the necessary preparations, including such technicalities as making sure we had bright fluoro lights to put behind bottles to check their fill level as we examined the cellar. We knew the lighting would almost certainly be below par, with absolutely no natural light and weak globes most likely only vaguely illuminating the bottles. Both Kevin and I had noted the condition of the cellar in the photos that Neville had shown us. As well as being wet, which could be good for the ageing corks, and cobwebby, the cellar looked dark.

Measuring the fill level of the bottles was an essential task, for several reasons. The height of the fill of wine in the bottles, as wine people call it, is an indication of the condition of the wine, and particularly how efficiently the cork has performed over many years. Poor corks will allow significant leakage when bottles are lying on their side, whereas with a very old wine, as many of these were claimed to be, a good fill level would indicate that the cork has held well, and the wine could be in good if not perfect condition. Over time, I had developed a technique to assess the fill level by taking photographs of bottles standing up against a bright white background, or with a bright white light behind, so that the fill level is clear. This also allows me to see the colour of the wine, which can also indicate the condition of the wine inside the bottle.

But it's possible to gather such photographic evidence only with a strong enough light to shine through the bottle, so I was determined we carry these lights onto the aeroplane. I wanted to be as self-sufficient as possible, because who knew if the Georgians would be helpful or across the need for such techniques, or if we could obtain the equipment once we were there. We had no plan B, heading into such an unknown region and cellar, so the more variables I could control before we even took off, the better.

It was those kinds of random details, legal necessities and worries about what we might have overlooked or forgotten that filled our minds that morning as we checked our luggage, wrestled Sydney Airport's brand-new electronic ticketing system, promised we weren't carrying any illegal cargo as we wandered through security and customs, then finally boarded a Qantas jumbo.

Kevin and I looked at one another as the final passengers got organised in their seats.

'Nothing ventured,' I said.

He replied, 'What could possibly go wrong?'

As the plane's engine roared and we built speed and lumbered into the sky, I began to be filled with a blood-pumping sense of adventure tangled up with the much heavier, more tangible dilemma of how to be certain of the authenticity of the wine before we had to hand over US$1 million.

For all of my wonder at the history of these wines, if they were real, this was very much a business deal and the amount we were being asked to pay was a big one, certainly more than I'd ever contemplated spending on a cellar of wine. I am okay at analysing the risk/reward aspect of a business deal and haven't gone too badly wrong over the years – with a couple of dinner-party-tale-worthy exceptions – but as we flew north-west, I couldn't shake the fact that if this escapade went really badly, I could lose a great deal: not only financially but also in reputation and, well – why lie? – in ego. In practical terms, could I lose my house or the Double Bay Cellars? Probably not: I was only on the hook for a quarter of the total investment. Nevertheless, I had the butterflies in my stomach that probably come with playing poker for the first time, for much higher stakes than you're used to. I tried to brush off the risk to my personal pride and reputation, or the financial landmines laid out in front of me, but there was no getting around the fact I was playing a game beyond any prior comfort level.

And then, consider that we were flying on the word of a man we barely knew called Neville, who had seen some bottles in the cellar but admitted he didn't know much about museum wine, and a couple of cheery phone calls with this George character, who had a charming English-as-a-second-language turn of phrase as he enthusiastically shouted down the phone – but was noticeably light on hard detail or specific information about exactly who owned the winery, which of the wines were Stalin's personal collection, or answers to any of the other key questions I had been pressing him on without success.

It wasn't just the million-dollar asking price, either. If we were to go ahead with the purchase, the costs would mount. We'd have to work out how to transport tens of thousands of potentially fragile bottles out of Georgia and safely to London, or maybe New York. There would be marketing and other costs. Hopefully, if we could establish the cellar was genuine with exceptional wine classics, a major auction house could help us through those later tasks and costs.

There were precedents for this. One of the bigger British auction houses – I'm pretty sure it was Sotheby's – had conducted an auction of the Massandra Collection, where the auction house's experts visited the official Russian winery in the Crimea, authenticated the old Russian and Soviet bloc wines (which were almost all missing labels), placed each individual bottle, standing up, in a cellophane bag, tied the top and added a Sotheby's label identifying the details of the wine. They then placed the bottles in solid cardboard carrying boxes and transported all the wines to London for the auction. What a logistical exercise and what an enormous expense! And now Kevin and I might be asking them to do exactly the same again with the mysterious, unproven bottles we were on our way to visit. No pressure at all. I didn't sleep well on the plane.

In Kevin's hand luggage, he was carrying three polystyrene packing cases for twelve bottles each, along with a lot of wrapping tape. We knew that this trip was not going to see us attempt to move any volume of wine, no matter how well things went in Tbilisi. Kevin and I were completely focused on discovering exactly what was in that cellar, and who we were dealing with. It was about exploring the cellar, not trying to lug it anywhere at this stage.

However, we had decided to make it a condition of a potential deal that we be allowed to take at least a dozen wines with us when we left, so we could check them for authenticity.

Neville had even put it in writing. I was carrying a letter of introduction to George that I was to give him on arrival. 'I would be most pleased if you could grant two of my colleagues the type of cooperation and assistance I have come used to during my seven-year involvement in Georgian business,' it said. He asked that Kevin and I be permitted to bring 'several bottles of wine . . . back to Australia, for scientific analysis,' and reassured George that these bottles would not need to be opened, so could eventually be returned to the winery.

George had already agreed on the phone, understanding that we would need to show the genuine bottles to various non-Georgian partners if the deal were to go ahead. But also, if things went pear-shaped, those twelve bottles would potentially offer our only return on our investment in the trip. If we could emerge with several pre-1900 bottles of French classics, we would be ahead, no matter what.

At worst, I thought as Kevin slept next to me, we'd have at least a dozen excellent bottles of wine for a dinner party to tell the story of our adventure and to rue what could have been.

And so we crossed the world, to London then back across Europe and the Black Sea towards Tbilisi. We landed, met George at the airport, were dutifully swept through customs, no questions asked – as promised by our jovial host – and were driven at crazy speeds through a dark, mysterious city. We pulled up at a bland 1950s-era hotel, like any tired Hilton you might find in any city in the world, and fell face-first into our beds.

It was Tuesday 15 June 1999.

And we were in Tbilisi. In the land of Josef Stalin.

PART II

GEORGIA

GETTING TO KNOW JOSEF STALIN

Let's be diplomatic and only call Josef Stalin one of the most divisive figures in world history.

Of course, most people will take umbrage at such a soft description. When there are entire books and websites devoted to answering the question of who was worse out of Stalin and Hitler, when it comes to mass murder – each responsible for many millions of deaths – it is clear that there is no place for flippancy or excuses.

Stalin was born Ioseb Vissarionovich Dzhugashvili, in December 1878, in Gori, a small Georgian town near Tiblisi. From an early age he answered to the nickname 'Koba', the hero of a Georgian novel who embodies morality. He cut his teeth as a revolutionary while young. The son of a washerwoman and a drunken cobbler who beat him, he read Karl Marx and quit school. He moved to Tiflis, as Tbilisi was then called, and first gained fame, or infamy, for being a ringleader in violent clashes between Russian Social Democrat protesters and police. He was then behind a major robbery in Tiflis, stealing funds for the Social Democrats' activities.

But it was as one of Vladimir Lenin's chief lieutenants in the Bolshevik Revolution in the 1910s and leading into the 1917 revolution that the man now known as Stalin – 'man of steel' – entered the world stage. His ruthlessness, capacity for violence and fanatical belief in the cause were precisely what the leader, Lenin, required. Only 1.63 m tall, Stalin wore stacked shoes and spoke softly with a thick Georgian accent, even describing himself once as a 'Russified Georgian'. One arm was longer than the other and he had scars on his face from having contracted smallpox as a child. In my reading up on Stalin, the clearest mention of his love of drinking I could find was that he liked getting other people drunk so they would spill secrets.

By the time Lenin died, and Stalin succeeded his mentor as Secretary General of the Soviet Communist Party and Premier of the Soviet Union, he had arguably the most political power of any person in history. Stalin was behind the ruthless modernisation and industrialisation of the Soviet states that saw Russia become a major world power and a nuclear state, yet the transformation came at a breathtakingly brutal cost.

His sweeping plans to modernise the Soviet Union led to mass famines in the 1930s, which are estimated to have seen five million people starve. Stalin followed up with the Great Terror, also known as the Great Purge, where political opponents, intellectuals, leaders of the armed forces and inconvenient groups like the *kulaks* – wealthy farm workers who were in the way of state-controlled agriculture – were removed, either to the gulags, from which roughly one million never returned, or through mass shootings. In the end, Stalin is estimated to have been responsible for the deaths of roughly six million people in his drive to make the Soviet Union's communist state supreme.

Yet only a few years later, as Stalin's army pushed back the advancing Nazi troops and went on to liberate the Auschwitz, Ravensbrück and Theresienstadt death camps, 'Uncle Joe' was photographed with other Allied leaders in their discussions of post-war peace settlements, which for many burnished his reputation after years of deadly and tyrannical behaviour.

Still seen in the late 1990s by many in the former Eastern Bloc, especially Russia and Georgia, as a champion of the people, a brilliant wartime leader and a Socialist star, Stalin is equally seen as a murderous dictator by those not enamoured by the cult of celebrity he has continued to enjoy. He was complex, devious, cruel and driven, and undoubtedly a giant of twentieth-century history.

7

SO, YOU'D LIKE TO BUY A WINERY?

Tbilisi, Georgia
July 1999

10.30 am, day one in Tbilisi, found us waiting in the hotel lobby after almost an hour, wondering why George was late.

'Johnny's pacing,' Kevin wrote in the diary he would keep throughout the trip. We agreed that we didn't feel too bad, given jet lag and our small amount of sleep, but I was tired enough not to take it well when George didn't turn up as promised. It didn't seem a great omen, although actually, we would soon discover that George generally had a pretty elastic take on the concept of punctuality.

I had the large bag of equipment we would need in the cellar to audit and check the wine. Kevin had a backpack with a camera and his notepad, along with whatever else Kevin carried around. The hotel foyer? Overwhelmingly burgundy with light brown wooden highlights. We could have been in Dallas, or Brussels, or a hundred other cities.

Except for the security screen between us and Telavi Street. We watched as Nino and another young man finally appeared, stalking through the front door. They both, as a reflex, reached to their belts and pulled handguns away from where they were tucked into their waists. We stared as they gave the guns to the bored-looking officer next to the security screen, along with car keys, and then wandered through the metal detector. I also noticed that the security people kept a very close eye on the man behind Nino, the guards more vigilant than usual.

'You know,' Kevin said, deadpan, 'if we *were* to run screaming to the airport and catch the first flight out of here, now would be the time.'

'Oh, come on,' I replied. 'If they were going to shoot us, they could have done it last night on the way in from the airport. Where's your sense of adventure?'

Nino was approaching us, his hand outstretched. Something strange was going on with his face but then I realised the hard man of last night was smiling.

'You sleep good?' he asked in his thick accent. 'You ready for winery?'

The man with him looked to be in his thirties. The standard leather jacket, this time in brown. He had a buzz cut hairstyle and the beginnings of a beard, more a multi-day unshaven growth on his chin. He was shorter than both of us but had a level gaze.

'This is Pyotr,' said Nino. 'He is helpful.'

We shook hands with Pyotr, who had a firm grip without trying to crunch our hands. In very passable English, he said he was pleased to meet us. He would prove to be very helpful.

'We can go,' Nino said. 'George is waiting.'

Kevin and I passed security, followed by Nino and Pyotr. Without a word, Nino was handed back his gun by the security guard, and Pyotr received his. It was amazing to us, as though they had handed over umbrellas and then retrieved them on leaving. Having said that, I noticed that the guards remained on high alert as Pyotr nonchalantly shoved the pistol back into his belt and headed out to the street where Nino's big black Mercedes with the tinted windows was parked right at the doorway of our hotel.

'Ah, yes,' said Kevin quietly. 'Of course. The mafia staff car.'

'You are allowed to park on a footpath?' I asked Nino.

He snorted and said, 'Parking restrictions are for aboriginals.' Kevin and I stared at one another as we got into the back seat. We didn't realise it at the time, but 'aboriginals' was Nino-speak for anybody who wasn't a high roller as he saw himself to be. I guess you'd call it his word for 'locals' or everyday people. It jarred every time, but he used it more than once during our stay. Approaching a red light, he would veer onto the wrong side of the road and roar straight through, often at a worryingly high speed. 'Red lights are for aboriginals,' he would proclaim, eye in the rear-vision mirror and grinning. Maybe he was right. The police never once lifted a finger as he lorded his way around Tbilisi.

What made all this even more terrifying is that Tbilisi is built around a gorge, carved by nature into the mountains, the river surging through the heart of the city. There are places where Tbilisi's streets are more like those of San Francisco, extremely steep and narrow. Not normally a place to rev through the gears, trying to get from nought to way too fast in a few seconds, you would have thought.

Nino disagreed. Instead, the car's engine screamed as we flew through the streets, speeding to the Savane Number One Winery for the first time. Pyotr sat silently in the front passenger seat as Nino drove, while Kevin and I tried to take in the view of the river as we headed through the city. The buildings were almost universally run-down but hinted at former grandeur. They were almost colonial in architectural style, with arches at ground level, shuttered windows, and huge balconies above, especially near the river.

We passed what appeared to be an opera house that had seen better days and several large buildings that in a former life might have been banks. Nino wove too fast between roadworks, which seemed to be happening everywhere or needed to be, as we bounced over crumbling bitumen. The day wasn't cold but the light was weak, the sky grey, which added to the tired, industrial feel of the city. The relief came from the Kura River (the Mt'k'vari river in Georgian, Pyotr told us), its path cutting through the city like a snake. We crossed it on a stone bridge before heading away from the water.

Through a gap in some buildings I saw a large construction site higher up the hill, of what looked like a cathedral of some kind. I wanted to ask Pyotr about it but with Nino driving, it was gone as quickly as I glimpsed it.

Mine and Kevin's jetlagged brains foggily tried to take in this strange town, and then we turned into a long driveway, with trees lining the way, and seemed to be heading through a large park. Nino tore up the road as though being chased by an unseen enemy and lurched to a halt outside a two-storey building with three ornamental arches and a high roof.

'We here,' Nino said and honked the horn.

Kevin and I climbed out of the back seat and took our first look at the winery. I believe its official name was the Sauplistsulo Mamouli Wine Bottling Factory but it was referred to variously by everyone we met as either the Savane Number One winery or the Georgia Number One winery.

Between us, we have always called it the Savane Number One, so let's go with that.

As well as the tall, arched building, there was a series of smaller, low-slung side buildings. An ornamental garden had been crafted in front of the buildings, including a central stand that might have been a fountain but on closer inspection was being used to dump cigarette butts. A light, with ten white globes like balloons, was an unexpected seventies touch to go with the main building which was a century old.

A red brick building with a tiled roof and a climbing plant starting to grow into the roof was off to our right. Several cars were parked in front of it, mostly sedans and all about ten or more years old. To the back of that building, we could hear noise, mostly people talking. As we gathered our bags from the boot of Nino's car, several men in polo shirts and jeans wandered across the driveway, disappearing behind a building here, to reappear over there. They gave us curious looks but didn't wave or engage, maybe in a hurry to get to wherever they were headed. Somebody was hammering something off to our left. This winery seemed to be a hive of activity. I was keen to discover what was being produced.

A door opened in the main building as we were taking in the scene and George and another shorter man appeared, George bounding down the stairs to the driveway and approaching us with a hand outstretched.

'John!' he said happily. 'John and Kevin! It's so wonderful. Welcome. Number One Winery – and number one for a reason! The best! In all Tbilisi. You will like it here very much. Welcome.'

'Hello, George,' I said. 'We're very happy to finally be here.'

'Ah, yes,' he said. 'There are some people for you to meet.'

'The winery seems busy,' Kevin said.

'Oh, yes, very busy,' said George. 'Lots of people here, working hard.'

'How much wine do you make here?' Kevin asked.

George looked confused. 'No wine. But soon.'

'Then why all the people?'

'Lots to do,' said George, with a wide smile, but didn't elaborate. 'This is Zurab. He's with me.'

Zurab gazed at us without saying anything as we took him in. He was wearing jeans, running shoes, a T-shirt with a buttoned shirt over the top. A dark and dangerous-looking handgun was stuck in his belt. The Georgian uniform, as far as we could tell. He'd been at the airport the night before but hadn't been introduced, taking a second car that followed our Mercedes into town. Zurab was slightly shorter than Nino, and stocky, and rarely left George's side over the next few days.

It only occurred to me later that his entire role was probably to be George's bodyguard.

Kevin and I gave each other looks as we were led away from the car, into the main building. The foyer's walls were painted olive green and hung with framed certificates in Georgian, speaking of achievements we couldn't decipher.

There were four men waiting for us, lined up as though to meet a member of a royal family, or maybe the president.

George did the introductions. First up was a paunchy middle-aged man with a bristling moustache and a comb-over hairstyle. He was the man from the airport, introduced again as Mr Revaz Rustaveli, the chief winemaker, who George had previously only called Mr Revaz. Next to him was Grigol Tsintsadze, the cellar manager, an older man with thick white hair. Then there was the marketing director, a slightly haggard-looking man whose name was Davit something, who wore a silver suit. He nodded, not even bothering to speak.

Finally, a silver-haired man in a blue suit with a pinstripe through it was introduced by George as the managing director of the winery, Mr Tamaz. He shook our now tiring hands and said that he was pleased to meet us.

George earnestly apologised that Nana Vorobieff, the union lady, was not able to be there to meet us but would drop by later. He also rattled off several other names as apologies, so that Kevin and I were left wondering just how much management a seemingly unproductive winery could need.

We were all guided into a small boardroom with a wooden T-shaped table. Mr Tamaz, Mr Revaz and the marketing manager sat at the head of the T, while we sat down one side of the stem, along with Pyotr to translate where required. George sat opposite us with Tamaz. Grigol seemed to have been excused, as he bowed and backed out through the door.

Once we were all seated, George spread his hands and said to us, 'Mr John and Mr Kevin, welcome to Tbilisi and welcome to Georgia. Our city is capital of Georgia and is historical place. East meets west, Asia meets Europe, right here. We bridge between Christians and Muslims. We once independent after Bolshevik Revolution but then

Red Army take over in 1921. Now we independent again and life is good.'

'Tbilisi is a fascinating city, George,' I said. 'We're delighted to be in Georgia and to explore its long and glorious history.'

George seemed like he would burst with pride. He said, 'Do you know how Georgia was formed? I will tell you a story.'

'A story,' said Kevin. 'We'd love that.'

'In the beginning, God, he say to the peoples of the world that they must choose their country; they must divide up the world into what part they want. But the very first Georgians, they busy at a feast when God sets deadline for choosing. They at table with lots of beautiful wine and lots of food. They sitting under pergola, having delicious meal and celebrating the bounty of Georgia's wonderful natural ingredients and grapes. Then God, he finished dividing up the world into, I don't know, you know, England, China, Kazakhstan, Greece, and he says, "I done now, job finished," and heads off for home. But then he sees the Georgians. They completely miss his deadline, they still having a nice time at their feast! And God, he mad about it. Say to Georgians: "What you doing? You don't respect me or my demand?" But the *tamada*, the toastmaster, he say to God, "No, wait a moment. You got it wrong. We don't care we got no place to live, to call our own. We love your world, we love all the beautiful food and wine. We toast you, God, we toast your creation. A toast for God. Another toast for the beautiful food. A toast for the grapes. A toast for the fresh water of this river. A toast for God!" And God, he so happy, he sees the Georgians love his world so much, he says to them, "You know what, I choose your country for you. I give you the one spot left, the one I be saving for myself but, you know, I got Heaven, I okay. You can have this place right here, called Georgia. It paradise, designed for God himself. But now it yours." And here we are.'

Kevin and I smiled broadly, so that even if the others around the table had no idea what George had been saying in his broken English for so long, they could see that we liked it. Everybody grinned and clapped. Happy that the meeting was going so well.

'We are extremely honoured and grateful to be in paradise, George,' I said, almost bowing. 'Thank you for that story.'

'Your pleasure,' George said, before turning to his fellow Georgians. He began to speak in a fast stream of Georgian language, speaking mainly to Tamaz and Revaz, but occasionally turning to Davit to emphasise a point. The Georgians nodded and Tamaz said something in reply, which made George nod furiously and gesture with his arms as he responded.

Then George turned to us and said, 'I was explaining to the leaders of the Savane that you are very experienced wine people from Australia and that you are excited and ambitious to hear about the history of the winery.'

I smiled and nodded towards the heads of the table, not knowing what else to do. Kevin sat like a stone, smiling slightly. 'Fantastic,' he said.

'Savane Winery has a brilliant history, dating back to 1896,' George said. 'Georgia, of course, is the home of wine, the cradle of making wine.'

'Yes, I believe there are wine jugs dating back 8000 years. Is that right?' I said.

'Some people say the Egyptians invent wine but no, it was Georgians,' George said passionately. 'The original wine grape, number one on globe, is *Vitis vinifera*, native to Caucasus region, which means native to here. Even our word for wine, *ghvino*, is original word. Other places take it and turn it into your wine, your *vino*, your *vin*, your *Wein*. Our word, *ghvino*? It first.'

'I didn't know that, George,' I said. 'Fascinating.'

'Lot of history, John. Very good history,' George declared. 'Savane Number One continues to be a proud maker of wine for all of Georgia and for international markets too.'

'What's your role in this, George?' asked Kevin. 'Are you the owner?'

George gave us a look that was loaded while never losing his smile. 'All will become clear, Kevin and John. Trust me while I pave the way for our mutual business.'

If those around the table who spoke English found that a strange statement, they gave no sign, and so George ploughed on with a long and elaborate history of the winery, including the fact that it employed seventy-five people and was on 0.77 hectares of land. It had the capacity to produce 40,000 hectolitres of wine annually, which George said equated to 5.3 million bottles. He admitted that in the last few years, such capacity had not been achieved, mostly because of a lack of working capital.

Kevin wrote on his notepad and pushed it slightly to the left so I could read it. *Iron Curtain fell. Capitalism. No cash?*

I nodded slightly.

George explained that the winery had found it hard to purchase enough actual bottles, while power outages had also affected production. Even so, the winery was confident of producing 100,000 litres of wine, or 1.3 million bottles, in the next calendar year. Sales would be made using direct consumer contacts, while the winery had a cellar door next to the plant itself. Cash flow remained positive, he said – Kevin wrote: *How???* – and there were no major liabilities associated with the Savane Number One, all of which was fully explained in documentation that we were welcome to see.

I wrote on Kevin's pad: *They think we're here to buy the bloody winery.*

George finally stopped talking and Mr Tamaz delivered an equally strident monologue in Georgian which Pyotr told us was explaining how our finance and production injection along with international marketing expertise would take Savane Number One to new global heights.

Kevin wrote in his travelogue: *If Johnny was standing right now, he would be pacing.*

As Mr Tamaz came to the end of his speech, I opened my mouth, unsure of what to say or where to start.

I was saved by George, who said quickly, 'It's okay, John. I know how excited you are but let me take it for now. All is well.'

I took that as a cue to not say a word in this meeting, unless specifically asked to. Whatever was going on here, George was in the driver's seat and we'd have to trust him.

Everybody kept talking for more than an hour. There were discussions about the Georgian partner in the proposed joint venture providing the necessary production facilities and required labour force. There were itemised lists of equipment that the Savane Number One venture currently owned and depreciation estimates.

Kevin finally couldn't help himself and asked politely if all assets above and below the ground would be included in the venture, such as any existing wines that may reside in the cellars, and George smiled broadly and said yes, of course, under Georgian law if you buy a property you automatically own everything and anything below the ground as well as above the ground.

But that's as close as we got to the rumoured cellar of wine tantalisingly said to be under our feet. Finally, the meeting was halted for tea and coffee and Kevin and I were able to stretch our legs as a weak sun broke through the grey clouds.

'So, congratulations on your decision to buy a broken-down winery a long way from home,' Kevin said as we wandered through the sculpted garden.

'Nobody has any idea why we're actually here,' I said. 'I mean, apart from George. What is this game that he's playing?'

'I think the big question is who is in charge here,' Kevin said. 'We've always been led to believe, from Neville and George, that it was George who owned this place and who we'd be dealing with. Who are all these other guys? Are they owners? Who are the decision-makers?'

'Look,' I said. 'We just have to play this game and see where it leads. Don't mention the rare bottles. Don't say anything at all if we can manage it. Let's follow George's lead.'

But once we were all back in the room, George said very little at all, apart from translating what was being said. He sat next to me this time, so he could pass on the odd comment or explanation of what was being said. Pyotr had disappeared. Kevin and I were handed a list of discussion topics, which started with wine, history of wine, any documentation and photos. I felt we'd already covered most of that in the first session, but my heart sank a little as I continued to read: what sort of wine used to be produced, production now, future production. A second list then itemised grape collection, date of starting harvests, sources, a review of winery history, inspections, marketing needs, ownership transfer time line. It went on.

Mr Tamaz held the floor, talking almost nonstop while ticking off all these items, according to the whispered translations George was providing. Every now and then Revaz would chime in and Tamaz would nod or shrug as if to say 'Of course' and then continue on. Grigol floated in and out of the room occasionally, and Davit spoke up during the items relating to recounting the winery's history, and marketing.

Clearly, Tamaz and the others were under the impression we were wealthy Australian investors, here to look at how to turn the Savane Number One Winery back into a successful producer. Nobody seemed to have a clue that we were only interested in the Tsar's and Stalin's wine collection. George kept his head down, only politely answering questions, when asked directly by Tamaz. Jetlagged Kevin and I nodded a lot, or smiled, and tried to appear to be listening, but as it was almost entirely in Georgian, we were a little blank about everything being discussed.

Finally, we broke for lunch and Nino appeared, handgun in jeans pocket as always, to drive us, George and Pyotr to a restaurant by the river. We were in the 'mafia staff car' Mercedes, hurtling downhill through Tbilisi at up to 100 kph, slowing only slightly when a red light loomed ahead of us. Nino veered and roared through the intersection, saying over his shoulder, 'Red lights not for us!'

What the hell had I got Kevin and myself into?

I had a long list of very pointed questions for George that I planned to deliver over lunch but not long after we arrived, Mr Revaz, Tamaz and Grigol also sat down around the table. George put a hand gently on my back as he poured me a glass of water and said softly into my ear, 'This will pass. Enjoy your lunch.'

I shrugged at Kevin and settled into trying to read a menu in Georgian, which is a language that, written, looks like a mix of Latin and Arabic.

The food was actually very good. The first plate served was *khachapuri*, a staple of the Georgian diet. It's a tasty cheese bread, with yeasty dough filled with grated cheese mixed with egg. Straight up delicious and a food that we would see often during our stay, served at tiny cafes in the old city or in restaurants like this. George told us the next dish, a stew, was *tevzis buglama*, translated roughly as salmon stew, and served with boiled potato and rice. *Kupati* was Georgian sausage, and I never discovered what the ingredients were, while there was also a *charkhlis mkhali*. Kevin ran the word around in his mouth, as though tasting it along with the purple puree itself. '*Mkhali*,' he said.

'Very famous, very traditional,' said George. 'We locals call it *pkhali*. Vegetables, herbs, walnuts. Got to be made by hand to be true good. This one made with beets.'

'Beetroot?' I asked.

'Yes, beets,' George nodded. 'Goes well with good wine of which, luckily, we have very much.'

Even better, this was our first chance to sample the Savane Number One's actual wine. Mr Tamaz produced a bottle of red, imaginatively titled 'Savane', and Kevin and I both eagerly offered our glasses, before sniffing, swirling and examining the wine. When I finally tasted it, the wine was completely unremarkable.

After we finished that bottle, a white wine was produced with 'GWC' on the label. George explained this was the Georgian Wine

Company, a joint venture a local Tbilisi entrepreneur had with a Dutch company. I guess it was presented to show us a glittering example of how international partnerships in the local wine industry can work. We tasted the white and, again, it was drinkable but nothing special.

Even so, an unspectacular wine can still do its job, to relax the tense muscles of Australians half a world away from Sydney and yet no closer to a fabled multi-million-dollar wine collection. I let the local wine flow through me and enjoyed the food and the spectacular view along the Mt'k'vari river. Everybody seemed to drop their guard over lunch, toasting our arrival and working hard to be friendly, to show they were glad we were in town. George was several people away from me, chatting with Tamaz and Grigol without appearing to be talking shop.

'George,' I asked, leaning forward to gain his attention. 'What are those big balconies that run almost between the houses or buildings on the other side of the river? It looks like people walk along them.'

The balconies mostly were timber, with struts underneath, so they ran on top of the footpath below.

'Is true, John,' George said. 'Balconies communal place for people to walk, meet, eat, hang out. Not private. For the people. You want to get together? Balcony a good option for us. The river, the city, it belong to everybody.'

Tamaz said something and George turned away from me again. I took a deep breath, sipped wine and served myself from a herb and egg salad that had arrived. Kevin was somewhat warily attempting to chat with Pyotr.

Handgun casually on the table, just like today you might put your smartphone next to your bread plate while you eat, Pyotr had perfect posture as he sat, and chatted in broken English.

'What's your background, Pyotr?' Kevin asked, to which Pyotr shrugged and said, 'I was originally from Chechnya. Now I am here. There were some interesting roads between the two places.'

'Chechnya,' Kevin said. 'You had to leave there?'

'Not something to talk about,' Pyotr said with finality, although no discernible annoyance. Just *end of discussion*.

George had returned to our conversation and so I pointed across the river to the huge construction site that I'd seen from the car, halfway up the opposite hill, and surrounded by houses.

'What is that being built?' I asked.

'The Holy Trinity Cathedral,' George answered. 'A major construction for Tbilisi. It is nine years since we were removed from the Communist rule. The cathedral is a symbol: that Tbilisi can build new churches, can take risks and has income.'

'Is there good income among the people?' I asked.

'No, is terrible,' George said, and smiled broadly at the juxtaposition of what he'd just said. 'Lots have no money. We need income from world.'

I opened my mouth to speak but George already had a hand up, saying, 'John, I know. Please. All will be well. Can you see up there, above the town? Narikala Fortress, very ancient, very interesting. Fourth century, John! We will take you for a visit while you're here.'

I sipped my wine and realised I couldn't force the issue, not here in a restaurant overlooking the river with everybody enjoying themselves.

Instead I asked, 'Is it true that Josef Stalin came from Tbilisi?'

'He born in Gori, small Georgia town, but, yes, he big man in Georgia before he join the revolution,' Pyotr said. 'He part of Messame Dassy, Georgian independence group. His name then was Dzhugashvili.'

'Not Stalin?' I asked.

'He became Stalin while exiled in Siberia, by Tsar. Stalin mean "steel",' Pyotr explained.

'How is he regarded here in Tbilisi?' I asked.

George sighed and shifted in his seat, taking a while to answer, softly, leaning forward. 'It complicated,' he said. 'Lots of people, here and in world, see Stalin as a monster, we know. But John, he also *big*

Georgian man, very famous. Not many Georgians so powerful. He has his supporters for that reason. You might see smiling picture of him in taxi or on wall of restaurant. He *our* champion, even if not a nice guy, no? Lots of death, John, under his watch, over many years. Sure, we like being a republic now, not part of Communist bloc. Stalin stays underground in his grave. That's good.'

I had so many questions, but George was clearly keen to change the subject.

Eventually, we made our way out the front door to Nino's Mercedes, parked half on the footpath right outside the doorway, and he roared back to the winery. We waited a couple of minutes until Grigol's car turned up, with Mr Tamaz and Revaz.

'It would be great to look around the winery,' I said brightly to George. 'We'd love to see what we're potentially buying into.'

'Of course, John. That's a wonderful idea,' he said, before turning to Tamaz and Revaz to chat briefly in Georgian. Grigol gazed, unsmiling, at us as we set off around the property.

The first few rooms we poked our heads into were abandoned storage spaces and what appeared to be old tasting areas. By the layer of dust and the scattered old equipment, it was difficult to know when they'd last been used. The afternoon light showed swirls of dust particles in the air as we walked through one room and into a larger inner chamber that turned out to be the bottling line.

'This hasn't been used in years,' Kevin murmured to me as we took in the archaic equipment. 'When did they last actually produce wine?'

'I'm starting to think many years ago,' I whispered in return.

We walked around the bottling line, nodding and showing great interest, as though with a quick wipe-down this would be churning out a million bottles per year within a day or so.

From there, we went to what looked almost like a large chicken coop – a flat patch of earth – but with what appeared to be enormous red clay vessels buried up to their narrow necks. 'You know *marani*?' asked George. 'This here is *marani*, place of burying *kvevris*.' He indicated the earthenware containers. 'Traditional Georgian winemaking, in clay, for making *machari*. Most winemaking now European method, but we have big *kvevris* buried, for traditional style. Do it right if we feel.'

'I'm definitely going to have to read up on that, George. It sounds fascinating.'

'Clay-made wine is different and good,' he said, opening what turned out to be the back door of the main building.

'Let's go downstairs,' said George and my heartbeat picked up. At last.

Revaz, the chief winemaker, reached inside a door to turn on a dim light that did enough to illuminate stairs heading down below.

He was followed by Grigol, the cellar manager, then Tamaz, George, Kevin and me. Pyotr brought up the rear.

The cellars filled several rooms, with rows of mostly identical bottles heading into the gloom. Occasionally we would pick one up and look at the label. The numbers 89 or 85 suggested the year of production, while the rest of the label was in Georgian but with the Savane logo at the top. There was a layer of dust over most of the bottles but nothing to suggest anything that had been lying in this vault for half a century or more.

As we headed back to the surface, Kevin asked mildly, 'Is that all of the cellars?'

'There is a second level, and a third level,' George said. 'Mr Tamaz would rather we talked some more in his office.'

And so it went, for another three hours. Tamaz and George trading questions and answers, almost exclusively in Georgian, with George occasionally leaning towards us to offer translated speeches about the history of the winery and the potentially glorious future. About the need for production recommencement and levels of investment. He handed us a document with speculative calendar dates.

George also tried to keep us abreast of endless, pointless questions from Tamaz to Revaz about past successes and the best vintages from the winery, as though Tamaz had never heard any of this information before and had just thought to ask while we happened to be sitting in the room. A strange and clumsy pantomime for two men who didn't speak the language.

The fight to not succumb to jet lag was mighty and I think I may have actually nodded my head once or twice shortly before they called a halt to the charade and we finally got to wander outside into the fresh air.

'George,' I said. 'The bottles.'

We were standing next to Nino's car, about to leave for the day. We hadn't seen a single bottle of interest and I wasn't about to climb into the back seat of the Mercedes without making that point.

'It has been a wonderful day, John,' George said, smiling broadly. 'My associates are very excited by the potential of our venture and have had a chance to say many things that they have been wishing to say to you. Let's talk some more over dinner, yes?'

'George, I'm just concerned that—'

'Yes, John, yes. It's all good and exciting, is it not? Mr Tamaz here could not be happier and I am happy too. Let's give you a chance to have a shower before we have dinner, yes?'

I stood there, feeling anger building. 'George, we are only here for four days and this is the end of the first day,' I said.

'Yes,' he said, with almost cartoonish pleasure. 'Four days. Plenty of time. Time for all kinds of things, John. So much to explore. Now, let's give you a chance to rest and freshen up.'

I felt Kevin's hand on my arm. 'Yes, that's a good idea, John. Let's do that. I could do with some downtime before dinner.'

'Okay, sure,' I said. I shook hands with Mr Tamaz, Mr Revaz and the marketing manager, who had reappeared towards the end of the day. Grigol hadn't come out to the car.

'Thank you for a fascinating day and for your kind hospitality,' I said in English, before George rattled off the words in the local language. 'I look forward to exploring the winery in even more detail tomorrow.'

Nino pulled his handgun out of his waistband and put it in the cup holder between the front seats as he slid into the driver's seat. Kevin and Pyotr climbed into the back and I got to sit in the front passenger seat for an even more vivid view of what it's like to drive at high speed through red lights in a crowded city. At the hotel, Pyotr and Nino nodded unsmiling goodbyes.

I went straight to the reception desk to ask about international dial codes, then went to my room, picked up the phone and called Neville Rhodes's office number, before my exhausted brain finally managed to do a rough time zone calculation. It was 6 pm in Tbilisi, which meant it was midnight in Sydney. No wonder he hadn't picked up. Despite the hour in Australia, I also rang Harry on his home number and his mobile but he didn't answer either.

I hung up, stared out the window at the gathering darkness and realised how tired I was, as well as frustrated and worried. I lay on the bed, set an alarm and almost immediately, in spite of my swirling brain, fell into a deep sleep.

8

TBILISI BY NIGHT

It took three rounds of the alarm before I finally climbed out of the fog. The shower was mercifully both hot and powerful, so I was dressed and vaguely human when Kevin knocked on my door at 8.30 pm.

'Did you sleep?' I asked him and he said, 'Yes, I got a couple of hours. Enough to hopefully get me through to the end of the evening. You?'

As he spoke, he walked past me to the bed and grabbed a TV remote off the side table, turning the power on and flicking channels until some kind of Georgian game show appeared on the screen. Kevin turned up the volume slightly louder than I would have wanted to have it and said loudly over the noise, 'Have you seen this show? It's hilarious.'

Now under the sound effects, fake audience applause and even more fake laughter of the host of the show, I said quietly to Kevin, 'You don't think they'd bug us, do you?'

He shrugged. 'Probably not but you never know.'

'I think you've been reading too many le Carré novels,' I said.

'Who's that?' he asked.

'Are you serious?' I said, narrowing my eyes. 'Kevin, don't you know John le Carré?'

'Is he Canadian? Does he write about ice hockey?'

'Okay, now I know you're winding me up,' I said.

'Who? Me?'

Somebody won a prize on the gameshow and the musical sting almost lifted the TV off its bench.

'Why don't we go to the lobby and see if we can find a drink,' Kevin said.

We killed the TV, headed downstairs, discovered the bar off the side of the foyer which sold a range of European and American beers, chose two bottles of Stella Artois and waited for Nino's inevitable screech to a halt outside. We were the only ones in the hotel bar apart from two businessmen in suits chatting in the far corner.

'I did have a short sleep,' Kevin said in a more normal voice. 'But only after I ducked to the US Embassy before they closed for the day.'

'The US Embassy?' I parroted. 'Why?'

'I asked them if they knew much about local wineries. Said we were a couple of Australian investors in town for mining interests but had a vague interest in local wineries, too, given the region's long history of making fun stuff out of grapes.'

'Had they heard of the Savane Number One?' I asked, sipping my beer.

'Better than that,' Kevin grinned. 'They had an entire document about it, as a potential international partnership option, I guess for US interests when they arrive in town.'

He pulled a piece of paper out of the inside pocket of his jacket and unfolded it on the table in front of me.

I read.

The masthead said: 'American Embassy Tbilisi'.

Then in bold letters it said:

The following leads from Georgia were submitted by the Bisnis Representative at the U.S. Embassy Tblisi. (sic) along with telephone and email details for the embassy executive responsible.

'*B-i-s-n-i-s-?*' I said.

'I know,' Kevin said, juggling peanuts into his mouth. 'It might be the same phonetic speller who compiled the labels on the Savane cellar list fifty years ago.'

'A long and glorious career,' I said, before continuing to read.

Company: Sauplistsulo Mamouli Wine Bottling Factory
Sauplistsulo Mamouli Wine Bottling Factory (Savane) was established in Tbilisi in 1896 and employs 75. The enterprise owns 0.77 hectares of land in downtown Tbilisi and can produce 40,000 hectoliters of wine annually (equivalent to 5.3 million bottles). Savane became a joint stock company in 1994, with the management owning the company's controlling stake. The capacity utilization has been low for the last couple of years because of the lack of working capital, bottles, and frequent power cutoffs. Savane expects to produce 100,000 liters, or 1.3 million bottles, in 1996. Savane sells its products through direct consumer contacts. The company has its own commercial outlets associated with the plant. The cash flow remains positive, though working capital is limited. Savane does not have any major liabilities. Savane is seeking a joint venture partner with financing and production marketing capability. The Georgian partner will provide all necessary production facilities and the labor force. Contact: Tamaz Akhmeteli, Managing Director, Georgia, 380062 Tbilisi, 1 Petriashvili St., Sauplistsulo Mamouli.

I looked up.

'Hang on, did they just literally read this to us this morning, as their pitch for our potential investment?'

'It seems so,' Kevin said. 'At least we know Mr Tamaz's surname is Akhmeteli.'

I shook my head. 'So, the winery is completely out of action, has ageing, decrepit equipment, no modern technology at all and

Departing Sydney airport with polystyrene boxes to pack the wine bottles in that we hoped to bring back. The cardboard box contained the lights and other equipment Kevin and I planned to use in the Georgian cellar.

The view of Tbilisi from my hotel window.

Top left: A page from the Georgian cellar book. With some imagination one can see how it corresponds to our translated list. *Top right:* Kevin with the well-armed Zurab and Ivane at Savane Number One Winery. *Bottom:* Myself and Kevin trying to be Georgian locals for five minutes.

Discussions on day one with (*left to right*) the marketing manager, chief winemaker Revaz and managing director Tamaz, plus George next to me, looking about as interested as George ever looked in these tedious talkfests.

Myself, Revaz and George discussing 'stuff' when we first went down to the floor of the cellar where the valuable bottles were stored.

In the cellar, including (*top right*) nursing an 1847 Château d'Yquem.

Walking between seemingly endless rows of supposedly antique wine covered in moisture and thick cobwebs was like visiting a relic of a bygone era.

Nino, our very own chief consultant in special issues.

Ivane helping himself to a superb century-old port.

Me and Grigol looking at wines towards the back of the cellar. It felt as though the racks went back endlessly into the darkness.

Tasting old Georgian wines at the Savane Number One.

Left and below: Kevin finding particular wines as we worked to check the translated list against the physical bottles, and (*above*) the staircase winding down to lower levels of the cellar.

The Savane
Number One in
more productive
times than during
mine and Kevin's
visit: *(top)* on the
bottling line; *(middle)*
securing wax seals;
and *(bottom)* some of
the winery's finished
products. © *AP Archive/*
The Footage Company

Inside a traditional Georgian *marani*, where the clay vessels – *quevri* – of wine are kept underground *(inset)*. © *Robert Grim and Magdalena Paluchowska / Alamy Stock Photo*

Khachapuri, the ubiquitous and delicious cheese bread and *(inset)* an example of a *kantsi*, a bull horn drinking vessel. © *Remo Savisaar and Fabrizio Troiani / Alamy Stock Photo*

George and his sweetheart at our dinner up in the hills surrounding Tbilisi.

'Enjoying' the Georgian speciality of a midnight sulphur bath.

Top left: Tsar Nicholas II with his wife the Empress Alexandra Feodorovna and their children at the christening of Alexi in the Grand Palace. *Top right:* Stalin photographed in 1901 in Georgia. © *Everett Collection Historical and GL Archive / Alamy Stock Photo*

The splendid Grand Peterhof Palace in St Petersburg. © *Sergey Borisov / Alamy Stock Photo*

Bordeaux's bustling Quai des Chartrons and the river Garonne, today and in the early nineteenth century. © *Andia and The Picture Art Collection / Alamy Stock Photo*

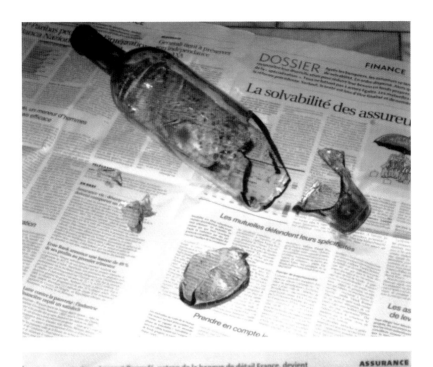

The broken bottle in Paris, with the cork and part of the capsule intact.

Château d'Yquem is one of the world's most celebrated producers of wine. Centuries of winemaking expertise and a unique microclimate, as well as low yields, lead to consistently outstanding quality that stands the test of time.

Left: Jean-François Bourrut Lacouture, who organised my visit to Yquem, and chief winemaker Sandrine Garbay.

Right: In prestigious company with (left to right) Sandrine, President and CEO of Château Yquem Pierre Lurton, and Jean-François.

At the end of a memorable day, with 375ml of nineteenth-century wine.

they're out hawking the whole thing to anybody who will listen. No wonder they got so excited when George said we were coming from Australia.'

'He probably told them about how he's already done a deal for mining with Neville, and we're the next suckers along to the party,' Kevin said.

'I still don't get it. We went the entire day and we don't even know if the Tsar's and Stalin's wines exist.'

'We've seen Neville's photos,' Kevin said.

'We've seen photos that Neville told us were at the winery,' I countered.

'But Neville put his money into the four-way partnership. Why would he do that if he was bullshitting us?'

'He probably wouldn't unless he had some other agenda. It doesn't make sense,' I agreed. 'Okay, so maybe we assume the wines are there, in those floors of the cellar they wouldn't let us visit today. But if we can't see them, we can't authenticate them.'

'And if we can't authenticate them, touch them, see them, even taste some, we have no reason to be here,' Kevin said.

'And George knows that because all our correspondence has been about those wines, not the winery.'

'So,' Kevin said, pointing the neck of his beer at me. 'He's playing some game with them and needs us to wait until he's done. Did you notice at times today it felt like he was just letting Tamaz and Revaz talk, just letting them prattle on? He wasn't guiding the conversation at all.'

'But how long is that going to go on for? I'm definitely ringing Neville in the morning, Australian time, to tell him to put a rocket up George. We only have three more days.'

We sipped our beers. Nino and George were due in a few minutes, which meant we probably had an hour to kill.

'What else do we have to think about?' I asked. 'What were your other impressions?'

Kevin waved for two more beers. It was a bad idea with the jet lag and the wine-drinking to come, but the beer did taste very good after the day we'd had.

He said, 'I'm trying to get my head around the winery's ownership structure. I have no idea who half the people wandering around that place are or what they do, but if you look at the senior management team that we're dealing with, it's very clear that Mr Tamaz and even potentially the winemaker, Revaz, have clout. Are they owners? Are they in a partnership with George? If it actually turns out the wine is there and we want to negotiate for it, who is going to make the call?'

'Yes, quite,' I said. 'We need to find that out and fast. Is Grigol somebody we need to factor in or worry about?'

'On the plus side, Pyotr seems friendly,' Kevin said. 'His translation is handy when George isn't around.'

'I don't trust him,' I said. 'I say we don't tell him anything more than we need to, and I'm not sure I believe anything he says. We can't afford to take anything said to us as gospel, no matter how helpful they are. We have to stay with facts that we know to be true. We haven't seen anything that we need to see, and in such foreign territory, to be safe, we have to remain mindful that this might all be a big con, until we can prove that it isn't.'

'Crazy day,' Kevin said. 'I can't believe we didn't even get to look at the wine.'

We heard a screech of tyres and a car door slam. No gunshots, but the noise was enough to make us believe that Nino had arrived.

'Crazy day and now here comes the night.' I smiled. 'Fingers crossed.'

Nino waited by the door, gun hanging at a jaunty angle out of his pocket as usual, as George came to get us. We left the hotel and wandered down the street to a restaurant that looked more pub than eatery. We took a table for four, and George poured us wine and ordered dinner for everybody but then, instead of sitting, announced he'd be back in fifteen minutes.

Kevin and I stared at one another as he and Nino stalked back out of the restaurant. The food began to arrive – more *khachapuri* cheese bread, a *lobio* kidney bean salad and *badridzhnis khizilala*, which turned out to be a kind of eggplant caviar. *Ikhvis chakhokhbili* was a duck stew, with hints of walnut.

There was no point sitting here with plates of food, wondering if Nino was coming back or whether anybody else would show up. So we ate, comparing our takes on the town of Tbilisi so far.

'Walking into the old town trying to find the embassy this afternoon was fascinating,' Kevin said. 'It's just such a classic post-Soviet landscape. The buildings were once impressive but now they're not being looked after. The vacuum that's left when the Soviet machine pulls away.'

'I can't believe the handguns everywhere,' I said. 'Yet everybody seems really friendly and relaxed. You could really imagine the Nazis marching through here, and the Ninos of the world turning into snipers on the rooftops.'

'Did the Nazis get here?' Kevin asked.

'Actually, no,' I said. 'I did some reading about it. Hitler invaded Russia, obviously, but didn't get down here. The Georgians were dragged into it, of course. Some estimates had 700,000 Georgian men heading off to the war and only maybe half coming back.'

'Jesus,' Kevin said. 'More than 300,000 casualties. That's a big hit of the young men in a small country.'

'Huge,' I agreed. 'The interesting thing is quite a few Georgians also joined the Nazis, because they weren't too fond of Soviet rule and thought the Nazis might liberate Georgia if they won.'

'How'd that go for them?' Kevin asked.

'Not well. Actually, Hitler initially liked them because the Georgians were regarded as an Aryan race, so he was all for that, but from what I read, as the war tilted and Hitler became more paranoid and had his back against the wall, he thought the Georgian divisions might be secretly working for Stalin after all and turned against them.

There was even a big fight between the Georgian divisions and the remaining Nazis, running beyond the official end of the war. It was the last actual fight of the whole thing.'

'How bizarre,' Kevin said. 'What happened to those Nazi Georgians once it all finished?'

'Stalin apparently wasn't impressed. Most of them ended up in Siberia or in gulags throughout the country. Never seen again.'

'War,' sighed Kevin. 'That shit would never happen in Canada. I can see Nino being in the middle of something like that.'

'What about Pyotr?' I asked.

Kevin laughed. 'Pyotr? I think he's the most dangerous one of all.'

'Pyotr? He's really calm and almost somewhat thoughtful,' I said.

Kevin looked me in the eye. 'John, I guarantee that Pyotr has some kind of military training. He said he got out of Chechnya, yeah? I really like him but he strikes me as the truly lethal person in the room. I think Pyotr would happily shoot you or just beat you to death with his gun if it failed to fire.'

I started laughing. 'More so than Nino?' I said, picturing Nino's dark eyes and sharp jaw, rarely smiling.

Kevin nodded. 'If Pyotr was unarmed and Nino had a gun,' he said, 'Pyotr would still easily win.'

'Speak of the devil,' I said, as George, Nino and Pyotr wandered in, accompanied by a very pretty dark-haired woman who must have been all of about nineteen years old.

'This is Nino's girlfriend,' George explained. 'Elene. She speaks good English. They learn at school.'

The pub was starting to find some energy as other Georgians arrived and the music was cranked up. I'd been wondering about Georgian pop culture and what kind of music they were into in this part of the world and so was mildly disappointed when the very familiar early beats of Michael Jackson's 'Billie Jean' came from the sound system.

Elene seemed to be more interested in Nino than the chance to practise her language skills with two middle-aged Australians, which seemed reasonable. Nino, for his part, managed to still look threatening in a general sense while talking quietly to Elene under the music. As always, his dark metallic handgun was on the table, next to his beer and within reach of his right hand.

'*Supra*!' said George. 'But only little *supra* because we got work tomorrow.'

'What is a *supra*?' I asked.

'How Georgians feast and drink, John. Great ceremony. We not dine casual. The *tamada* in charge make the toasts. I be *tamada*. You see.'

Pyotr arrived at the table with some drinks. Firstly, of course, a round of vodka, and George led the toast in which we all toasted one another. Then we were toasted again, this time with some Georgian rosé, which he explained was a gift from another table.

We waved at a couple of men and a young woman at that table, with no idea who they were, while George went over and said something quietly to them.

When he returned, he started pouring the rosé into glasses. I noticed that he poured the wine carefully towards us, and always with his right hand.

'You have a deliberate way of pouring, George,' I said.

'Georgia take how to pour seriously, John. Never left hand. Never away from body. Very rude. Western pouring, too casual. Not cool.'

'I'll note that,' I said. 'Please remind us so that we follow the rules.'

'All good. You guests,' he smiled, then added, 'These are traditional Georgian wine. Different production technique to the west. You remember big *kvevris* at winery? Red clay? This them. See if you like it.'

We all raised our glasses and sipped. The wine was sweet, with an unusual finish. Honeyish, perhaps? A slightly oxidised, almost sherry flavour? I took another sip, getting my taste-buds acclimatised.

'It's interesting,' said Kevin.

'Does that mean you're longing for Crown Royal?' I asked him.

'Not quite but getting there,' he said.

The music had gone up another notch. Michael Jackson segued into Prince. Kevin and I huddled in to talk with George.

'An unusual day for you, yes?' George said, with his customary boyish smile and a bit of a laugh. 'You discover that the entire winery can be yours! What an honour and a delight, no?'

We both laughed. How could you not?

'We do have a few questions,' Kevin said drily.

'George,' I said. 'I never thought this trip would be boring, and you're not disappointing me on that front.'

'Look, gentlemen,' George said, spreading his hands in front of him. 'We need to play a few little games to get to the real wine. That is all. These men, these ones who talked all day, they need to believe that there is a future for them and their winery. They need to believe that you have an interest in Tbilisi and our future, beyond the wine in the bottom levels of the cellar.'

'So, the wine does exist?' Kevin said.

For the first time, George looked genuinely shocked. 'The Tsar's wine? Stalin's wine? Of course it exists, Mr Kevin.'

'Well, that's a relief,' Kevin said. 'I don't mean to be rude, but we have come a long way to only hear about the giddy potential of a rusted bottling line.'

I looked at Kevin in surprise, because he was usually a lot more diplomatic than that. I mean, hell, he's Canadian. But he was looking pleasantly at Pyotr, who, in turn, had leaned back in his chair and was giving Kevin an equally measured look, a slight smile on his face. Kevin reached for his drink and whatever was going on between them was broken.

I said, 'I think the point Kevin is trying to make, George, is that we are mildly concerned that we have already spent one day of the four days we're here and we haven't seen any physical evidence that the wine is there, let alone done the appraisals of what might be in the collection, as we need to do.'

'I understand,' George said. 'Of course I do, John. But you have to realise that the bottles you will see – and you'll see them tomorrow, I am sure,' he said, looking meaningfully at Kevin, 'they are not just bottles to the managers of the Savane Number One, or to the people of Tbilisi, for that matter.'

George looked over both shoulders to check we were not being overheard before he leaned back to us, his face earnest. 'These wines belonged to Nicholas the Second, the very last tsar of Russia! They actually belonged to Josef Stalin, the most famous Georgian to ever live! He held some of these bottles in his hands. We could not just walk in today and say, "The Australians have come to pay cash for the wine." John, you need to understand, this thing today had to happen. Those guys, Tamaz and Revaz and them, they want to do overall deal, make winery big. Not think this is Australians come to snatch wines and sell them.'

'You make it sound as though we are trying to take precious treasures from your people, George. Wasn't it you who first raised the idea of the sale with Neville?'

George laughed. 'Yes, absolutely, because who cares about the bottles? The way I see it, the French wines were bought by Russians. They mean nothing to us Georgians. They just got sent here by Stalin and now we make money and sell them. It's only Tamaz and co who we need to please.'

'But we do only want the antique wines, George. How are they going to feel when that becomes clear?'

George had lit a cigarette and held it between two fingers as he waved his hand dismissively. 'Trust me, I know these people and how to play this. I will explain that you were keen to see all the cellars tomorrow, to help decide if investment is worthy. They will get bored with all the talking and drift away. You will get the time you need with the bottles, and with Pyotr here to help you. After your time here is up, we will tell them that you are still considering the overall winery production proposal, but there is a separate potential opportunity here, to raise some much needed capital for the winery's revival by selling the wines in the cellar. They will not stand in our way.'

'Who exactly are the owners of the winery, George?' I asked. 'Neville indicated to me that it was yours, but clearly some of these other men have a share at least in the Savane Number One?'

George waved his hand again. 'They do but Neville and I have discussed this. When the time comes, I will move to buy their shares, then we start to shift the wines. You not need to worry about that. Just be polite, smile and shake their hands for now. I promise I will clear the way for to look at the wines in the cellar as soon as I can.'

'Okay,' I said, giving Kevin a glance. 'That would be a relief. We're very aware of the short amount of time we have here.'

'It is short,' said George, 'but not so short we cannot share a vodka.'

On command, Pyotr stood and went to the bar, eventually returning with a large bottle of vodka and small shot glasses. It was not what we needed, still less than twenty-four hours off the plane and with jet lag ever present. But George was pouring.

'Time for another toast, my friends. To our future success.'

'I'll drink to that,' Kevin said. 'I mean, it might be as close as we get.'

WHEN IS A WINE TOO GOOD TO BE TRUE?

In a lot of ways, forging antique wine has the potential to be the perfect crime.

Graphic design programs such as Photoshop can easily replicate a label, especially from 100 years ago when labels were less 'designed'. Paper can be aged so that the label looks worn and damp and as though it's been lying in a cellar for decades.

Many potential purchasers of an old bottle would unlikely be expert enough to truly understand the most subtle differences of the shape, type of glass, or other telltale idiosyncrasies of a winery's product from fifty years or more ago.

And then there's the wine itself. Very few would know what a wine should taste like after so many years. One of the things I've always loved about wine and been fascinated by is that wine is a living, breathing thing. 'When collectors do open fraudulent bottles they often lack the experience and acute sense of taste to know that they have been defrauded,' wrote Patrick Radden Keefe in *The New Yorker* in 2007. 'To begin with, even genuine old wines vary enormously from bottle to bottle. It's a living organism,' says Serena Sutcliffe, Master of Wine and head of Sotheby's international wine department. 'It moves, it changes, it evolves – and once you're into wines that are forty, fifty, sixty years old, even if the bottles are stored side by side in similar conditions, you will get big differences between bottles.'

She is right. Two bottles of the same aged wine of the same vintage can have noticeable differences. When faced with a very old wine, even a château's chief winemaker may only be able to assess that yes, that's what we would *expect* our wine to taste like after so long.

Wines can be chemically tested, for certainty, and bottles and corks can be forensically judged for authenticity, but your usual buyer of such wines doesn't have access to, or the appetite for, such measures.

Plus, the victim of a wine forgery crime is unlikely to come forward and chase the forger. There's a romance in buying old wine, a connection to the great labels of the world. But in some cases there's also often a large chunk of ego involved in paying huge prices for such wines, with no certainty of whether the wine itself is still drinkable, before you even get to the fact the treasured bottle may turn out to have been filled with something different. How embarrassing to admit that you were duped; that wildly expensive antique wines in your cellar are fake.

Look at the purchasers of the fabled Thomas Jefferson wines. In hindsight, the backstory – found in a wall in Paris, but without the address ever being shared for authentication – was sketchy at best, and the original source of the bottles, a German called Hardy Rodenstock, mysterious and unlikely. Yet a US billionaire, Bill Koch, paid US$500,000 for four of the bottles, to add to his astonishing collection of treasures, such as General Custer's rifle. Did he intend to open the bottles? I doubt it. Like a hunter keeping the heads of kills on the wall, many collectors like Koch, it seems to me, may just amass trophies as a symbol of their wealth and business success. Even when the Jefferson bottles were proven to be fake, Koch kept them on display. 'I used to brag that I got the Thomas Jefferson wines,' he told a reporter. 'Now I get to brag that I have the fake Thomas Jefferson wines.'

It would be reasonable to then turn to the auction house that facilitated the sale. Shouldn't it have authenticated the wine before offering it to the buying public? Well, yes, but some forgers will build strong relationships for years with the sellers, or the paper trail will appear convincing enough to satisfy an auction house, especially one that is – how to put it? – a little too comfortable? Asleep at the wheel? Auction houses can receive a healthy seller's percentage from antique wine sales, so they'd like the wines to be real. I wonder if that nagging question in the back of the mind is overpowered by the financial benefit of a sale going through and no questions being asked?

But even if an auction house is sharp, and alert, and looking for anomalies, the task of definitively confirming a wine is authentic can be difficult.

With bottles a century old, you rely on wineries having kept meticulous records of each harvest's production. You need to consider the state of the wider world at the time. During wars in the nineteenth century, for example, the best glass was often diverted for military use, meaning lesser-quality glass and different-shaped bottles were used for some of the French wines back then.

As Kevin and I arrived in that cellar in Tbilisi, to discover seemingly endless rows of supposedly antique wines, covered in moisture and thick cobwebs, labels deteriorated clean off most of the bottles, all of these thoughts were swirling in our minds. Could the Georgians have faked bottles on this scale? Could they have done the work required to forge an entire cellar, along with the cellar book, dates on the corks and Nicholas II's crest on the French bottles created specifically for him? Were they only showing us a small percentage of the bottles which might be real, banking on us assuming all the others were therefore also real, as we handed over US$1 million?

Given the fantastic (in every sense of the word) story of the wine belonging to the last Tsar and then Stalin, I walked into the cellar acutely aware that this could all be a grand fraud by these potentially shady Georgian players.

The cellar was going to have to work very hard to prove my scepticism wrong.

9

THE CELLARS

The only good thing about jet lag is that it often sees you awake far earlier than you need to be, which is handy if you are trying to plan a huge day of antique wine analysis in a foreign country, in a cellar you've never visited, with a support crew who don't speak your language.

I was out of bed before 5 am, checking and double-checking I had everything I needed to be productive in whatever time period we were going to be given to make judgements on this alluring yet so far untouchable wine treasure.

I was counting the spare batteries for the lights for maybe the third time when my phone rang. It was just after 6 am, Georgian time, which made it roughly noon in Australia. I figured it was probably Kevin, also awake, as I answered. But no.

'John?' said a voice down a crackly international line. 'This is Neville. I just wanted to see how you guys were going over there.'

'Neville! Thanks for calling. You were certainly right about this place being the wild west,' I said.

'How does the wine look? Is it all there?'

I pondered briefly if Kevin's fear that the rooms might be bugged had foundation. Did it matter? All I wanted to do was emphasise why we were in Tbilisi, but George's words of caution from last night also echoed.

'We're not sure,' I answered Neville. 'We had a frustrating day yesterday, sitting through endless meetings with all the high-level executives of the winery, and we didn't actually lay eyes on the antique wines. I'm hoping and assuming that today will change that. In fact, if you felt like calling George to emphasise how important it is that we be allowed to spend some time in the cellars, that could be very helpful.'

'I'll see what I can do,' Neville said. 'So, you don't have a read yet on what the bottles are worth?'

'That's kind of difficult when we haven't actually seen that the bottles even exist,' I said.

'Oh, they're there, all right,' Neville said. 'I didn't invest in this to give you a holiday.'

We both laughed. 'Well, we've only been here a bit over twenty-four hours, but I can see the attraction of Tbilisi. It's a fascinating town.'

'Is George treating you well?'

'He goes missing occasionally and he's playing a mysterious game with some other men who apparently have a share of the winery, but yes, he's looking after us.'

'That's good. Doing business in Georgia is a tricky endeavour, John. I warned you. It will be okay. George knows what we're about.'

'Well, if you do get a chance to call and remind him, I'd appreciate it.'

'As soon as we hang up,' he said. 'Have you had a bath yet?'

That stopped me. 'Um, I have had a couple of showers.'

Neville laughed down the line. 'That's not what I meant. You haven't experienced the real Tbilisi yet but that's okay. You've got a few more days. Talk soon.'

Nino's driving out to the winery was maybe even more hair-raising than the day before. At one point, a police car siren started wailing behind us and Nino frowned into his rear-view mirror but roared on.

'You're not going to stop for the police?' I asked.

Nino waved an arm, hurtling along a suburban street at roughly 100 kph. 'Why should we? The police should know better than to pull me over! Am I man who stops for the police?'

Kevin and I exchanged looks, trying not to be white-knuckled in the back seat. But Nino seemed to be right. After a minute or so, the police turned off the siren and then dropped away. One law for some, one law for others in Tbilisi. Nino seemed to be in the protected bracket.

Somehow we arrived alive, just in time to be ushered back into Mr Tamaz's office for another round of winery discussions.

'Did Neville call you?' I asked George as he greeted us.

'Who?' he said.

'Neville, from Australia.'

'Neville? He's here?'

'No, did he telephone you?'

'When?'

'It's okay, George. Never mind.'

With a sinking feeling, we took our usual places around the T-shaped table and, sure enough, we had an hour or so of monologues about the future potential of the Savane in particular and Georgian wine in general, according to George's occasional translations. I was shifting around in my seat in frustration, unable to even pace, and thinking of ever-more expansive ways to torture George when he finally spoke up, saying something to Tamaz that made the older man bark at George, waving his arms in anger.

'What's happening?' Kevin asked Pyotr.

'George just suggested it might be worth letting you into the cellar, to assess the value of the bottles there, but Mr Tamaz doesn't want you to look at the collection. He's worried you might touch one of the bottles.'

Revaz picked up a phone and dialled a number, said something briefly, and hung up. Everybody sat silently and then Tamaz and

George started debating again. Kevin and I looked at one another as the Georgians bickered in front of us.

Grigol appeared with a big wad of paper in the shape of a loosely bound book. He walked over to the desk we were sitting behind and laid it out. Kevin and I leaned over the pages and saw it was the original cellar book. The list we'd been given by Harry in Sydney had clearly been translated from this, but this one was in meticulously scripted Georgian language, that weird cross of Arabic and maybe Latin with curves, serifs and flourishes.

We carefully turned the pages, noting dates where we could, and wondering how we were supposed to make any sense from it.

Revaz came over and picked up the book, handing it back to Grigol, who immediately left the office again. Then Revaz turned and said something to us in Georgian, hands spread.

Pyotr said, 'Mr Revaz says you've seen the cellar book and you know the collection is there, you saw the modern bottles yesterday, so now you don't need to see anything else.'

I said, 'Do we need to answer that?'

George had started speaking and so Pyotr said quietly, 'No, I'd just let George handle it right now.'

Tamaz was now into another monologue, with pointing fingers and occasional waving for emphasis.

George turned to us, shook his head slightly in exasperation, and said, 'Mr Tamaz is making the point that the Georgian wines in the cellar are national treasures. Mr Tamaz says these wines are so important that we couldn't possibly let two Australians look at them or try to assess their worth or value.'

'George . . .' I said.

But George shook his head, smiled slightly and said in English, 'The "national treasure" speech is an aboriginal tradition, John. You know, in Georgia, you see a dog shit on the street, nobody wants to know about it. But as soon as someone says it important and tries to pick it up, it's a fucking national treasure.'

Mr Tamaz had watched this exchange in English and started asking questions of George, in Georgian. George raised a hand to silence him and apparently said something succinct and definitive, because Tamaz stopped talking as though George had pointed a gun at him.

'What did George say?' Kevin whispered.

Pyotr said quietly, 'George said if you can't see the wine right now, you're walking out, heading to the airport and won't discuss any investment in the winery for another second.'

'Wow, the truth!' I said. 'What are the chances that could work?'

Revaz didn't look happy. Tamaz looked even grumpier. They murmured among themselves and then seemed to come to a decision. There was some nodding and Tamaz shrugged and Revaz stood. As if by magic, Grigol, the cellar manager, appeared in the doorway.

George also stood with a slight smirk and said to us brightly, 'John and Kevin, Mr Tamaz thinks it would be a good idea for me to show you the cellars. There are some remarkable old, big old wines in the second and third floors of the cellars and I have mentioned that you probably would like to see them for sure.'

'At last. Well done, George,' I said.

I turned to Kevin and, poker-faced, asked, 'Are you up for that, Kevin, or would you rather wait here?'

'No, I think I'll come. It would be nice to stretch my legs,' he replied, equally poker-faced. George completely missed the exchange, but Pyotr grinned. It seems our Chechnyan military man got the Australian sense of humour.

Mr Tamaz led the way as we went back out to the courtyard and over to the taller main building, with the arches. Several people we didn't know joined us, so it was a party of ten as we went inside. One of them, Ivane, would become a regular assistant to us over the next few days. A woman we hadn't seen before, in a green cardigan, used a set of keys to open a large door leading underground, and then stepped aside so we could all walk down a narrow flight of steps to the first floor of the cellars, with all the unremarkable modern bottles, where we'd been allowed to peer around yesterday. Grigol headed across the landing and opened a door hidden in shadows that revealed wider steps, leading further down. He found a light switch and a weak globe illuminated the stairs as we all trooped down.

It was hard to fit so many people into the small space at the bottom of the stairs. Revaz looked around, as though he had no idea where the light switch was, until Grigol stepped over to an alcove and flicked on several rows of dim overhead lights. The cellar lit up.

And there they were. The bottles.

The cobwebs were intense in all directions, endless white strands of thick webbing completely covering entire racks of bottles that were otherwise dark and gleaming. It felt like the room should be full of dust but actually, as Neville had promised, the cellar was almost wet, the air heavy with moisture, which the wine lover part of my brain instantly recognised as good news for the chances of the corks still being in working condition in 100-plus-year-old bottles.

Most of the racks were tall, made of nondescript grey metal, apart from one separate unit of five shelves in front of us which appeared to host spirits and other jars and bottles, not wines.

Kevin was taking a few steps here, a few steps there, seemingly browsing the room with no real purpose, but I knew him well enough to see the calculator in his brain working overtime. Missing nothing. I watched as he tilted his head slightly and scratched his chin, looking up and down the closest of the main racks, and I could almost hear his internal thought track: 'A width of two bottles of wine, with one bottle stacked from each side. Maybe twenty bottles of wine high and how far into the darkness? Even if the horizontal count is 100 per rack that makes 2000 bottles per side, per rack.'

As our eyes adjusted to the gloom, we could make out the shelves disappearing towards the back of the cellar, and in one corner a tangle of broken metal and glass where shelves had collapsed, smashing who knew how many potentially valuable bottles. From what Harry, Neville and George had told us, there were several such collapsed racks, with maybe 20,000 bottles destroyed. Yet maybe 40,000 total bottles remained, in this enormous and damp underground cavern. I had to take a moment. All these bottles.

A couple of the mysterious winery workers who had joined us wandered back up the stairs while Kevin and I walked the aisles between racks. As warned, many of the bottles no longer had labels, or the label that was left was just a fragment of the original. I would have loved to have pulled out the torch from my bag but I was aware of Tamaz and Revaz's ongoing hostility to the idea of us making ourselves too familiar with the wines at this stage. I didn't want to appear to have come suspiciously prepared.

While Kevin was carefully brushing spiderwebs off some bottles, trying to see what kind of wine it was and how full the bottles were, I pondered the enormous task of matching these endless shelves to the translated list that Harry had initially sent me of the original cellar book.

But as I stood there, I also became aware of one thought fighting its way to the surface of all my impressions of the cellar. If this *was* all a giant con, designed to rob us of US$1 million, I thought, looking around, it was an incredibly elaborate one. These spiderwebs and the soaked-in dampness of the cellars felt very real. These wines felt very much as though they'd authentically been lying here for fifty-plus years. And how could anybody fake-fill this many bottles, even with the inexplicably large workforce of this dormant winery? To be honest, it felt deeply like the most genuine old cellar I had ever visited, an absolute relic of a bygone era. Nevertheless, I tried to remain focused, looking for any sign of deceit.

But as I pondered these logistics, Mr Revaz appeared out of the gloom, carrying a damp, dark bottle. He had a lazy gait, like an old man or somebody who wasn't very active, so that he sort of lurched out of the darkness, reminding me of an old vampire film.

I glanced at Kevin, to see if he had also been startled, but he was looking intently and exclusively at the bottle in Revaz's hands.

The chief winemaker said, in a surprisingly passable attempt at French pronunciation: '1899 Château Suduiraut.'

'That is a good wine,' said Kevin.

I took a moment to savour this scene. Look at us, I thought, Kevin and I from Sydney, standing in a dimly lit cellar in Tbilisi, Georgia, a place we could not have visited a decade before because of world politics. But here we were, apparently surrounded by tens of thousands of bottles that individually I would have been stunned to see in my lifetime, let alone all together in one cellar. An 1899 Château Suduiraut? A 100-year-old Sauternes from one of the great producers of France? This was a bottle that you might see at Christie's or Sotheby's auction houses, or maybe behind solid glass at the château itself. Worth maybe tens of thousands of dollars. To have Revaz wander along the shelves and just pick one up, from among how many others that might also be there, felt truly incredible. Yet maybe it was real? Could these cobwebs have been faked? Could this entire thing have been set up? It just didn't feel possible.

And, hell, I so wanted it to be real. Because if it was real, I was standing in the middle of history. Nicholas II! These wines that may carry his seal might have actually been held in his hands. And what of the wines that Stalin had reportedly added to the collection? Was this Suduiraut one of them? Had Josef Stalin brought this wine from France? Tasted it, decided he liked it? Or had it been in St Petersburg during the Revolution? Had it witnessed the Nazi advance and felt itself smuggled by night out of the Russian capital, to Georgia? Lugged down those big steps into this secret place. Sitting here, breathing quietly in its bottle, for more than fifty years, wondering what was happening on the surface, up above. Patiently sitting in its rack as the world turned, with epic battles to decide the world war, feeling the faint tremors of Hiroshima and Nagasaki, then the reordering of Europe and the Soviet bloc, plus the endless march of the west, to modern life, to man walking on the moon.

I felt almost overcome. This bottle wasn't just a bottle of wine, it was a piece of history. And its value took on a life of its own in my head. How much would you pay at a major auction house for an 1899 Suduiraut? But how much more if you knew that it had belonged to the personal collection of Josef Stalin, or the last tsar, had survived so much Russian history, had this incredible backstory in a remote Georgian winery? What was all that worth?

I was still wrestling these questions, taking it all in, as Mr Revaz shifted the bottle from his right hand to his left and I could sense the instability of the slippery, wet glass in his hands.

I watched as the chief winemaker, supposedly the king of this world, mishandled the bottle and dropped it.

The bottle plunged to the floor and broke.

10

A TASTE OF HISTORY

I've been around wine, and fine wine, for many years and have instinctive muscle memory when I see gravity take hold of an expensive bottle of wine.

Even in the brief moment of the Château Suduiraut falling, I began to move, and while I couldn't stop the bottle hitting the hard stone floor, I got my foot under it, trying to break its fall. Then I scooped the bottle up, like a good slips fieldsman in cricket, so that I saved the wine that was in the still intact bottom half of the bottle.

Holding what was left in my hands, I could see that the bottle indeed still had a partial label and it was definitely the Suduiraut, one of the great Sauternes. Revaz looked bright red with embarrassment, even in the gloom, and everybody was speechless.

We all stared at one another until Kevin smiled and said, 'That was a brilliant idea, Mr Revaz! We would not have dreamed of being so rude as to ask you to open a bottle, but now we can taste some wine.'

Pyotr translated and Revaz smiled with relief, ignoring glares from Tamaz. George boomed his big laugh and agreed it was wonderful that we could try the Suduiraut. I watched for signs that anybody was nervous that we were about to test an allegedly century-old classic.

Grigol and Pyotr got busy, finding some tumblers and a bottle of water, to wash them. They used some cloth to dry the glasses and

I took over to strain the remaining wine from the broken bottle through the cloth and into a jug, in case shards of glass had found their way into the liquid.

I peered at the wine that was now lying in the jug. It was a deep golden colour, even in the gloomy light.

Kevin and I gave each other a look as Grigol poured each person a small serving of the Sauternes. This was the moment that would give us a pretty good idea if this entire venture was vindicated or for nothing. Was this the real thing? Excitement and wonder or shattering disappointment?

I was handed my tumbler and put it to my nose, breathing in. God, it smelt wonderful.

I swirled the liquid and then smelt it again. A hint of a very delicate apricot character and lovely richness.

I closed my eyes and took a sip.

The Suduiraut had a silky fineness with shades of the apricot that I had detected. Oh wow. It had retained some fine acidity, wonderful harmony and gorgeous Sauternes sweetness. The wine was elegant, almost ethereal. It was magnificent.

The wine was superb but the orchestra was deafening. I had to pause as my head was almost exploding with the delight of the exceptional wine and what this might mean. If I was serious about this venture before, I was doubly so now.

Kevin was writing a note in his book and I took a few steps so that I could read it from over his shoulder. He'd written: 'Exceptional apricot, quince character, finesse, very alive'. Because I was there, he underlined the 'very alive'.

I stepped back and took another sip of the 1899 gem. Kevin and I were determined to remain poker-faced, in the art of the bigger deal, but we found a moment to lock eyes.

It had to be real.

The 1899 Château Suduiraut was outstanding and surely had to be genuine. Did that mean that the entire cellar might be legitimate?

I'm not sure a wine has ever tasted so good.

And I still don't know if it was the spectacular wine itself, or the moment and its significance, that gave it that power.

Either way, I enjoyed that glass.

Tamaz and Revaz seemed to have loosened up as George spoke to them, occasionally pointing at us, and finally the executives trooped back up the stairs, leaving us, Pyotr, Grigol, George and Ivane alone in the cellar.

'What did you say, George?' I asked.

'I said you had to take some notes and make some assessments of individual bottles, and it might take some time,' George said. 'I indicated it would probably need several hours but it would be wonderful if they could stay to assist you and be available if required. Or, I then suggested, Pyotr, Ivane and I could do that for them if they were busy. And they looked big relieved and left immediately.'

He laughed his happy chuckle.

'I also am going to leave now,' he said. 'I have some urgent matters to fix but will be back for lunch. You can finally look at your precious wine, John. Please try not break anything, despite the fine example of my colleagues moments ago.'

We all laughed and then George left. We huddled around the cellar book. Grigol stood by, waiting.

I showed Pyotr our version of the cellar book, translated into English, although we weren't sure who by. I explained that what we would like to do is try to find select wines out of the racks, to see if the cellar book and our translated list were accurate about the contents of the cellar. We wanted to see if the bottles in specific racks matched what was written down.

He understood and spoke to Grigol in Georgian, consulting the book. Watching the body language of the conversation was funny, because it was clear that Grigol was trying to explain how the book worked without any real idea of how the book worked, and Pyotr was gradually picking up the system on his own.

Kevin got involved and there was a lot of cross-language debate and finger-pointing, with Pyotr heading to a nearby rack to look at the markings, numbering etc. and then returning to the book to find the same details. After maybe twenty minutes, he and Kevin seemed to have cracked the system and even Grigol looked cheered that the book made sense.

The four of us worked our way through shelves five to twenty-six, categorising the wines as dry or sweet or by label if one existed, just generally to get a feel for the wines in relation to the cellar book and our translation.

Grigol said to Pyotr that he didn't think any of the dry wines would be drinkable, which was not encouraging, but at this point, I just want to know which dry white wines existed on these ageing racks.

I felt we were finally getting our heads around the system of the racks and interpreting the book when suddenly the middle-aged woman in the green cardigan appeared from the stairs, jangling a set of keys. She said something almost harshly to Pyotr, and stood with a hand on her hip, scowling.

'Who is this, Pyotr?' I asked.

'Mrs Nana Vorobieff,' he said. 'Union lady.'

'What does she want?'

Pyotr shrugged. 'Time to lock up, she says. Union rules. Lunch-break.'

'You're kidding. We were just getting going.'

'John, we're no longer under Communist rule here but the union holds a lot of power. There are ways things are done and nobody can change it. Believe me. Nana here has the keys to the cellars and she won't let us stay.'

Kevin looked confused. 'She has the keys?'

'Yes, the only set,' Pyotr said.

'Not Grigol or Revaz?'

'No, Nana. She is the union representative.' Pyotr said more quietly, 'It's in our interests to keep her happy, if we want to get back in here without fuss.'

And so we found ourselves in Nino's mafia staff car, racing through Tbilisi to another restaurant by the river, where Nino of course parked across a pedestrian crossing at the front door. George hadn't reappeared from wherever he'd gone, so it was just Kevin, me, Pyotr and Nino, who ate quickly and then excused himself and went to another table where three other similarly swarthy and dangerous-looking characters sat – all, naturally, with their handguns on the table.

Pyotr's presence meant Kevin and I couldn't really discuss the morning, the wine we'd tasted or where we were at. We tried to make small talk and enjoyed the food but I was dying to get back into that cellar. As soon as we could, we pushed back our chairs and headed for the Savane Number One.

It was hard to sneak back into the winery without alerting Tamaz and the other executives, especially when Nino locked up the brakes on the gravel drive and slid to a stop, giving the powerful engine one final loud rev.

Maybe they were all still at lunch because the executive offices remained quiet as we almost crept back into the main building and into the foyer where the union lady used her exclusive keys to unlock the door to the cellars.

Even Grigol wasn't around, which meant Kevin, Pyotr, Ivane and I were able to really get to work. Finally, I was able to pull the bank of lights out of my bag, the notepaper and pens, a camera with flash and the other equipment we'd carefully packed.

The pre-lunch analysis had done its job. Pretty quickly, we were able to work out a system of validation.

I had our translated Sydney list and would pick out a wine. In fact, still curious about the fact Revaz had been able to just go and pluck out a bottle of 1899 Château Suduiraut that morning, I started with that one. 'Shelf one,' I said to Pyotr. 'Château Suduiraut, 1899. How many bottles do you have?'

Pyotr examined the cellar book, found the first shelf and located the 1899 Suduiraut, with a little help from Kevin. 'Yes, it's number thirteen wine on shelf one. There are twenty-nine bottles,' he said, returning to the original cellar book.

I'd been careful not to tell him how many bottles my list said there should be, but sure enough, the figure was thirty bottles. Now minus one, as of this morning.

'Okay,' I said. 'Can you please show us those bottles, Pyotr? Point them out to us.'

'Here,' he said, stepping back and pointing. 'It starts here,' he indicated a point, 'and ends here.'

Sure enough, there were identical bottles between those two points. Kevin, Pyotr and I counted twenty-nine – so it would have been thirty, as listed, before one bottle was unfortunate enough to end up in the clumsy mitts of 'Magic Hands' Revaz earlier that day.

Kevin and I carried a couple of the bottles carefully to the table where we'd set up the lights. We took photos with the fluorescent lights behind the bottles in order to see the level of fill. In bottles this old, it would be normal for some of the wine to have evaporated or leaked, but these ones were up to the base of the neck, which is exceptional for a 100-year-old wine. Assuming they were the real thing, their corks were still doing their job after exactly a century.

We carried them back to rack 1. A few of the bottles we hadn't taken still had mostly intact labels on them, if badly deteriorated. We could clearly make out the words, though, or enough to discern 'Ch Suduiraut 1899'.

Kevin and I didn't know how long we would have in the cellar before Nana would come jangling her keys or the executives would appear and usher us out. George was still nowhere to be seen, but that was okay because Pyotr was both helpful and smart.

We decided we had better try to get to the really important bottles, but we had to be a little subtle about it, as I was sure our interests and activities would be reported back to management.

Having used our system now on a few bottles, I ran my finger down my list, seemingly randomly stabbed my finger on a line, and said casually to Pyotr, 'Shelf fifteen, Pyotr. Is there a Château Ikem?'

Pyotr peered at the book, ran his finger down the columns, and said, 'Yes, Ikem is number forty-four wine. It's 1847, and there are three bottles.'

Man, that's exactly what I've got, I thought to myself, trying to maintain my poker face and not to show any anticipation.

'Could you get those bottles for us, please, Pyotr?' I said.

Kevin was paying close attention, watching silently, as Pyotr went to the shelf, checked the numbers and where the bottles lay, then clambered onto a stool, and carefully extracted three bottles, carrying them to the table in front of the lights. I was willing Pyotr to please not drop any of these three!

We gazed at them. The level of fill was high-shoulder in one, mid-shoulder in the next and almost mid-shoulder in the third. That seemed about right and was actually quite encouraging for bottles of such a grand age. There was a chance they had been recorked at some stage, although by whom I couldn't begin to guess. But maybe not. None of them had labels but the shape of bottle looked correct for a 150-year-old Château d'Yquem and they were the right colour. At first pass, they certainly looked genuine. I tried to look casual as I took a photo.

Kevin and I hadn't exchanged a word but we didn't need to. We both knew a single bottle of 1847 Yquem, one of the best vintages from the nineteenth century of one of the world's absolute greatest wines, had recently sold for US$75,000. (In 2014, a bottle of 1847 Yquem became the most expensive wine ever sold in the United States and the most expensive white wine ever sold worldwide. Today, a bottle of 1847 Yquem, if you could find one and it was genuine and it was in an acceptable condition, may cost in excess of US$200,000.)

We were looking at three. Potentially three-fifths of the price of the entire cellar, in a trio of label-free bottles.

'Great, thanks, Pyotr,' I said breezily. 'Let's carefully put them back and move on.'

Taking a deep breath that the three great bottles had been checked without any hiccup, I calmly went back to my list and asked Pyotr and Kevin to find a wine on the number nine shelf that was spelled 'Heresbrin' in the translation that I held.

I didn't give Pyotr any more information, or clues. He turned a few pages and frowned at the cellar book, consulted with Kevin, and finally said, 'Ah yes, it's wine number seven and there are eight bottles.'

It was extraordinary how precise whoever had put the cellar book together had been. My list matched exactly what Pyotr was telling me. He went to the rack, worked out their position and got the bottles. We took photos of wine number seven from shelf nine. Eight bottles of red wine, unlabelled, with a few tufts of label left here or there.

Kevin was standing next to me and said quietly, 'Haut-Brion?'

'That's what I'm thinking,' I said.

Kevin tilted one of the bottles and we could see the wine inside and importantly, thanks to our lights, the colour. It was a brownish brick red, which fitted this château at this age. They could absolutely be 1889 Château Haut-Brion. I would have adored to open one and taste it.

Kevin said quietly, 'Ka-ching.'

'Pyotr, can you have a look in your cellar book at shelf number two, please?' I said. 'There's a wine there from 1909 and it's down on my list as "Clatesterne". Can you find it and tell me how many bottles you have and what size, if it's on your list?'

I had intentionally selected a wine that was not an obvious one; if these wines were fake, this was a more obscure one to have perfected the look and feel of. But Pyotr didn't blink, went to shelf number two in his book, found the wine and, heading to the actual shelf, examined the bottles and said, 'Yes, there it is. I've got something like that at position number 102 and there are thirteen bottles.'

'Is that so?' I said, trying to sound slightly bored. 'Well, let's have a look at it, just to be thorough.'

He pulled out the thirteen bottles and they took their place in front of the lights.

The bottles looked exactly right to be the great second growth Château Cos d'Estournel. They had the red capsule over the top of the bottle and the end of the cork that would be correct for that maker, assuming that had also been the case so long ago. So they had the capsule and the right shape and look of a Bordeaux bottle, if only bits of labels.

A single bottle of the 1909 vintage being worth, well, hard to say, but certainly some thousands, if it was a genuine Cos. And here were thirteen bottles.

It was about here that Kevin gave me a look, as though to say, 'This is very impressive.'

I had been trying everything to find a flaw in the system, any kind of sign that this whole thing may have been a fraud. Kevin, of course, had an even sharper eye, missing nothing as he looked for fakes or holes in their system. But we'd been at it now for a few hours and had yet to find a single thing that flew in the face of what was becoming the otherwise overwhelming evidence that maybe this was all genuine.

Still poker-faced, we had Pyotr find a '1919 Margot' in the cellar book and then on the shelves. This is one of my favourite wines, a Château Margaux: one of the first growth classics, the epitome of charm in Bordeaux. Again, it checked out, looking exactly how the bottle should look. We also inspected several vintages of Yquem, just because we couldn't quite believe we were in a room with so much century-old or even older Yquem.

It wasn't particularly extraordinary that the English list I had matched the Georgian cellar book, because it was merely meant to be a translation of the original document. What we found remarkable was that the wines on the shelves matched exactly the list I'd been given. They were all there, intact, apart from the bottle Revaz had dropped. We couldn't fault the list or the apparent authenticity of the bottles we were selecting and inspecting.

Kevin had been watching like a hawk how the shelving system worked, how the numbers worked, how Pyotr was finding the wines from the book, and he told me that everything looked to be completely in order.

Meanwhile, Pyotr had finally become bored with playing fetch with ancient wines and wandered away to light a cigarette. He then casually took from a shelf what turned out to be a probably very valuable Portuguese port that was more than 100 years old, found a corkscrew and unceremoniously pulled the cork. We stared briefly, unable to believe how cavalier he was about it, and then dived for tumblers to taste the port. It was superb.

Importantly for us, it tasted exactly how you would hope a century-old port would taste. It tasted genuine.

We'd had a good few hours, but I was still concerned on a few fronts as we savoured the port. George was still missing in action, and Pyotr had no idea where he was, beyond 'on business'. I was slightly irritated that George was not around and had not shown any sign of giving me a promised extra list of Stalin's personal library of wines.

Nevertheless, at least I felt we were finally up close and personal with the wines and how the cellar worked, authenticating some of the important bottles. We were making headway in validating our list and the contents of the cellar. We decided to press on while we could.

However, the Georgians had other plans. It was mid afternoon when we heard footsteps on the stairs and the executives filled the room. Tamaz and Revaz were there, and Grigol was back, chatting with Pyotr, who clearly explained what he had been doing, as he pointed to the cellar book and indicated the wines.

Tamaz looked at our lights and other equipment but didn't seemed concerned. Instead, he said something to Pyotr, who explained to us that Mr Tamaz would like us to join him in his office to taste a selection of the fine, old Georgian wines from the collection.

This was no small thing, because of the estimated 40,000 bottles in this cellar, our list suggested that up to half of them might be the local produce. While we reluctantly packed up our equipment, knowing that Nana of the Keys – or 'the Union Lady' as Pyotr called her – would almost certainly be along to lock the door to the cellars before we could come back, we were also keen to have a taste of the Georgian bottles to see if they were still alive and whether they would be a genuinely valuable part of the potential purchase, or simply a waste of time and energy.

The cellar book said the Georgian wines were mixed through parts of shelves five to twenty-six and Kevin suggested we pick a selection of the local wines, particularly where there was a quantity of bottles. We chose old reds, old whites, and some sweet wines. The Georgians were amenable and collected everything we requested to carry up to the surface and across the courtyard to Tamaz's office.

Revaz began opening bottles and Kevin murmured to me, 'That guy is a butcher with a corkscrew.'

It was as we were waiting to be served the first wine that George suddenly appeared, with a big smile and a hearty query into how we were, how our day was going, and whether we were having a productive time. No word of explanation of why he'd been missing all day or any hint of an apology. Just his big laugh and a clap on the back as though we were old friends, reunited at last. Zurab, as always, at his back.

I should have been annoyed but there was something about George that was impossible not to warm to. He was such a likeable rogue, a bear of a man and so happy the whole time that you just found yourself smiling along with him. Having said that, these were all traits that made the wary businessman in me uncomfortable in believing all that he said, as I continued to look for possibilities of an underhanded play. And I was 100 per cent sure that my travelling companion's antenna was tuned even more intently to see through the bonhomie for anything fraudulent. Yet again I was grateful that I had Kevin along as an expert second pair of eyes and ears.

Maybe it was the opening of bottles that drew a crowd but even the marketing guy, Davit, turned up.

Kevin and I were more focused on the wines. Given Georgia's many-thousand-year history of wine production, our first taste of genuine Georgian aged wine was no small matter.

The first one offered was from shelf six, wine number five. It was listed as a Tsinandali, from 1978, making it twenty-one years old at the time. We peered at the liquid in our glasses. While it was a white wine, it had almost a greeny-brown colour to it. We sniffed it and I thought it was not unlike an aged Chenin Blanc: almost a sweaty, sheep's wool sort of nose. Kevin and I gave each other a small smile, enjoying the adventure, and then took a sip.

'Clean palate,' I said to Kevin.

He nodded, and added, 'Good acidity, too. A sort of almond nut character.'

'Yes,' I said. 'And it develops a sort of honey nose and palate with the air.'

Kevin gave a slight shrug. It was okay, but nothing remarkable, especially from an international sales perspective.

We moved on to shelf number seven, wine number six. 'A Napareuli,' Revaz informed us solemnly.

It was another white wine but this time had a brownish colour, almost like weak Chinese tea. There was a hint of honey on the nose, but not very distinct. I took a sip and tasted nutty flavours again but they faded quickly on the palate. Whatever this wine once was, it was past its best.

Tamaz obviously picked up our vague lack of enthusiasm because he barked something at Revaz, who reached for a new wine, number twenty-two, from shelf number twenty-one. This was a red, another Tsinandali apparently, from 1945. The colour was exceptional, especially for a fifty-four-year-old wine, but as soon as we smelt and tasted it, we could tell it was corked. It was a pity. I would have liked to have seen that wine in its prime.

Tamaz and the others also registered that the wine was corked, so there was a slight edge of rising tension as Tamaz asked Revaz to pour shelf twenty, wine number three, which George announced was a Kvareli, a red wine from 1949. Again, the colour was great but the wine was corked. I wandered out from my spot behind the desk and looked at the bottles Revaz was pouring from. Generally the corks looked shorter than usual and of questionable quality. There was a good chance, if they were standard Georgian corks, as I imagine most were, that a number of these bottles were going to be undrinkable, and therefore unmarketable.

But Tamaz and co weren't beaten yet. Revaz poured wine number eight from shelf number twenty-four, and it was announced as a dessert wine from 1932. 'A Khikhvi,' George said, raising his glass. 'Very old, very beautiful. Like my mother, God rest her soul. Well, actually, she's alive.'

We all laughed dutifully and tasted the Khikhvi, and finally we had a real wine in our glass. It was a superb fortified wine, very much like port, and extremely alive despite its age. Kevin's eyes gleamed.

Opting for a port, which was more likely to have held its ground against the years, had been a good idea. Tamaz looked pleased with himself and his wines, now that we had enthusiastically greeted the 1932 Khikhvi.

Revaz moved on to some of the wines in ceramic pots, the 1000-plus-year-old local tradition. Shelf number four, wine number two, was another Tsinandali, from 1920, a dry white. It had a yellow tea colour with a sherry nose and a hint of honey caramel. This was promising and I took a sip. The palate was light, almost tasting like butterscotch.

'What do you think?' I asked Kevin.

'Interesting,' he said. 'Actually, it's pretty outstanding for a seventy-seven-year-old white wine.'

'Normal, we drink from horn,' George said.

'A horn?' I asked.

'Oh, yes. A *kantsi*. Can be big, lots of wine. Even better than a *deda-khelada* for serving the very good *ghvino*,' he said.

'Okay, I'll bite. What's a *deda-khelada*?' Kevin asked.

'It mother-jug,' George said and smiled as he saw our reactions. 'I am serious. It big jug with little jugs on side, like many breasts.'

'Sure it is,' said Kevin. 'I'm not buying it.'

'You want to buy?' George said. 'Mother-jug very historic tradition in Tbilisi.'

Kevin looked extremely unconvinced but the banter had been productive as we were all friends now, sharing wines and laughing.

Revaz reached for the next ceramic pot. Shelf number four, wine number five, another Tsinandali, from 1945. You could feel the confidence in the room that whatever investment we were going to eventually make in the Savane Number One Winery, these old Georgian wines were pleasing the 'executives' and I'm sure in their minds adding dollars to the value of their operation.

Right up until I smelt the 1945 Tsinandali and peered at the dirty yellow colour of the wine in my glass. The wine was clearly oxidised, but I took a sip, getting a trace of honey and maybe sherry. But my face gave away my reaction to the oxidised liquid and Kevin put down his glass, saying a simple 'No.'

The Georgians lost their smiles.

We tried a few others and most were drinkable, some really good, and another couple were okay but maybe past their best. We made encouraging noises and tried to let Tamaz and co know that we really rated the good ones. George worked hard to keep the mood in the room light and happy, before ushering us out.

As I suspected, we weren't getting back into the cellars that day and so we were driven back to our hotel.

We stood at the front door, watching Nino's tail-lights hurtle around a corner and disappear. It was late afternoon and the first time

I had surfaced from being at the winery or dining with the Georgians since we'd arrived. I became aware of the jet lag still nagging at my energy levels, and how intensely I'd been concentrating from what felt like the moment we'd arrived.

'Want to get a coffee in the lobby?' I asked Kevin, but he shook his head.

'No, John, let's walk a bit. We've been sitting or standing in that gloomy cellar all day. Let's grab some fresh air and what's left of the sunlight.'

11

A STROLL THROUGH
OLD TBILISI

It was a good idea. We dropped our bags with the concierge and headed back onto the street. Kevin led the way, having worked out where the old town was on his embassy search.

And he was right, it was wonderful to actually stretch our legs and breathe in some air that wasn't from the stale cellar. We could hear the river roaring somewhere off to our right, as we watched a local mother with two young children step onto a balcony and walk past several open doors, waving to neighbours in their living rooms before reaching the door of her apartment. As we approached the centre of the old town, I could hear music somewhere up ahead, and was fascinated by the variety of shops and hole-in-the-wall food options available, most seeming to sell the *khachapuri* filled bread. Street vendors were spruiking *khinkali* dumplings and broth, and I was fascinated by what appeared to be some kind of Tbilisian milk bar, offering long vertical cones full of different flavours.

Coming from Sydney, with its multicultural population, I was struck by the uniformity of the faces on the street. I had read that Hitler thought of the Georgians as Aryan, but based on the features and hair colour of the people we passed, I couldn't see it. The shops also reflected Tbilisi's long-time fame as the meeting point of east and west, of Christianity to the west and Muslim empires to the east. I could have poked around this place for days.

Kevin even nudged me as we went past a shop selling what appeared to be clay drinking bowls, single-handed pitchers, labelled *kheladas*, and jugs shaped like animals. Kevin was laughing at a large jug right in the heart of the window display that featured several smaller jugs attached to its sides.

'I don't believe it,' I said. 'The mother-jug was real.'

'See,' Kevin said. 'These lovely Georgians would never tell us a fib.'

'Ha,' I said. 'I'm not sure I'd go quite that far just yet.'

We kept walking, and I breathed deeply. I could feel my bones starting to register that tonight was a night off and I'd be able to soak in a bath then lie in bed, undisturbed. After such a decent stint in the cellars, logging the historic wines, and even tasting that 1899 Suduiraut, I felt slightly more relaxed that we might be on track and I could let myself unwind into the task ahead.

'So, what do we deduce from that tasting?' I asked Kevin, as we mingled among the locals and looped slowly back towards our hotel.

'It was certainly an experience,' he said. 'Did you notice that Davit the marketing guy didn't taste any of the wines, apart from the excellent port?'

'No, I didn't,' I said. 'Where does he fit in? I still can't work it out.'

'I guess he fits in the same way everybody else wandering aimlessly around a dormant winery fits in,' Kevin said. 'What did you think of the actual wines, the drinkable ones?'

'You know what I found most interesting?' I said. 'Almost all of them had a slightly butterscotch or honeyish finish to them. Did you pick that up? It's a very strange character, especially once we got away from the dessert wines. I noticed it across the dry whites and even the dry reds. Some wines had no fruit character left but did have some acidity and were not oxidised, so were still sort of drinkable in a way, and they had this hint of caramel on the finish. Now I think of it, even the rosé we had last night at the hotel had hints of it.'

'No idea,' Kevin said. 'We'll have to remember to ask George or Revaz, although I'm not sure I'd necessarily trust him on much to do with the delicacies of winemaking.'

'The bigger question is with regard to the sale,' I said. 'Do the Georgian wines have any value?'

Kevin frowned as he walked, thinking on it for a while.

Finally he said, 'They were interesting but their value is questionable, really. I think it would come down to the marketing campaign by an auction house, you know? If it's a big marketing campaign and a story can be built around them as the back end of the wider collection, you could probably sell them. Old wines from the Massandra Collection sell for big money, so these might too.'

I nodded. 'Yeah, you could have a few open for tastings at the auction, especially if it's in New York or London. That would be unusual, driving publicity, and if we can have some of the better wines available to taste, it would drive sales to the more unusual Georgian varieties.'

'So they're stocking fillers, at worst,' Kevin said.

'Okay, so as part of the million-dollar sale price, we take the Georgian museum wines, but we understand that the real value is in the French masters,' I said. 'I still can't quite believe there are 217 bottles of Yquem from the 1800s and 1900s sitting in that cellar. We really have to check as many of those bottles as we can. So much of the value is tied up in that wine.'

'Agreed,' Kevin said.

We were back at the hotel and collected our bags from the concierge. We walked over and pressed the button for the elevator.

I sighed deeply. 'Man, it's been quite the day,' I said, regarding my slightly haggard-looking partner in this crazy venture.

'It sure has.' Kevin nodded. 'And now, if it's okay with you, I think I will go and die in my nondescript hotel room.'

'Do you want dinner?' I asked.

'Why don't we call each other a bit later, once we've had a rest?'

he said. 'If I don't answer, it means I've passed out properly, for the night, and I'll assume the same for you.'

'That sounds like a plan,' I said. 'I am dying for a bath and silence.'

12

SUPRA!

At about 9 pm, I was annoyed that I hadn't been able to fall into a deep sleep, having crawled gratefully into bed after a long soak in the bath. My brain had been fighting off jet lag all day but was now refusing to succumb completely to my desperate need for slumber. Instead, I kind of drifted in and out of a light doze, slightly annoyed every time I realised I had come back to the surface.

So when the phone rang next to my bed, I was half-asleep but aware enough to assume it was Kevin, proposing dinner. I lay there, midway between alertness and drowsiness. Hmm, bugger, I thought. Kevin will understand if I'm not the best company and a bit of a zombie. I may as well stagger out and grab something quick to eat, then try again to sleep.

I picked up and said, 'Kevin?'

'John!' said George's voice, booming down the receiver. 'I think it time for you to have an adventure! Kevin already on his way down. We're here to take you to nice dinner in the mountains. You ready to go?'

'Now? For the mountains?' I said.

'Yes,' said George happily. 'We show you a very good time.'

'You're downstairs in the lobby?' My brain was still catching up to reality.

'Very soon. Any minute. Leaving now. See you almost immediately,' said George, and hung up.

I lay there, blinking at the ceiling, and then rolled out of bed, got dressed and headed to the lobby. Kevin was indeed already there, in a neatly pressed polo shirt and charcoal-coloured jeans. He looked cool and unfazed, as Kevin does, as though getting unexpectedly dragged out of jetlagged sleep to be summonsed to a mystery dinner in the Georgian mountains by a bunch of gun-toting locals was just a normal Wednesday night.

'You look fresh,' he said, and I swore softly.

'Anything to keep this fantasy moving along,' he continued happily, and I shook my head but couldn't help chuckling.

Of course, George's idea of almost immediately meant Nino came swaggering through the door thirty minutes later. He did the usual gun-check at the security door, as did Zurab, who had the same scowl as Nino but with maybe 5 per cent less menace. Maybe he was a trainee thug? Nino said, 'George in car,' and jerked his head, showing the international diplomacy we had come to love him for. I found myself hoping Pyotr was coming, for his interpreter skills and because I had come to think of him as the one man besides George who might offer a genuine account of whatever was happening.

Sure enough, Pyotr waved to us from the passenger seat of a second car, as Zurab settled into the driver's seat. In the black Mercedes, we were greeted by after-hours George, in a light-blue collared shirt with a dark vest over the top. He greeted us with typical George enthusiasm, saying, 'Too much time in hotels and offices, my Australian friends! It's time we show you real Tbilisi.'

He held a bottle of vodka and poured us a glass each. Brilliant! I thought, as I raised my glass and let the alcohol wake me. When in Tbilisi . . .

The car roared through the city as usual, except that mercifully there were fewer pedestrians at this time of night.

As we drove, George leaned in and said to us, 'You like the old Georgian wines? They're the real thing, hey?'

I said, 'They appear to be, from what we've seen, George.'

'A good addition to the imported wines, yes?'

I shrugged. 'We can't really tell yet. We need to look at a lot more of them tomorrow, and we still haven't seen a list of Stalin's personal collection. We need that extra list, George.'

'No problem. It will happen,' he said, leaned back against the seat and waved a hand dismissively. 'You're going to be very happy. And we do good deal. We're all going to be very happy with good deal.'

'We're trusting you, George,' I said.

'You're right to. I make you good deal,' he laughed. 'You know what else Georgia is famous for, apart from wines?'

'Cheese bread?' Kevin guessed.

'No, much better. Amazons! Did you know the Amazons of legend live in Georgian mountains? Cut breast off so to fire arrow well, or at least, that's what they say. Fierce warrior women. Big, very beautiful.'

'Are you serious?' I asked. 'Amazon legends originated here?'

The car was slowing down.

'You don't believe,' George said, 'Just look out window. We got some Amazons of our very own, right here.'

We craned our necks to see where he was looking, outside on the street. Three girls in nightclub gear – very high heels, short skirts and black tops, with little coats over their shoulders – were waiting at a bus stop and climbed into the car as soon as Nino pulled up. They were maybe in their early twenties. One was Elene, Nino's girlfriend from the previous night, while another was introduced as George's girl, and the third was Natascha, a very attractive red-haired woman wearing a lot of make-up. If she was nervous as she said hello to two middle-aged Australians lurking in the back of a Mercedes with blacked-out windows, she didn't show it. George's girlfriend sat on my knee, to my surprise, while Natascha perched on Kevin's knee. Elene had taken the passenger seat in the front, alongside Nino.

'Cosy,' I said to Kevin.

'Very,' he said. 'All those spare seats in Pyotr's car.'

Nino took off, the second car following in convoy, and we left the city and tore through the night, into dark countryside. It occurred to me that George wasn't carrying a gun and actually never seemed to. Maybe having guys like Nino, Zurab and Pyotr around meant he didn't need to. Was there some kind of hierarchy here, in terms of potential violence and protection, that I hadn't really factored in yet? Was the second car for convenience because there were a few of us, or to keep an eye on the Merc? As I pondered all this, George's girlfriend shifted in my lap so she could kiss George on the lips. Kevin was trying to look as casual as you can with a glamorous Georgian woman sitting on top of you and asking about Sydney in surprisingly decent English. I almost laughed. Neville hadn't been kidding: Georgia was indeed the wild west.

The restaurant was high in the hills overlooking Tbilisi. We walked into a grand foyer with deep purple floor-to-ceiling curtains and large statues of heroic-looking figures, one wearing a huge coat.

'Gold,' Nino said proudly, pointing at the figure.

'The statues are gold?' I asked. They definitely looked to be made of bronze or another duller metal.

'No,' Nino shook his head. 'Coat is gold.'

'The guy in the statue is wearing a golden coat,' Kevin said carefully.

Natascha appeared and put a hand on Kevin's shoulder. 'The statues are of Jason and the Argonauts, and the golden fleece,' she explained. 'That all happened in Georgia.'

Her hand stayed on his shoulder.

'Is that right?' I said. 'The legend of Jason finding the golden fleece is set in Tbilisi?'

'Almost,' Natascha said. 'Actually, Kutaisi, another city, off to our west. But Georgia still calls itself The Land of the Golden Fleece.'

'First Amazons, now Argonauts. Georgia is full of surprises,' Kevin said, before moving subtly away from Natascha to more closely examine the statues. To watch him, you'd think he had never seen anything so fascinating as these works of art. He was still examining them as we were greeted by a man in an immaculate suit, who I assume was the head waiter, and George murmured something that clearly had an effect. The waiter looked startled but then nodded and almost bowed, as though greeting royalty, before indicating we should follow him.

The restaurant's dining room was large with tables spread generously around, so there was plenty of space between them. Six or seven tables towards the back of the room had couples or groups of four diners, talking quietly. All alone, right at the huge full-length window with the best view, several tables had been pushed together.

The waiter ushered George in that direction, with the rest of us following.

'Look at that view,' said Kevin, walking to the window. 'John, come and look at this view.'

'I can see it from here,' I said, but Kevin gave me a look.

'No, you really should see it from where I'm standing.'

I wandered over, checking none of the Georgians had followed me, but they were all settling into their seats and looking at the drinks menu.

'Wow! This *is* a lovely view,' I said loudly.

Kevin said very quietly from beside me, 'What do you think the deal is with these women?'

'I have no idea,' I said. 'They seem to be girlfriends, don't they? God, I hope they haven't been brought here for us. That's going to be an awkward discussion.'

'They wouldn't have been, would they?' he said.

I looked at the view and exhaled. 'Kevin, we really don't know the rules of this place. From Nino's lawless driving to the guns everywhere to pretty much everything else going on. I honestly wouldn't assume anything either way.'

'How do we play it?' Kevin asked, still quietly. 'Just be polite, friendly? Be vague if there are any moves made?'

'Exactly,' I said, putting a hand on his shoulder where Natascha's had been. 'Play it completely naturally, you Canadian hunk.'

Kevin carefully made his way to one end of the table, near Pyotr and Zurab, while I took the empty seat next to Natascha, with George on my other side.

Laid out below us were the lights of Tbilisi plus the huge black mass of mountains in all directions. Occasionally there were a sprinkling of lights where a small village must be perched in the foothills. The night had a half-moon which was just strong enough to reflect on the river winding through the valley and the slopes of Tbilisi far below.

'I'd love to see this view during the day,' I said to George. 'Tbilisi is really beautiful, isn't it?'

'Why would Ioseb Dzhugashvili ever want to leave?' he said. 'Apart from to be boss of Soviet Union and the world, obviously.'

'Ioseb who?' I had to ask.

'Stalin,' Kevin said. 'That was Josef Stalin's Georgian name before he headed to the big show.'

'How do you know things like that?' I asked.

Kevin shrugged and grinned. 'A life well read. Also, Pyotr mentioned it at lunch yesterday.'

'Amazing,' I said. 'You miss nothing. I thought if locals from here hadn't played for the Canadiens in the NHL, you'd have never heard of them.'

'Firstly,' Kevin said, 'I'm a Winnipeg Jets guy, and you know that, and secondly, you've probably never heard of the KHL.'

'You're right, I haven't,' I said. 'Should I have?'

'Kontinental Hockey League . . . Russian,' Nino said, sparking up. 'Very good hockey. Skill and fights!'

'You like hockey?' Kevin said, and Nino nodded enthusiastically. Who knew, pucks were the key to unlocking George's chief hard man.

Plates of meat began to arrive, along with bottles of vodka and smaller bottles of beer. Everybody relaxed and we had an excellent meal, with Nino and George posing for photos with the women, who seemed to be having a good time.

At one point, George stood and announced the meal was officially a *supra* and he was *tamada* for the evening. All the locals cheered. Kevin and I looked at one another, trying to catch up. They were the same words he'd used the night before, but now George was emphasising them much more.

'*Tamada* makes the toasts,' Natascha explained to us. 'Georgian tradition, at weddings, celebrations, occasions. He is like the dictator of the table, making jokes, agreeing to toasts and leading. There are excavations, pots and statues showing *tamada* from the seventh century. Big Georgian tradition.'

George was holding up a full glass of wine. He rattled off a long speech in Georgian but then turned to us and said, 'I just say a toast for us all, for our ancestors, for our families now, for our future descendants. I say a toast for our visitors from across the world, our Australians, for you, John and Kevin. I say a toast for our success.'

'Hard not to drink to that,' I said, and raised my glass towards him. We all drank.

And that, of course, turned out to be only the first of many toasts. Various members of the dinner party would stand and address George, who would nod and laugh and make comments that made everybody else laugh. Then he would briefly translate to us what the toast was for and why. And we'd obediently drink to whatever it was.

Between all these toasts, Natascha turned out to be good company. She said that she was at university, studying accountancy as a potential pathway to international business, and had studied English for almost a decade because she saw how vital it would be to her plans.

She said she was excited to have a native English speaker with whom to practise her language skills and so we talked about Australia and how different it was to Georgia, before I returned to the statues in the foyer, asking her about them, and she explained how the legend of Jason and the golden fleece was believed to have a basis in an ancient

Georgian tradition. Apparently, centuries ago, alluvial gold could be found in mountain rivers and was collected by using sheep fleeces. Natascha told me that the fleeces were thick enough to trap any slivers or shards of gold, while allowing the water to pass through, with the result being that the gold-seekers would end up with a sheep's fleece hopefully covered in pieces of gold.

'It might be that Apollonius, who wrote the original Greek poem, may have heard of that tradition and used it as the basis for Georgia being home to such a magnificent treasure in his story,' she said.

'What about Medea?' I asked. 'Is she based on a real Georgian woman?'

Natascha looked directly at me with a spark in her eye as she said, 'You definitely want to watch out for us Georgian women, Mr John. We can enchant any man, from Argonauts to Australians.'

I laughed and raised my glass to that and then started talking slightly faster about how great the weather had been since we arrived. Natascha sipped her vodka with an amused, almost smug expression on her face that left me quiet.

The meal wound down as the Georgians posed for photos with the women, talked more and more loudly and had several final vodka toasts, still led by George as *tamada*, to celebrate the wonderful partnership between Australia and Georgia.

I could see Kevin sharing my relief that our female companions were apparently no more than girlfriends or friends of our hosts and so we unwound and let ourselves have one more vodka toast that we probably didn't need, before we all headed for the cars and were driven back to our hotel, Georgian pop music blaring from the front seats. George and his girl had gone in Zurab's car, so it was just Kevin, Natascha and myself in the back seat of the Mercedes. She sang along to the music, dancing in her seat and smiling at me and Kevin, while occasionally leaning forward for snatches of conversation with Nino and Elene up the front.

Along the way, we stopped at a nondescript apartment building where George's girlfriend got out of the other car, giving him one long kiss before she waved and ran up the steps and inside the building. Natascha opened her door, went to the other car and got in the back seat where we could see her sit on George's lap.

We took off again, with Kevin and I laughing silently in the back seat as we approached our hotel.

We thanked Nino for the ride, got out and George and Natascha also climbed out of Zurab's car to say goodbye. Zurab and Pyotr took off, with a single wave in our direction.

'Thanks for a really fun night, George,' I said. 'Tbilisi is never boring.'

'Don't get too fond of it, Mr John,' he said. 'If you decide to move here, we would no more be international partners.'

'Fair point,' I said.

Kevin and I gave Natascha a carefully chaste kiss on the cheek and then watched Nino drive her and George off into the night, a trail of pop music fading in their wake.

'Well, so much for an early night,' said Kevin as we stood alone on the pavement. It was almost 1 am.

'I think I'm going to dream about Medea,' I said as we headed to the lobby. 'Actually, I think I'm going to dream about impossible tasks worthy of Greek mythology, like us actually getting that bottle of 1847 Yquem out of that cellar.'

Kevin laughed. 'Yes, I'm still worried enough about this whole deal that I would have been much happier if everybody hadn't used the word "fleece" quite so often tonight.'

Up in my room, I decided I was sober enough to make some phone calls. I rang Harry and then Neville, explaining that we'd finally seen some of the antique wines but were concerned we had yet to receive a list or any details of Stalin's personal collection. I asked them if they could call George and emphasise how important that was. Both promised down the echoey line that they would definitely call him before we got to the winery the next day.

Excellent. I could relax, lie back and wait for whatever the next day's games would turn out to be.

It was now hours after I had last tossed, turned and dozed in this poky hotel room before being snatched off to the mountains. I gratefully fell back into my bed, now with a full stomach and ever so slightly drunk. I had six hours until the alarm would sound.

I was deeply asleep within seconds.

13

STORMS IN THE CELLAR

Of course, when we got to the winery on day three, Nana, the Union Lady, was not there. Nobody could open the cellar.

Of course, George was missing as well. Who knew what time he and Zurab might turn up?

And it goes without saying that, of course, when George finally did arrive, fifty minutes later, he said that no, he hadn't received any phone calls from Australia, from Harry or Neville. Should he have?

'I spoke to them last night and they were also concerned that we still haven't received the details of Stalin's private collection,' I said.

'All in good time, John,' he said. 'All in good time.'

'George, we do not have unlimited time here,' I said.

He looked briefly as though this was a surprising revelation but then nodded. 'Yes, I know,' he said. 'I'll make it happen. You'll be happy. All will be well.'

A small, slightly battered car came puttering up the long tree-lined driveway. It creaked to a halt and Nana Vorobieff slowly hoisted herself out of the driver's seat. I breathed a sigh of relief as she disappeared into the main building. We could look at wines after all.

We had a rough plan. Over breakfast, Kevin and I had compared notes and decided on an agenda for the day, obviously headlined by 'Information re: Stalin's personal collection'.

'What do you make of "the basement" in the cellar,' Kevin had asked me, as we ate eggs, bacon, toast and jam, with filter coffee; a very western hotel selection.

'It's definitely there. I heard Pyotr and Grigol mention it, and Tamaz talked about it during one of his rants, I mean monologues,' I said. 'When we first went into the cellar, they indicated the stairs kept going to the basement level, yes? Looking at my list from Sydney, I think I can see where level one finishes and the basement begins.'

Kevin nodded. 'I went over the list again as well, looking at what we discovered in the cellar book yesterday and what appears to be on the shelves on the level we were on yesterday,' he said. 'If my calculations are right, there's roughly 8424 bottles in the basement, which are not included in the 30,000 that we were focusing on yesterday on the floor above.'

'Roughly,' I said.

'Well, I didn't want to assume the list was completely correct,' Kevin said.

'Except that we haven't found a hole in it yet,' I said. 'Isn't that the strangest thing? We're working overtime, looking for any single sign of fraud or "holes" in comparing the physical bottles to the cellar book and our translated copy, and there hasn't been one. We can't fault it.'

'We only had one day,' Kevin said. 'Let's see how today goes.'

I loved it. Kevin with the perfect brain to refuse to quit looking for traps, looking for the scam.

'Well,' I said, 'if that figure of 8424 is close to correct, it would bring the total number of bottles in the two levels of the cellar to close to 40,000 bottles, which is the figure Neville originally quoted us in Sydney. According to my list, most of those wines in the basement are going to be Georgian or Crimean.'

'But there is also supposed to be some 1938 Margaux,' Kevin said. 'Although I'm concerned it says there are fifteen bottles, at 800 mls. That seems unlikely.'

I had pushed my plate aside and was also looking at my list.

'There should be more Yquem, according to this. Maybe forty-five or fifty bottles, with some 1924 and a couple of unknown vintages.'

'And 639 bottles of Tsinandali, the Georgian white wine we tried, from 1915 to 1968. If they're in good shape, we should definitely be looking to get those bottles for the second-level part of the auction we talked about.'

'Hey, look at this,' I said as a thought occurred to me.

'What?' Kevin asked.

'The Yquem listed in the basement is 1924. Some of the Tsinandali dates to, what, 1968? It's after poor Nicholas the Second got taken to the basement.'

'So, it might be Stalin's personal collection down there,' Kevin said.

'Although when did he die? In the fifties, yes?'

'Early fifties, I think,' said Kevin. 'Maybe 1953.'

'How on earth can you know his original Georgian name but not when he died?'

Kevin shrugged. 'It's early. I'm slightly hungover.'

'Fair enough. Anyway, that 1968 date means wine has been added beyond Stalin's death, so we still can't know that the wine in the basement is his. We've really got to sort this out today.'

Now, at the winery, executives absent, as the Union Lady jangled keys below us and we headed down the dimly lit stairs back into the cellar, we were ready for a big day of cross-referencing.

Things started off well when George said, 'John, I finally have the list you wanted. Stalin's personal collection. Those shelves there.'

He pointed down towards the back of the room to one shelf that stood slightly apart from the others, now I took in the layout. I could see some half bottles on there, but cobwebs covered most of it.

'That's an excellent start to the day, George. Thanks,' I said, taking the sheets of paper from him.

I looked for a moment. The paper read:

სტალინის IV გრებული ბიბლიოთეკაში

'Um, George,' I said. 'It's written entirely in Georgian.'

He looked, as though he'd never seen the paper before. 'Oh, so it is. That says, "The Collection of IV Stalin with Library".'

'IV?' I asked.

'Ioseb Vissarionovich,' said Kevin, clearly having shaken off his hangover.

'George, we need it in English,' I said.

'Ah, yes, of course,' he replied, before rattling off some Georgian to Grigol, who took the papers and left the room. 'Grigol is going to my office where it can be translated, very fast,' said George. 'By lunch-time, I promise.'

There was nothing to be done so I said, 'Okay, thanks, George.'

'So close and yet so far,' Kevin said to me quietly.

I shrugged. I was unhappy that the list had been there and was now gone, but what could I do? We just needed to get back to the rest of our work.

George and Zurab left and Pyotr, Kevin and I got down to the business of validating more of the lists and the wines.

We had a good morning. I poked around some of the French classics, looking for any hint of subterfuge, in the corkage, the shape of the bottle or the colour of the wine. Meanwhile, Kevin and Pyotr inspected the Georgian wines, including heading into the basement for the first time. It was much like the room above although with slightly fewer bottles. There seemed to be more cave-ins, too, with who knows how many bottles destroyed.

By lunchtime, Kevin was satisfied that the Georgian element of the general cellar list and book was pretty much exactly as it was written, which was astounding in its own right. I hadn't found a single bottle that raised an alarm bell for potential illegitimacy. We needed to get some sunlight and fresh air and so we headed back to the car park, where Zurab was sitting in a red delivery van. We took that to one of the usual restaurants overlooking the river where Pyotr and Zurab ate enough for two men each. Zurab didn't even take his gun out of his belt as he sat at the table. It just stuck out from his shirt like a growth.

After we had eaten, we took the delivery van back to the Savane Number One.

'We must be slipping,' Kevin said. 'No Mercedes.'

'Maybe Natascha was disappointed in us,' I said.

'She wouldn't be the first,' Kevin replied, watching Tbilisi out the window.

The next few hours were fantastic. We had our system really working and checked dozens of listed wines and vintages that were important, if we did buy the cellar. Numerous vintages of Yquem, Palmer, Madeira, and so many more of the all-time greats, ticked off and more than once – often a dozen bottles or more of a vintage. These wines were monumental in the history of wine. We counted seven vintages of the sublime Château Margaux with forty-three bottles of 1910 and twenty-four bottles of 1911; seven vintages of the aristocratic Château Latour from 1874 to 1914, with thirty-four bottles of 1912; Lafite Rothschild 1877 and 1878. This was starting to border on the impossible, I thought to myself. Even the actual wine libraries of these imposing châteaux may not have some of these vintages, let alone quantities like this. To count four cases of 1910 Margaux and on the next shelf three cases of 1912 Latour was ridiculous. Yet we inspected a lot of these wines and couldn't find a fault with the bottles or the numbers corresponding to our translated cellar list. Kevin had dollar signs in his eyes. I was certainly warming to the possibilities that the cellar presented.

Grigol turned up, but not with Stalin's list, translated.

'Pyotr, can you ask Grigol where the translated list is, please?' I said, trying to keep any note of alarm or anger out of my voice.

Grigol and Pyotr spoke for a few moments, arms waving.

'Grigol says the list is still being translated,' Pyotr said. 'Any minute now.'

'Do you believe him?' I asked.

Pyotr gave me a long look, a half smile on his face.

'This is Tbilisi,' he finally said. 'I trust my fellow Georgian worker.'

'I think that's a sign to let it drop for now,' Kevin said, but I had got the message. We returned to cross-checking the wines, with Grigol wandering around, half-heartedly trying to help.

At about 3 pm, Grigol's concentration was clearly slipping. He looked bored as Kevin and Pyotr went, bottle by bottle, over rack twenty-three, and finally we turned to see that Grigol had opened a bottle, like Pyotr had the day before. This bottle turned out to be a 1933 Spotikach, a coffee liqueur, and so of course we had a taste. And it was interesting.

Just as we were finishing our glass, there were footsteps on the stairs and Revaz and Tamaz walked in. Tamaz looked red in the face, and I wondered if he'd been drinking at lunch. The pair of executives took us all in, each with a glass in our hand, and started barking words at Pyotr, who spoke urgently in return.

'What's going on, Pyotr?' I asked but he ignored me, concentrating on Tamaz, who was waving his arms around and shouting. Revaz pointed at the bottle of Spotikach and demanded something from Grigol, who shrugged and looked miserable, then spoke quietly, pointing at me.

Tamaz looked at four bottles of Château d'Yquem that we had in front of our lights, for photos and to check the level of fill, and said to me in English, 'Why you touching the bottles?'

'Because George said we could,' I replied, thinking I had no intention of getting involved in winery politics.

Tamaz and Revaz swung back around and had a heated discussion with Pyotr, who seemed to give as good as he got, but the executives didn't look happy and stomped out of the room.

'What was that all about?' we asked Pyotr.

'They're not happy we're drinking from the cellar,' he said.

'The bottle Grigol opened?' I said. 'You told him it wasn't us who opened it?'

'Of course,' Pyotr said. 'But they'll believe what they want to believe, no? Loyalty to fellow Georgian workers means I can't really say what Grigol had to say.'

'You don't need to. I already know,' I said, remembering Grigol's finger pointing straight at me.

Kevin and I exchanged looks, wondering what was going on here, the deeper rivers running, but didn't have time to discuss it because there were more footsteps and here was Nana Vorobieff, the Union Lady, jangling keys and indicating, whether you knew the language or not, that we needed to leave so she could lock up. It wasn't even 4 pm.

Up at ground level, we stood in the car park and waited for George. Nobody said much. Kevin and I clearly weren't happy and none of the Georgians seemed to be into small talk at the best of times. This was not the best of times.

George finally drove up, being chauffeured by Zurab in the red delivery van, and listened as Pyotr outlined what had happened. George raised a hand in our direction, fingers spread: a universal symbol of 'stay calm, I'll deal with it'.

He headed in and we could hear a lot of loud Georgian arguing for what felt like half an hour.

'Screw this,' I said to Kevin and marched into Tamaz's office, with Pyotr and then Kevin in my wake. Tamaz, Revaz and George all stopped arguing in surprise as we barged into the room.

'What's going on, George? We're losing time,' I said.

Tamaz let rip with a burst of Georgian staccato.

'Mr Tamaz wants to know why you were drinking the wines,' George said.

'We haven't been drinking,' I said. 'Well, we had that 1899 Suduiraut that Revaz dropped, and Pyotr opened a port yesterday. The only thing we've drunk today was a bottle that Grigol opened, a Spotikach coffee liqueur. I'm pretty sure he's told them it was me who opened it, which of course I didn't.'

George turned back to Tamaz and Grigol, and spoke forcefully in Georgian. Grigol looked shifty but argued strongly back while Tamaz just looked angrily at us.

To hell with this, I thought and edged my way past Pyotr and Kevin back out of the room and into the car park. We still didn't have a complete list, or even the details of Stalin's list, we had one day to go and we had to sit through this bullshit among the locals. Even worse, I couldn't threaten that I was ready to head to the airport, because the tantalising treasure of that cellar had me in its hold. We were too far in to fly away now.

After a while, I couldn't help but notice that the building behind me had become quiet. No more loud ranting or arguing. I stood quietly, leaning against the delivery van, wondering what was happening in there.

Kevin was the first to emerge, with that quiet smile on his face that says even though shit has been going on, he's actually been having quite a lot of fun watching the world burn. It was a look I'd seen many times.

Pyotr and George followed him, and then Tamaz and Revaz. Everybody was smiling and Tamaz said something lightly that made him, George and Revaz break into laughter.

'We're all friends again,' I said to Kevin in amazement.

'I think you might find that somebody might have paid somebody something,' Kevin said. 'But yes, I believe we're good.'

'Then let's get back down there and do some work.'

14

SELECTING THE DOZEN

Kevin and I had a working dinner alone that night. We only had one more day to spend in the cellar – Tamaz, Revaz and union ladies permitting – and so we wanted to make sure we didn't waste it. This night was a chance to take a breath and reconcile our thoughts and impressions, compare tasting notes and reflect on where our strategies and agendas were at. We half expected another phone call from George, telling us to be out the front for another crazy night-time adventure, but it didn't come. Maybe George needed a night off as well. Maybe George was at the opera with Natascha and his girlfriend. Or maybe George had a wife and five children that we hadn't heard about.

Kevin looked across the table at me, our plates pushed to the side to make way for all our notebooks and paperwork.

He said, 'You realise we still haven't broached the most fraught subject of them all.'

'Whether the people we're dealing with are the Georgian mafia?'

Kevin snorted. 'Oh, I'm way past that.'

'Okay then, who actually owns the cellar and who can negotiate the sale of the wines?'

He laughed. 'That is a good one, but mine is more immediate than that,' he said.

'Okay, then what's the other fraught question?' I asked.

Kevin said, 'How do we convince everybody not named George to honour our pre-trip deal, that we can take at least a dozen antique bottles with us when we leave?'

I sipped my Georgian rosé. 'Yeah, I've been thinking about it a lot. It's essential that we have those bottles. I guess it's going to take money. That's what seems to solve every other issue around here, like today with that tasting fiasco.'

'We need to have a decent amount of American currency on us tomorrow, just in case,' Kevin said. 'And we need to have a list of the wines we'd like to take, so that there's as little room for debate as possible.'

'We talked about all this before we even got on the plane, remember?' I said, shuffling through my notebook. 'Here it is. I wrote down that we'd agreed on several criteria for choosing them. The first is to pick bottles that have features, characteristics or ways of being authenticated as completely as possible, so that we can reduce any ambiguity on whether the collection is genuine. We certainly want some Yquem as it is the basis of the value in the cellar. The list says there are 217 Yquems from the 1800s and 1900s, and there may be vintages that the château itself may not have in their own library.'

SHELF	ROW	NAME	VINTAGE	SIZE	BOTTLES	
1	9	Chateau Ikem	1881		10	
1	19	Chateau Ikem	1874	0.75	10	
1	21	Chateau Ikem	1854	0.75	6	
1	43	Chateau Ikem	1891	0.75	11	
1	44	Chateau Ikem	1847	0.75	3	600,000+
1	45	Chateau Ikem	1888	0.75	2	
2	19	Chateau Ikem	1864	0.70	18	
2	27	Chateau Ikem	1861	0.80	4	
2	28	Chateau Ikem	1864	0.80	1	

SHELF	ROW	NAME	VINTAGE	SIZE	BOTTLES
2	63	Chateau Ikem	1861	0.75	1
2	96	Chateau Ikem	1877	0.75	3
3	28	Chateau Ikem	1851	0.75	6
29	4	Chateau Ikem French		0.40	46
29	16	Chateau Ikem	1924	0.70	15
29	17	Chateau Ikem	1924	0.40	18
29	37	Chateau Ikem		0.70	12
29	51	Chateau Ikem	1924	0.70	9
30	22	Chateau Ikem	1940	0.80	3
30	30	Chateau Ikem		1.00	6
30	38	Chateau Ikem	1858	0.75	21
30	41	Chateau Ikem	1859	0.75	5
30	42	Chateau Ikem	1874	0.75	7
					217

'The second is to pick bottles that show the range of the cellar to a potential auction house like Christie's.

'The third is to choose bottles that are valuable in their own right, so that if this entire venture goes belly up, which, let's face it, it still very well might, we have in our possession some bottles that on their own could sell for enough money to cover the costs of this trip, the expense of setting up the partnership and other costs incurred so far.

'My final note in my notebook,' I said, pretending to squint as I peered at the page, 'was a comment from one Kevin Hopko, Esquire, who said we should retain the right to not sell all twelve bottles, because they could also be the basis of a really spectacular dinner party with friends.'

'And I stand by that comment,' Kevin said. 'You're lucky to have me, for my mature and sensible alternative viewpoints.'

'So, if we look at the bottles we'd like, we should start with two dozen and potentially get talked back from there to twelve,' I said.

'Further, we don't want Georgian wines, we want old Bordeaux or Yquem because ideally we want to have ones that can be chemically tested to establish that they're genuine, and anyway, with so much century-old Yquem in that cellar, we really want to take some with us.'

We sat and went through the wines that we had cross-referenced as matching the cellar book over the last two days. A list began to take shape.

We decided that an 1877 Lafite would be a solid choice, for individual value, impressing an auction house and the ability to be authenticated. An 1884 Margaux made the list and then we pondered the various Yquems. Those three tantalising bottles of 1847 Yquem hovered in my consciousness. Was there any chance the Georgians didn't realise the rarity of that trio of bottles? Would they let even one fly away?

We agreed we didn't need to choose another 1899 Suduiraut, as much as I'd have loved to have that bottle sitting in my cellar at home, not only because of how good it was but also for the memory of the moment we tasted the dropped wine and the lights went on that the cellar may be real. However, the fact was that we had already tasted it and felt there was no question it was genuine, so maybe other bottles could tell us more?

As we tried to put our two dozen dream bottles together, we realised that we still had some important wines to inspect on the last day, representing sizeable amounts of the value in the cellar, as far as we could tell from our translated list.

Kevin and I went over the pages for the thousandth time.

'Shelf number two, wine number twenty-seven is four bottles of 1861 Yquem,' I said. 'We definitely need to check those.'

'Shelf number three, wine number twenty-eight is also Yquem, 1851,' Kevin said. 'We also need to check those.'

I smiled. 'Shelf number thirty, wine number thirty is *also* Yquem but doesn't have a vintage listed. I guess we should check on those and see if we can discern the vintage from the corks.'

'I think we should,' Kevin said. 'What do you think the chances are of us actually receiving a list of Stalin's personal collection tomorrow, in a language we can read?'

'About the same as us walking onto the plane with two dozen bottles of 150-year-old Yquem,' I replied.

Kevin lifted his glass of rosé. 'I think you might be right.'

'Do you want dessert?' I asked him. 'They have crème brûlée.'

Kevin shook his head and looked wary. 'I never trust a dessert that wobbles,' he declared definitively.

What do you even say to that? I ate dessert alone.

Pyotr picked us up in the delivery van the next morning. As soon as I saw him, I noticed that he seemed coiled like a spring. While he had been hugely helpful to us and mostly friendly, Pyotr definitely had a steelier edge to him. We watched as he argued with the hotel security guard about leaving his gun behind to join us in the lobby. He'd left his gun without complaint before, so it made me wonder about his mood today. As before, the security staff all tuned in to Pyotr's presence in a way they didn't when Nino or Zurab came through the front door.

We saved the guards from a potential stand-off by walking through security to meet Pyotr on the street, and he seemed friendly enough to us. His driving was more sedate that Nino's as well, which was another relief.

We exchanged pleasantries with Tamaz and Revaz at the winery and headed for the cellar. All rancour from yesterday's umbrage at our alleged brazen drinking of the collection seemed to have evaporated, but Revaz indicated he'd be coming with us today, which annoyed me because we were on the clock, with only today to dive into the collection, and the chief winemaker was incredibly slow and ponderous to have involved.

I asked Pyotr to gently explain to Revaz that we were deeply concerned not to have seen details of Stalin's personal collection, after several days of asking, and a full day since we sent a Georgian version to be translated. What I didn't ask Pyotr to translate was my urgency to assess the collection because those bottles were no longer just bottles of wine. They were Russian memorabilia, a true collectable with Stalin's provenance. They were essential to our endeavour.

The temperature of the cellar on that final day was really chilly, so we found ourselves in thick jumpers and wondering if we could see our breath in better light. Possibly shamed by the fact that they had failed to hand us the Stalin list, Revaz produced a more detailed list than we'd ever seen of the wines in the lower basement. We spent the morning down there, ticking off several Yquems, a Lafite and other classics.

As per the previous two days, I was still on high alert for a sign, any sign, that this cellar was not legitimate. Kevin and I only needed one bottle of alleged Bordeaux that was in the wrong-shaped bottle or the wrong colour or had a suspicious cork, and internal alarm bells would have gone off that this may not be all it appeared or was alleged to be. However, the lower basement seemed as well chronicled and legitimate in every way as the main cellar above.

We had lunch at a cafeteria not far from the Savane winery, with Pyotr and a friend of his, a guy in a large overcoat which he didn't take off, even in a warm restaurant, for the duration of the meal. Kevin had a quiet word in Pyotr's ear as we were getting ready to head back and so we drove away from the winery. 'I thought we had better get some money,' Kevin said to me quietly, as we sat in the back, with Pyotr and his friend up the front. 'Pyotr seems to know where we should go.'

We stopped at an antique shop and Pyotr said a few words to his overcoat friend, who got out of the car and lounged against the wall of the shop, by the front door. I wondered if he had a submachine gun under that coat. Nothing would have surprised me.

The antique shop was fantastic. I, but particularly Kevin, could have stayed there all day in other circumstances. It had everything from the standard terrible vases and lamps, old books and trinkets that seem to be in antique shops the world over, to a large collection of rifles, pistols, swords and other military hardware. Some of it looked to date back centuries, while other guns and uniforms were much more modern, either from World War Two or even more recent, to my untrained eye.

'We might need one of these,' Kevin said, pointing to a small novelty pistol with two barrels that diverted halfway down the gun and would apparently shoot at 45-degree angles to one another. 'In case Tamaz and Revaz charge us at the same time,' he said.

Pyotr had gone over to the counter and was having a quiet word with the owner, who disappeared into a back room. Pyotr called Kevin over, and asked for his traveller's cheques. As I checked out revolutionary swords, they went into a huddle and then Pyotr shook hands with the owner and we all marched out of the shop. Overcoat Man had barely moved a muscle and stayed at his post, both hands still hidden in the folds of his coat, until the three of us were safely in the car. Then he sauntered to the passenger seat and got in, for Pyotr to drive away.

Kevin leaned over to me and said, 'We either just robbed that antique store or my traveller's cheque receipts just lit up on international cybercrime networks across the globe, or maybe both.'

'How much money did you get?' I asked.

'One thousand American dollars,' he said.

I lifted my shirt slightly so Kevin could see the bandage-brown line of a pouch hidden under the line of my jeans. 'Then we've got two thousand dollars if we need it,' I said.

Kevin looked genuinely amazed.

'Have you been carrying that around the whole time?' he asked. 'Surrounded by guns and hoodlums and in a town like this?'

'Without blinking,' I said.

When we returned to the winery, a miracle occurred. George was there and handed us a stapled collection of pages that turned out to be the translated English version of Stalin's personal collection.

'This is what you needed, yes?' he said. 'Just remember that I, your favourite George, am here to help you. Forever, and always, at times.'

'That's good to know, George. Thank you,' I replied. 'And on that, while you're here, we need to talk about the wines we're leaving with tomorrow.'

'Leaving?' He looked confused.

'Remember, in the deal, before we came to Georgia, we discussed that we would need to take some of the antique wines home with us, to have them tested, to prove authenticity and to convince our partners that this entire cellar is legitimate and that we can feel safe in buying it.'

'What kind of testing?' he asked.

'There are a couple of ways,' Kevin said. 'All organic materials, whether in wine or not, contain a radioactive isotope carbon 14, and it decays at a known rate, meaning chemical testers can measure wine, measure the rate of decay and know roughly how old the liquid is.'

'Okay,' said George.

'It's kind of cool because when nuclear tests happened in the 1950s and 1960s, that pushed the worldwide levels of carbon 14 up at that time, so really, the wines in your cellar shouldn't reflect that. If they do, they're younger than the fifties and we have a problem.'

'Okay,' said George again.

'Tritium, too, is another measure that shouldn't register as particularly high if the wines are genuinely more than a century old,' Kevin continued.

'Okay,' said George, nodding.

'Of course, there is also a scientist, Hubert, in France who uses low-frequency gamma rays to test wine without even opening the bottle,' Kevin said. 'By directing the gamma ray at the wine, he can detect whether the radioactive isotope caesium-137 is present, which can only happen as a reaction of nuclear fallout so, again, if the wine here is genuinely dating back to pre-1900, that isotope cannot be present.'

'Okay,' George said.

'Kevin, I don't want to burst your scientific bubble but I think George understood about 3 per cent of what you just said,' I pointed out.

'Oh, okay, sorry,' said Kevin. 'George, the short version is we *really* need to test the wine.'

'Yes, I not understand specifics, but I can see the need,' George said, frowning. 'However, this might be difficult.'

'George,' I said. 'You never mentioned that there were other owners of the winery or that we'd have to deal with people like Tamaz. You need to make this happen. I'm not being overly dramatic when I say that if we don't have bottles with us when we leave, this entire deal will fall through as we won't be able to prove that the wines are genuine. No million dollars from us.'

'How many bottles do you want to take?' he asked.

'Ideally, twenty-four.'

'Twenty-four!' He sounded as though I'd said half the cellar. 'That's a lot of bottles.'

'We need to show the variety of wines within the cellar. We need to show that they can test any of these wines and they are what we claim them to be. We need a show of faith from you and your people, George.'

George thought for a long moment and then sighed. 'John, I understand. I remember our earlier discussion. I did not realise you were talking about so many bottles, but first things first. I will start the explanation to Mr Tamaz and the others.'

'Thank you, George. It's very important.'

'I do not think you'll be able to take any of the Stalin collection,' he said, pointing to the pages I held.

'Okay, well, let me see what's in there, and what else would be best to take as samples from the wider cellar,' I said.

'Also, John,' George leaned towards me and said in a quiet voice, 'There may be some need for a little cash to persuade certain parties.'

'I hope not but I'll leave that with you, George. We're partners, remember?'

'Well, I thought you were a buyer and I was a seller, but in this yes, we have a mutual interest,' he said. And then laughed that big laugh of his. 'It will be okay, John. The sale will happen, and it will be wonderful. All will be fine. Hopefully.'

I headed down to the cellar and to the shelves that we'd been told contained Stalin's collection. My misgivings about the negotiations about us taking bottles home was mixed with excitement that we could finally be face to face with Stalin's personal favourites.

We huddled by torchlight in the gloom to read the translated Stalin list. It was titled 'The Collection of IV Stalin with Library'.

The list had a lot more spirits than the general collection. Stalin had broader tastes than the Tsar – and even being able to discern that from the list was a thrill, like we were that much closer to the actual man, instead of the historical figure. Stalin had bought some Yquem, including a 1924 bottle that was listed as 400 ml, which was unusual. There were another fifteen bottles of more standard 1924 Yquem, and then another entry for even more 1924 Yquem, eighteen bottles. But then he had collected eighty bottles of Hennessy Jubilee Cognac. I didn't know what that was. He had French Chartreuse, whisky and a vodka listed as '50 degrees', which we took to maybe mean 50 per cent proof. There was 1923 Bols gin, from England, and 104 bottles of Chacha brandy, again 50 per cent proof.

As Kevin put it poetically, looking at the list: 'When old Josef decided to hit the bottle, he didn't fuck around.'

I went over the list several times, caught up not only in the brands and labels, but also just in the story it told of Stalin, the man. His tastes, his preferences. How he came to like Bols gin over other gins, as the list seemed to suggest. How he got a taste for Chartreuse, if that was true.

Kevin was poking around, examining the bottles themselves, and was intrigued by some other bottles, almost completely hidden under cobwebs, that had mostly lost their labels, although one fragment of label mentioned *miel*, the French word for honey. They didn't seem to be on the list so we weren't sure what they were or where they fitted.

'Why do you collect honey among a wine and spirits collection?' Kevin wondered.

'I'm not sure,' I said. 'Is it related to a spirit?'

'I'll have to do some homework,' Kevin said. 'Also, what are these references on the list to "hardened" wine? What does "hardened" mean?'

'And while we're at it,' I said, laughing, 'did you notice this little section on the back of the list?'

Kevin came and peered over my shoulder, reading: "King Alexander the Third Collection". You're kidding me.'

'Nicholas the Second's father,' I said.

We spent a couple of hours working our way through Stalin's personal collection, taking photos of a few bottles and wiping cobwebs off many others. Now that we had the list and were able to substantiate the important bottles, I was able to relax, and we just enjoyed being in the presence of history. I couldn't help but imagine Stalin, in St Petersburg, wandering the racks of these bottles when they were recently arrived from France, labels fresh and wine vibrant inside.

I mentioned this to Kevin who said, 'Yes, and I want to do the same thing with them in my office in Sydney, just before I sell them. Let's work out which ones we can take home.'

As soon as we mentioned that we were looking to collect some bottles for authentication, the Georgians started paying much closer attention to our movements.

Grigol immediately said, through Pyotr, that we were not to touch or remove any foreign wines. We nodded and said, yes, Grigol, of course, and then as soon as he drifted upstairs out of the cellar, we began collecting our predetermined list. We put small tags on them, attached carefully to the neck with rubber bands, noting the wine and year, the shelf and number, as most had no labels. One Yquem that we pulled aside had a cork that showed it was from 1870-something, but the final number was obscured. We shone torches at the cork inside the bottle, and could read 187.

We took it anyway. The whole point was to have wine experts, even from Yquem itself – in fact, especially from Yquem if we could organise it – authenticate that it was genuine and which year it was from.

Without our little labels, attached by rubber band, it was hard to know what the bottles were. Removed from the shelf, and therefore the list, each was just a dark bottle filled with liquid. Most didn't have labels and their corks were often obscured, like that Yquem. Our tags were going to be vital, so we made sure they were securely attached.

We gathered twenty-four bottles, a greatest hits of the collection, you might call it, including an 1847 Yquem and one of Stalin's personally collected 1924 Yquems.

'Why the hell not? Let's see what happens,' I said.

It was soon after when Revaz, the chief winemaker, came down the stairs into the cellar, followed by George. Revaz's face was beetroot red, even in the bad light.

Kevin said quietly to me, 'Let the games begin.'

George did most of the talking on our behalf. Revaz shook his head a lot or waved his arms.

For over an hour, it went to and fro. George was smooth, rarely raising his voice, all reason and explanation, occasionally pointing a hand in our direction as he made a point or indicating the bottles that stood like a silent jury on the table next to our now-cooling LED lights.

Maybe ninety minutes in, George indicated to us that it might be wise to offer the winery executives a gift to 'smooth things over'. A figure of US$1500 was mentioned, we suggested US$1100 and George played along until we landed on a figure of US$1250. Kevin and I combined our secret stashes and gave George the cash.

I was hopeful that this was the end of it, but of course there was still a problem. Revaz kept saying Tamaz's name and eventually we all trooped upstairs and George and Revaz disappeared into Tamaz's office.

We were sitting in the boardroom where we'd had all the interminable meetings a few days before. Pyotr went and got us a beer, which was much needed by this point.

Kevin wrote in his notes, 'John's getting edgy.'

And I was. I was pacing now, while sipping my beer. We were so close yet this bunch of suits, running their defunct winery, could kill the entire project on a whim.

Eventually I said, 'I need some air,' and walked out to pace the winery's car park and long-neglected garden. Kevin, Pyotr, Ivane and Nino joined me and it was Kevin who asked Pyotr to fill in the time by taking some photos, of us with each of them, of Kevin and I together, of the winery itself. It hadn't occurred to me until Kevin produced his camera that this would almost certainly be the last time we'd be at the Savane Number One, on this trip anyway, and so I was pleased to record the moment, even if I was apprehensive about the outcome of the negotiations inside. Nino and Pyotr insisted we pose for photos with handguns in our waistbands, doing our best to look just like Tbilisi-style hard men.

Towards the end of all this, George emerged and updated us on what was happening. It seemed that Tamaz wanted some kind of contract and approval from 'the authorities'.

We had no idea who 'the authorities' were.

Phone calls were made, discussions were held. We went back inside and finished our beers.

An hour later, we were brought back into the negotiations. We agreed that we would leave with 'six or seven' bottles, only. Kevin and I immediately took that to mean a dozen.

Revaz was clear that they didn't want us to take anything of which there were only a few bottles.

I still didn't want to signal how valuable the entire collection might be, but I also wanted to give us the best chance of flying out with some of the golden bottles.

'George,' I said. 'Just because of its age and condition, the 1847 Yquem is the best possible bottle we could take to impress an auction house.'

He looked down the list and said, 'But there are only three of them, John. I honestly do not think these men will let you take that one. There is many other Château d'Yquem to choose from, yes? With many more bottles.'

We did have others among our twenty-four bottles, so I decided to let go of the tantalising 1847 for the greater good. I replaced it in the collection with a winery now considered to be one of the iconic first growths, a Château Mouton Rothschild, listed to be from 1874. Our translated list actually had it as a Buton-Rothschild but I was assuming somehow Mouton had become Buton along the way.

In the end, as far as I could tell, Revaz got to keep the $1250 in US currency. I'm not sure Tamaz even knew about the deal.

And to be honest, I didn't care. We managed to take our dozen bottles out through a side door to Nino's Mercedes.

'I wonder if the mafia staff car's return is linked to the US dollars we just paid them?' Kevin wondered.

George said he was going to stay behind for a while to do some work but would meet us afterwards for a drink on our final evening together.

'George,' I said. 'Can you please hang on to the other twelve bottles we chose? We're going to need them, but we'll have to work out how to get them from you later, at the hotel.'

We drove back and Pyotr joined us in Kevin's room, where we carefully washed the cobwebs and dirt off the bottles we'd liberated.

We washed them with extreme care, making sure not to dislodge anything important, like the hint of a label, or smudge the hand-written tags that we'd attached. Finally, we packed them into the polystyrene container carried all the way from Australia, hoping for this moment. Then we wrapped bubble wrap around it and put it into a cardboard box, which Kevin expertly taped shut. They were as secure as they could be.

15

THE LAST NIGHT IN TBILISI

By the time we had done all this, I looked out the window and saw dusk was falling.

It occurred to me that our work was finished. I could finally relax, a dozen bottles of amazing antique wine safely in our possession and the cellar logged, as much as we could hope to.

It was Friday night and our final night in Tbilisi. We could drop our guard enough to enjoy dinner without having to wrestle disputes with winery executives or solve other problems.

Pyotr still seemed to be our assigned assistant and appeared happy enough to hang out for dinner. He took us to a restaurant called the Mirage, across the road from our hotel. It had beautiful views across the river, and we could make out large squat buildings, probably government offices of some kind, on the other side and downstream. Way up on high, on top of the hill looking down over Old Tbilisi, I could see the enormous Kartlis Deda statue – the silver Mother of Georgia – with a bowl of wine in her left hand and a sword held across her stomach, representing freedom and what Georgians were prepared to do to keep it.

'To Mamma Georgia,' I said, toasting the statue.

'To Mamma Georgia!' Pyotr and Kevin said, and we drank.

Kevin had felt the same lightening of tension that I had, and we finally got to enjoy a night in a city we still barely knew. Pyotr, catching the mood, ordered caviar and sturgeon, fried goats' cheese and what he said was the finest Georgian wine on the list, a nicely aged red. I took a sip and immediately noticed the same butterscotchy character I had detected all trip – among the museum Georgian wines we had tasted at the winery and more everyday wines we had tasted during meals.

And then it finally hit me. There was sugar in the wine. The Georgian winemaking technique must include slightly sugaring the wine as it's made, which is why even those very old ones had this slightly candied finish to them. How had I not realised this before? It was so obvious, once I realised. I suppose I'd had many other more important things on my mind all week.

We decided to share playing the role of *tamada*. We toasted sugary wines. We toasted Georgia. We toasted Tbilisi. We toasted Nicholas the Second. We toasted Pyotr for his help and he toasted us. As the wine flowed, Pyotr seemed pleased to have learnt how to toast in English. We were pleased with the view of the river at night. We were pleased with the food. We were pleased with the universe.

Which made it the perfect time for George, Zurab and Nino to walk through the door, along with Nino's girlfriend, Elene.

There was nothing for it but to toast George, Zurab and Nino, and Elene, and then Australia and Georgia one more time.

We even toasted the Mother of Georgia all over again.

'When was she built?' Kevin asked.

'In the fifties,' George replied. 'She celebrate 1500 years of Tbilisi. I love her and I love this city. We live in heaven, abundant in all we need.'

And so we had to toast that.

George was smiling at me during the toasts and I couldn't work out if it was a smile of happiness that we had made it through the visit and were still on track for a potential sale, or whether it was some other kind of gotcha smile. I had to admit he had handled today very well, ensuring we left the winery with any bottles at all.

I told him so and he shrugged, laughed and said, 'I understand the big worry of Mr Tamaz, of Mr Revaz. They see the wine, they know it is more than wine. It is a cultural artefact of Soviets, of so much history. It has lain there, protected, for so many years. Then some Australian men come, only vouched for by me, nobody else, and you say you want to take some of the best wines, on a handshake. This is history! You know and I know that this is wine bottles with a price tag in a big auction house, yet they are also beyond price, if you know what I mean.'

Pyotr was leaning forward, listening intently.

'Is that a problem?' I asked.

'A problem? Is what a problem?' George asked back, looking confused.

'The fact that the bottles are seen as cultural artefacts and history. Tamaz and company.'

George waved a hand, dismissively. 'Those men are no problem. We do not have any problems. I take care of everything over here. You take care of the money.'

'To partners you can trust,' I said, raising my glass of red.

'To us,' said George. 'You know, John,' he said, leaning forward. 'There's the wine you want, sure, but the winery itself is important too, for us. Tamaz and all his meetings on that day one and two, about wanting investments, make Savane great again? Not all warm air.'

'Hot air?' I asked.

'That too,' he said. 'Even I, with an eye for American dollar and the worth of those wines in the cellar, even I like the idea of Georgia reclaiming number one place on the world wine stage. It's important to my country that we build, that we have exports, that we have industries to take to the world.'

'I understand, George,' I said. 'In fact, I promise that I'll help you in any way I can, but running wineries is not something I do. Putting in the kind of funds required and sourcing the equipment is not my business. But there are plenty of people in Australia who do that and I'd be very happy to try and make the connection, if that would help.'

'Thank you, John,' he said, looking serious. 'Look, there is pressure on me. From others. But obviously, it will help our business with the wines go better if Tamaz and co see you a friend of the winery as well, but the two things are separate. We can sell the wine anyway, but any assistance you could offer would be very welcome to us.'

'What pressure, George?' I asked.

'You need not to know. Just pressure.'

'Well, here's to getting rid of that and selling the wine,' I said.

I raised my glass and we toasted one another, eyes locked. George was not smiling now.

As I tuned back in to the wider table, Nino was managing to convey through his limited language that he was excited to watch the Olympic Games, coming up the following year in Sydney.

'You be at Games?' he asked.

'I suppose,' I said, although I'm not that much of a sports fan. To be honest, I was more interested in selling wine to all the Olympic parties that would no doubt be taking place at that time.

'I'm predicting fireworks off the Sydney Harbour Bridge,' Kevin said, deadpan.

I asked whether Georgia had an Olympic team and Pyotr told us that after the fall of the Soviet Union, some Georgians had competed for a 'Unified Team' at the 1992 Barcelona Olympics: a kind of place-holder team for athletes from the various former Soviet states while their newly liberated countries sorted themselves out.

It wasn't until four years later that Georgian Olympians were finally able to compete in the Games under their own flag. This historic and symbolic moment for the Georgian people had happened three years before our visit, at the 1996 Olympic Games, coincident-ally held in Atlanta, the capital city of the US state of Georgia.

'We had Georgians, for first time, competing, and – look at that! –

in Georgia, but a long way from Tbilisi,' George said, butting in to Pyotr's explanation. 'Instead, Georgia, USA: home of Coca-Cola, not the original home of great wine and Stalin. Still, there it was, in the opening ceremony parade. Our flag.'

I looked out the window to where the Georgian flag was flying on top of those government buildings on the other side of the river. At this time, in the late nineties and early 2000s, the then flag of Georgia was a distinctive mostly deep red colour with black and white horizontal stripes in the top left-hand corner, where the Union Jack would be on the Australian flag. It had been the flag of the Democratic Republic of Georgia for three years, from 1918 to 1921, before the country was swallowed by the Soviet Union.

I asked what sports Georgia was best at and Pyotr shrugged that the team usually did best at judo, boxing, weightlifting, all the grunt sports. Archery was popular too, he said.

'No shooting?' Kevin asked, again deadpan.

'We see that more as a way of life than a pastime,' Pyotr said and smiled at Kevin, who laughed back. The Chechnyan hard man got our sense of humour.

It only took that burst of laughter for George, now firmly if wordlessly re-established as *tamada* at the *supra*, to launch into another round of toasts.

In fact, he went further, leaping from his seat and yelling something in Georgian to the restaurant manager. A staff member was summoned who darted into a back room and returned with a long horn, laced with silver. Wine was poured liberally into the open mouth.

'To this glorious *kantsi*!' George roared. 'To wine!'

And we all had to take turns drinking from the *kantsi*.

'Can I make a toast?' I asked when the *kantsi* made its way to me.

'Of course, John,' George said, bowing his head.

I raised the horn. 'To the friendship and hospitality of you wonderful Georgians,' I said.

'John,' George said, only half smiling. 'We have a saying here in Georgia. It go like this: "An enemy may come as far as the door of your house. But once he enters, he is friend."'

Before I could think that through, George was on his feet. He clapped his hands and said, 'I have a wonderful idea. Come on, we are leaving.'

'Where are we going, George?' Kevin asked.

He smiled and said, 'I want to have a bath with you.'

'Excuse me?' I said.

'A magnificent Tbilisi tradition! You cannot leave without enjoying a sulphur bath after dinner.'

'You're kidding,' Kevin said.

We looked at one another, a slightly drunken challenge in the air.

'When in Tbilisi . . .' I said, trying my best not to laugh.

Kevin shrugged and grinned back. 'In for a tetri, in for a lari,' he said.

'I will drive,' George announced. 'Nino, the keys.'

We piled into the back with Nino's girlfriend, as Nino looked worried, sitting in the passenger seat of his own Mercedes. Following our car was Zurab with a guy in the passenger seat who I didn't recognise. Maybe he'd been waiting while we were all in the restaurant.

In the whole visit, we had never seen George drive, and now it was clear why. Where Nino was a maniacal and fast but technically highly skilled driver, George was simply inept behind the wheel. Maybe it was all the toasts – nobody ever seemed to worry much about counting how many drinks they'd had here – or maybe he just didn't drive much. Luckily, it wasn't a very long trip. We lurched through the streets, Elene tumbling into Kevin or me every time we veered dangerously around a corner, after which she would give us a slightly shy, apologetic look and then let fly with a burst of loud verbal abuse in George's direction, which we didn't need to be able to translate to get the gist of. Meanwhile, George had the radio on and sang happily as he drove.

Finally, mercifully, he pulled up on Abano Street, just down from a large cathedral, and outside what appeared to be the sulphur baths.

We all staggered out of the car. The spoiled-egg smell of sulphur filled the air, so that I screwed up my nose. Nino grabbed his keys back, and he and his girlfriend drove off into the night.

'Ah, he's no fun,' George said, amiably. 'Come on. You'll love this.'

Zurab and the other guy sat in their car, slightly down the street. I saw cigarette smoke emerge from the window.

'Where are we, George?' Kevin asked.

'Abanotubani,' he said. 'Bathhouse Number Five. Very famous. This is most ancient part of the city. In fifth century, big king, Vakhtang, discovered these hot springs while hunting and built the whole city from there.'

Pyotr said, 'The word Tbilisi translates as "warm place".'

'Because of these hot springs?' I asked.

'So the story goes,' Pyotr said.

'Lots of bathhouses in this part of town,' George said. 'This one is the best. Locals, not tourists. No offence.'

'None taken,' I said.

Kevin and I took in the building. It was entirely red brick, from the walls to the roof where a series of brick domes poked towards the sky like Salvador Dalí–inspired breasts.

Inside, the walls were completely covered in intricate mosaics, made from little tiles of all different shades of blue.

George had a quick chat with the attendant behind the counter and we were shown to some private rooms where huge baths were made of giant stone walls, like a garden rockery.

The springs definitely lived up to their name. They were seriously hot. Pyotr told me, as I turned red and gasped, adjusting to the scorching water, that the temperature can nudge 40 degrees. The four of us sat naked in the chest-high water until our bodies started to cope better with the heat.

About twenty minutes in, the door of our private room opened and a man, aged in maybe his sixties, strode in. His face was one of those lived-in European faces that tells you without a word that you cannot imagine the things it has seen. It was also a totally blank canvas, and he couldn't have looked more bored as he walked into this room of naked men. Without speaking, he indicated with a business-like air a long marble slab off to the side of the bath.

'You first, John,' said George, no doubt enjoying the confusion on my face.

'Really?' I asked.

'Of course. Come on, don't be scared. Is just old Georgian man. He not bite.'

I laughed. When in Tbilisi . . . I got out of the bath and approached the stone.

'Facedown,' called Pyotr from within the steam of the spa, and so I lay on my stomach.

The man proceeded to scrub my body, vigorously and with some kind of coarse not-quite-steel-wool material that reminded me of an oven mitt. He started with my back, but then moved to my legs and arms. It wasn't quite painful but it felt like the skin was almost being scrubbed off.

The scrubbing stopped as he went to the bath where the others lounged, dipped in a bucket and then threw the contents over me. I gasped but it felt amazing.

Then the scrubbing started again. This time unashamedly on my backside, and into my legs. Another bucket of water and then a massage, the man's hands pushing mercilessly into my shoulders and neck, my back muscles and lower back.

I breathed deeply and relaxed into the pressure of the massage. Just like the temperature of the bath, it was all only just on the manageable side of excruciating, to the point of being fantastic. I could feel my muscles loosening and started to appreciate why this crazy late-night activity is a centuries old pastime in Tbilisi.

After I'd been scrubbed and pounded, the old man filled some kind of bag with a mysterious substance and started rubbing my now scalded skin. It was a kind of soap, bubbling with suds and smelling delightful as he expertly doused my whole body. Finally, what was left of me was allowed to stagger back to slip soapily into the spa, which somehow felt welcoming despite the heat. The others took their turn on the stone slab while every muscle in my body unwound after almost a week of intense concentration, tension and an almost levitating combination of success and 'where do we go from here?'

When it was all over, we dressed, made our way to Zurab's car and all piled in. The mysterious man was gone, meaning there was enough room for George, Pyotr, Kevin and me to sit comfortably. I guessed the mystery man might have been some kind of bodyguard. I never found out.

None of us felt much like talking, full of food and wine and slightly zoned out from the traditional sulphur bath experience. Kevin and I were practically poured out of the car at our hotel entrance and we waved goodbye to our never-boring local hosts.

'See you in the morning, John and Kevin,' George said out the window as Zurab prepared to drive away. 'Tonight, you will sleep. I promise you.'

He was right. Those baths do the trick. I barely remember hitting the pillow.

⚒

The next morning was Leaving Day.

Pyotr turned up early, just to hang out as much as anything, from what I could tell. For all of his dangerous persona schtick, and the way he unconsciously put every security guard in our hotel on edge just by showing up, Pyotr had been good to us.

I fully respected Kevin's observation that, even unarmed, Pyotr was actually more lethal than Nino, Zurab and the rest of George's hard men combined. But, when I thought about it, he had remained helpful and polite through it all, even given we were, as I've said, ever alert for a huge con, and had our walls up.

On this final day, we finished packing our gear and gave Pyotr whatever we weren't carrying home, as a souvenir of the trip. He seemed genuinely pleased to receive our lights from the cellar and other equipment we didn't need to carry back to Australia. We also asked him to keep our spare polystyrene packaging for bottles, on the chance that he was able to somehow package up the remaining twelve bottles we'd left with George and have them sent over to us. As part of that, I gave Pyotr my business card and said if he ever made it to Australia, to please call me. I told him I would like to return his hospitality in Sydney.

George and Nino turned up to drive us to the airport. One more terrifying car trip, as we wove through Tbilisi traffic at speeds of up to 120 kph, among mutterings about 'aboriginals' and how dare they get in our way. Some parts of being in Tbilisi I wasn't going to miss.

When we'd last been inside Tbilisi Airport, it had been the middle of the night. In daylight, it was a different beast. In fact, there literally were beasts, with several people walking goats or other livestock through the check-in area, and then through security to where the departure lounges were located. Surely they couldn't fly with a goat, I thought, incredulous. Other passengers were loaded up with those blue, red and white hessian zipped bags, loaded with who knew what contraband or cheap Georgian delicacies to fly up to Moscow.

Everywhere, people were smoking indoors, including flight attendants, looking bored and shooting smoke at one another, so they must have reeked of cigarettes, pre-flight.

I shook all this strangeness off to concentrate on the task at hand. We had our luggage to check in, or carry on, including the carefully packaged dozen antique bottles. Kevin had signed paperwork – a *carnet* – allowing him to take the bottles as hand luggage and without paying any duties on the plane, sitting next to him on an empty seat. We had done as much to protect them as we could.

Our Georgian hosts had been lurking, waiting for us to complete our ticketing, and now we sat down for one last coffee at the departure lounge.

'George,' I said. 'It's been a lot of fun.'

'For us as well, John. You have been wonderful guests,' he said. 'I look forward to the next phase of our business.'

I laughed. 'Well, that's certainly what I'm hoping as well. We have a couple of issues to sort out but here is probably not the place to try and solve them.'

'Of course,' he said, graciously, smiling. But then asked, 'Such as what?'

I shrugged. 'Mostly, it's about the ownership, and my nagging worry about the cultural significance of the bottles. We can't give you your money, even get the wines out of the cellar to London or New York and then have a representative of the Georgian government turn up, announcing they own the wines, either through shares in the winery or because the bottles are cultural icons, not just wines for sale.'

George was already looking pained and waving a hand. 'John, please, don't worry about any of that. I have an uncle in the government. I will take care of all of that. There will be no problem.'

'Well, that's good to know, George. That's what is standing in the way of a deal.'

'That, and us scientifically confirming that the bottles we have with us are genuine,' Kevin pointed out.

'Yes, Kevin, I understand,' said George. 'Don't you worry either. The bottles are real. You know in your heart that they are real. All will be well. We'll all be rich!'

There was nothing else much to say. We shook hands one more time with George, Nino and Pyotr, made our way through the gates to our flight and nestled in for the long trek to Heathrow.

Kevin said, 'Should we ask the flight attendant for wine or just crack one of the bottles next to me?'

'I am so relieved we managed to get the dozen,' I said. 'I feel like it was touch-and-go for a while there.'

'With all your talk about them being cultural icons, I was worried we'd be pulled up at the airport,' he said.

'Who knows. Anything seems possible in Georgia,' I said. 'It's good we're safely on the plane.'

'Yes, safe, sound and ready to fly,' Kevin said, left it a beat and then added, 'Until they arrest us at Heathrow.'

I love Kevin but he can be a real prick.

PART III

AFTER GEORGIA

AFTER GLORIA

16

KEVIN MAKES A FRIEND

Kevin and I separated at Heathrow Airport in London. I had some meetings, there and in France, to discuss stock purchasing from some European distributors. I would have loved to have turned up at Sotheby's or Christie's for preliminary discussions on the Georgian cellar, but I knew it was too early and that I wasn't anywhere near prepared or advanced enough to mention it to anybody.

Kevin was tasked with nursing our precious dozen-bottle cargo safely back to Sydney.

We stood at the intersection of two corridors within Heathrow's international arrivals, where Kevin would head to transit and a flight home, while I would take the other corridor to baggage reclaim and the exit.

'Well,' I said. 'We wanted an adventure.'

Kevin laughed. 'I have to say, after all the tricks we've got up to over the years, that was one of our wilder escapades.'

'I think we did well, though,' I said. 'We did a pretty good job of auditing the cellar, we pretty much confirmed it's all real and the cellar list is accurate, or accurate enough, *and* we managed to bring these dozen bottles away with us, to cover the costs of the trip, if nothing else. It's a better result than we could have hoped for when Neville first told us the background to this venture.'

'And we got to pose for photos with guns in our belts,' Kevin said.

I laughed. 'Yes, we did. Man, what were we thinking?'

'When in Tbilisi, do what the Tbilisians do,' he said, and held out his hand.

Kevin and I have never been much for hugging. We shook hands warmly and smiled at one another. It's lovely when the people you work with can be genuinely counted among your better friends.

We wished each other safe voyages from here, although maybe I was directing those sentiments more to the large box full of bubble-wrapped bottles that Kevin was wheeling on a trolley than to the man himself. He would understand.

It wasn't until we reconnected in Sydney a couple of weeks later that Kevin told me what had happened in the transit lounge after I'd gone.

He'd wandered into the duty-free area, as you do when you have a few hours to kill between flights. There was a fine wine merchant among the usual parade of 'exclusive boutiques' that seem to exist in every transit lounge in the world.

Of course, Kevin poked around within the wine shop and was intrigued to see they had a bottle of Château d'Yquem in a glass display case behind the counter. Kevin squinted and could make out that the Yquem was a 1985 vintage, so roughly fourteen years old at that point.

'Can I help you?' The man behind the counter looked, to Kevin, to be in his late twenties, maybe. His name tag read: 'Manager'.

'Can I have a look at that Château d'Yquem, please?' Kevin asked, indicating the bottle.

The manager looked over his shoulder and gave Kevin a dismiss-ive kind of look as he said, 'Look, I'm sorry, sir, but I'm afraid we don't allow customers to handle such precious wines as that lovely French classic.'

Kevin stared at him. 'What year is it? It looks like 1985 from here.'

'That's right, sir,' said the manager. 'An exceptional vintage. I'm afraid we really have to treat such a precious wine like that with the utmost care and respect.'

Kevin smiled, imagining what this 'manager' might have to say if he could peer into Kevin's carry-on luggage. 'I would have loved to have said, "Well, while we're on the subject, what do you think of this 1870 Yquem, a hundred and ten years older than yours, that I just carry around for fun?"' he laughed, telling me the story.

But he didn't do that. Instead, being Canadian polite, Kevin thanked the manager for his time and walked on, only laughing on the inside.

17

THE DUST SETTLES

Sydney, Australia
August 1999

And so, loaded up with stories like that, among all the other crazy tales of Tbilisi, we got back to work in our everyday world. We had enough dinner party tales to last a lifetime from those few days in Georgia.

From my point of view, the work was just beginning. Having been there and actually seen them, touched them and even tasted some of them, I had to now, somehow, from my desk in Sydney, 13,500 km away, get 40,000 bottles of the world's rarest wines out of that cellar.

I had barely dropped my bags inside the front door before I was on the phone and computer, trying to firm up our potential purchase.

George was obviously equally keen. He had sent his first email within a day of my return home, more or less asking when he could expect us to confirm we would like to buy the cellar.

I wrote back to say that we had a few issues to work through at our end, but to stay tuned.

The next call I had to make was to Neville. My answering machine at home had been busy while I was away and in the last few days there had been two calls from Neville.

His voice on the messages had been friendly and enthusiastic.

The first one said, 'Hi, John, Neville Rhodes here on Tuesday 22 June. Just wondering if you're back and how the trip went? I'm very interested to hear whether the cellar passed muster for you and Kevin. Talk soon.'

The second message was from two days later: 'John, Neville again. I guess you're not back yet. Just wondering if we could chat about the bottles and whether you think they're authentic. Hope all is well and talk soon. Cheers.'

Then, the day before I got back: 'Hi, John. This is Paula Stanford. You might remember me from the meeting we had in Neville Rhodes's office, to brief you on the cellar in Tbilisi. Neville and I would like to organise a meeting, if possible, as soon as you're back. Please call me through Neville's office. Thank you.'

Well, it would seem Neville is still an energetic partner in the venture, I thought, as I rang back. Of course, I got a personal assistant who promised to pass on a message.

I didn't hear back for a day, so I emailed him, writing,

Hi Neville, it's John Baker here. I just landed back in town and have some stories to tell. Yes, we have some wines to discuss and the interesting time we had with your Georgian friends. I even had a bath. Let's have a chat when we can, to discuss the next steps. Talk soon.'

I rang Harry and told him the brief story, of how we had managed to audit most of the cellar and hadn't found any faults. I imagined him rubbing his hands together with glee like a pantomime villain on the other end of the phone. After all, money was in the air.

But not quite.

As is my way, I cleared the whiteboard in my office and wrote notes to visualise what lay ahead.

US$1 million, I wrote. Then a tick.

I wasn't actually concerned about the investment of such a large amount. Between four of us and with almost certain confirmation that the bottles weren't fake, we knew we'd sell the entire cellar for much more than the cost price, plus expenses. Kevin was doing a rough valuation now that we were confident that the cellar list was mostly accurate. He'd get back to me soon.

I then wrote: *Give George the money?* And a cross.

Laughing and friendly as he'd been, I could hardly afford to trust George any more than I had to, or Tamaz and the other executives. We obviously couldn't transfer US\$1 million to them in the hope that they would hand over the wine. The contents of that cellar and the executives of the winery could vanish as mysteriously as the cash.

I wrote a question mark next to the cross and decided to come back to it.

Next up was: *Title to the wine?*

Who actually, legally owned the cellar and all the bottles? We still weren't sure, despite George's bluster. Did Tamaz and Revaz have shares? Did others have a stake? Before we could do a deal, we needed to clarify that George had a legal right to sell it. It bothered me that I still wasn't clear on this, even after spending a week there and all those long, boring hours in pointless meetings about future development and ownership of the winery. Another question mark went up on the whiteboard.

Underneath, I wrote: *Customs?*

George's words at the airport came back to me. 'Don't worry, John. I fix it, I fix it. We can fix all that.' His alleged uncle within the government who could make any customs issues go away, apparently. Even for what might be construed as historic and significant bottles. To be honest, I wasn't even sure what George meant by 'fixing it'. This needed clarity. A third large question mark.

Finally, I wrote: *Men in suits.* Underlined. Twice.

This was my nightmare scenario and, strangely, it could only play out if we paid George the money and everything went well.

I stood back from the whiteboard and ran through it in my head: George's mysterious parliamentary uncle has a word and actually does convince Georgian customs that 40,000 bottles of old wine leaving the country is totally okay. Superb. Hypothetically, because we wouldn't actually move the wine this way, but say we managed to pack and cart the bottles safely to London or New York. They're in place with Sotheby's or whoever, and ready to be auctioned. Our auction house runs a major marketing campaign and a large, rich crowd turns up on the big day, cheque books at the ready to buy these famous, rare, historic wines. Stalin's wine! Nicholas II's wine! Even Alexander III's wine!

Kevin, Neville, Harry and I are standing there, clinking glasses and moments away from watching the wines slowly go under the auctioneer's gavel when some men in suits appear and announce they are from the Georgian government, in charge of cultural affairs and historic artefacts. They announce we have no legal right to sell the wine. They declare that the wine is not actually just bottles of wine; it is a cultural treasure and they therefore have a legal right, according to Georgian law, to claim it for the state. In reality, maybe we could split hairs on this point, because really the cellar was whisked out of Russia by Stalin, making the wines more Russian than Georgian, but that would hardly carry the day when push came to shove. Hell, maybe it would be Soviet men in suits showing up and delivering a cultural heritage speech.

What does the auction house do? Either way, the auction is cancelled, and by this stage we are all a lot of money out of pocket.

I mentally chewed on this for a while, as I stared at the words I had written. **Men in suits.**

I realised it all came down to title. We still had an amazing collection of wine with questionable ownership. We simply had to clear it up and be squeaky-clean before we could approach any of the major auction houses. George had to prove, legally and unequivocally, that the wine was his to sell and that Georgian customs authorities would definitely permit the wines to leave the country. The government needed to agree to our purchase, before we would pay a cent or attempt to lift another bottle out of that cave.

A couple of days later, Neville, Harry, Kevin and I met in Neville's shiny office with the big view and I ran through the same list for the partners. Beforehand, over the phone, I had given both Neville and Harry a brief outline of how things went in Tbilisi, so when we arrived at the office, it was all handshakes and backslaps and celebrations. I felt like the Apollo 11 crew arriving home. Neville in particular was all smiles, telling us what a great job we'd done, and how excited he was to hear our findings.

But now, as I laid out my list of concerns, the mood became slightly more circumspect.

'It still all comes down to the bottles and whether they're real,' said Harry.

'We need to do the chemical tests,' agreed Kevin. 'We would like to consult some of the châteaux whose wines are in the cellar, and particularly Yquem, as so much of the value is in the Yquems, if they will talk to us. But every indication is that they're legitimate.'

'Do we need to pay the money up front for the Georgians to release the bottles for the sale?' Harry asked.

'Well,' Neville said. 'John, as you have just found out, it's a bit the law of the gun over there. George will be thinking that if he and his partners have the bottles, then they're theirs. If we want them, we need to give them money. There's no trust involved in this. It will be a transaction for US dollars, in their minds.'

'But John has made it clear that we can't be sure we would receive the bottles or be sure of being able to sell them once we hand over the million,' Harry said.

I waited my turn and quietly suggested, 'Well, actually, I might have an idea. It seems to me that out of the issues we face, the three biggest problems are the unclear ownership of title, the ability to get the bottles out of Tbilisi and then our right to sell them, free of Georgian government, customs or cultural officers' intervention on the day. Am I right?'

'That's my reading of it,' said Neville.

'Then how about we offer George a partnership, instead of a straight-out purchase price? My thinking is that, and I agree, we do have to give him some money, as you said, Neville, or we'll never see the bottles. But what if we offered to pay him half the agreed amount – 500,000 US dollars – as a sign of good faith, as a confirmation of the partnership? In effect, we would then own half of the cellar and he would retain half. In the partnership, we would then be in charge of moving the bottles, preparing them, running the marketing campaign and handling the actual sale. All the stuff we have to do anyway. However, and this is the key, *George* would retain ownership of the bottles and be contractually and formally in charge of all the things he keeps saying are no problem, such as clearing customs, confirming title, and waving away the Georgian customs officers, if it came to that. For the sale to be completed, he has to sort that stuff out, not us. Our contract and partnership with him would need to state that he is the owner of the wines and we have been engaged to sell the wines for him, for which we get half the profit.'

I took a breath to let everybody digest what I'd said so far, then dived into the second part of my plan.

'Obviously, this would all need to be worded so that our share is cast-iron yet we are not construed as a part owner. I'm sure a decent solicitor can work that out. Should any problems arise, George's the owner of the wines, not us, so, hey, if anybody tries to talk about us having ownership or exporting wines that we shouldn't have, we are just his agents, selling the wine for him.'

Everybody pondered it.

'We are potentially giving up 50 per cent of a large profit, though, John,' said Harry.

'We are. It's true, Harry,' I said. 'But I'm honestly not sure we can manage the potential minefield we might have to cross if we don't have George chained to the logistics side of the venture. He needs to have very tangible profit-related reasons to come through for us. And, look, maybe I *am* being too cautious and none of my fears actually happen, but what if they do?'

I took a sip of water and finished by saying, 'So we're clear, I can't see myself being involved in handing over half a million or a million dollars of US currency without some assurances that we can execute the sale and get to the profit.'

Everybody pondered this for a while.

'It has a lot of merit,' Neville said. 'We're telling George that we're happy to take the commercial risk but we're not happy to be under the cloud of the title risk.'

'What do you think, Kevin?' I asked.

'I think it sounds like an interesting plan,' he said. 'Almost every bearpit in front of us is actually in Georgia and needs that local handling we can't do. George only gets half of his million bucks but he is half of the selling exercise and knows he will get a lot more than 500,000 dollars for his share of the sale of the wine.'

'It's a major departure from where George started,' Harry said. 'He might just want the money.'

'Well, that can't happen,' I said. 'I think I can convince him that he can end up with a lot more money by going down this road, and I think George might actually enjoy being a partner in an international endeavour like this.'

'And we can be sure the sale won't be sabotaged.' Neville nodded.

'But look, we all need to digest this, because we're potentially going from maybe being 100 per cent owners of the cellar to half that. You need time to make that decision.'

We broke for coffee and small talk. But actually, the small talk didn't last long with such a major proposal in the air. Very quickly, Neville and Harry declared that they didn't really need much thinking time and the 50 per cent plan sounded like the safest and most sensible way to go.

'Okay, great,' I said. 'If we're all agreed, I might propose it to George and see what he says. He's also very keen to have investment in the winery itself, to re-establish it. Neville, I don't know if that's something that interests you?'

'No,' Neville said. 'I only want mining rights over there, and a cut of this wine treasure because I was the one who found it. I only want to buy into that ageing old vineyard if it turns out there's coal or gold underneath it.'

'Fair enough,' I said. 'So, we're agreed that we'll propose a partnership to George, instead of a straight sale?'

'Okay,' said Harry, 'but let's cut to the chase. Assuming they are real, all 40,000 or so bottles, what is the cellar worth?'

'Kevin is still working out that figure,' I said.

'You must have a rough idea,' Harry said to Kevin. 'In your head, there must be an estimate.'

'I'm uncomfortable putting a dollar figure out there before I've finished my work,' Kevin said. 'I have to look at comparable sales globally, how many other bottles of a particular rare vintage are in known collections, or available through major auction or retail channels. I also have to estimate what this provenance of Stalin and co might add to normal market prices. I will be doing a fair bit of guesswork.'

Neville looked slightly exasperated. 'Kevin, nobody is asking you to sign in blood. We just want to know that if we are going to invest half a million US dollars plus costs, we can expect a decent return.'

Kevin shifted in his seat and frowned. 'Well, sure. If I really had to pin a number to a board right now at this moment, I'd probably say two and a half to three million US dollars.'

We all considered this. 'As a total auction sale price?' Harry said.

'It might be more if the Georgian-made wines happen to catch the public imagination,' Kevin said.

'We really need to talk to a major château and show them some bottles,' I added. 'And choose an auction partner to get their view on potential costs and issues.'

'Okay, then let's move forward on that basis,' Neville said. 'I'll wait to hear a more formal estimation once you have one. Harry, can you stay behind for a moment?'

Neville led us to the elevators, shaking hands again, smiling and telling us he was so glad we were on board as partners, with so much expertise to share. There was talk of a barbecue at his Hunter Valley farm as a more social way to meet next time. We said that sounded great.

And then Kevin and I were alone, heading silently down to the ground, both staring at the inside of the closed elevator door.

'Was that your actual figure?' I asked quietly, almost certain that Kevin was playing with them a little. 'The estimation.'

'Of course not,' Kevin said. 'I have no idea what the actual figure is yet. I'll let you know when I get there but yes, it's going to be a lot more than I just told them.'

I laughed.

As we exited the building and headed to the car, Kevin said, 'They really went for your 50 per cent ownership idea. I was surprised. Neville is pragmatic so I could see him following your logic, but I didn't think old Harry would so readily step away from 100 per cent ownership.'

I shrugged. 'Harry is in a lot of deals and loves making profits but he also doesn't like to have his funds at too much risk. George's half share is like an insurance policy on Harry's invested capital so I think he found comfort in that. Without George fully committed, what we're about to attempt would be much more fraught.'

The staff at the Double Bay Cellars wanted to know everything when we returned. We had a big dinner one night after closing the shop where Kevin and I took turns telling parts of the adventure, with

Frank and Jillian particularly tuned in to the bottles in the cellar and the details of the collection.

I mentioned that on one shelf of the cellar we'd found mysterious bottles mentioning *miel*, which had confused us.

'*Ah, oui. Chouchen*,' Jillian shrugged.

'Excuse me?' I said.

'*Chouchen*. It's Breton: a honey-based liqueur, from Bretagne, or Brittany in English, the most westerly part of France. You know, the Celtic part? The fishermen drink *chouchen* when they return from the sea. Lots of honey. But it is dangerous stuff, *mon ami*. It used to be made with honeycomb, bees, venom, everything, and legend has it the venom fermented and made *chouchen* super potent. The hotels in Brittany still have hooks at the bar for the fishermen to attach their belts to, because too much *chouchen* affects a man's balance and they can fall clean backwards off their stools.'

Kevin and I looked at one another.

'I feel like our valuation might have missed a trick there,' he said.

'We'll have to look them up again if we go back,' I agreed.

'And make sure we never drink whatever that is.' Kevin laughed. 'It sounds lethal.'

'Like everything in life, Kevin, it's all about moderation,' Jillian said.

Kevin nodded. 'Okay, that's good to know. I'm not bad at moderation.'

Late in the first week after my return to Sydney, George emailed again, addressing the email to Kevin and me.

Dear Kevin. Was pleased to get that info that all the wines got home safe for you. Please let me know if you need any more detail about the winery or wine industry of Georgia. John, can you please provide me with draft of any winery development? I want to use it as draft to make one quick one for Winery Number 1, regards George Aramhishvili.

This became the theme of our email exchanges over the next couple of weeks: George kept throwing out requests for winery redevelopment leads while we asked our own questions, such as Kevin wanting to know about the 'hardened' wines we'd found in the list when we finally received details of Stalin's collection, and, more importantly, could George please send the other twelve bottles we'd put aside?

George replied:

I will find out about 'hardened'. I think in Georgian it is *shemar-grebuli*, which is a sort of port wine. On the bottles, I have Tamaz received permission from God to give next 12 bottles. He loves Chato Ikems especially. He is telling bullshit me about prices 10,000 for 10 bottles of Chato Ikem. Kind regards, George.

Kevin and I both digested that email, and George's turn of phrase. In the end, it was Kevin who wrote back, saying he was still pulling together information about rebuilding wineries and equipment that might be required, and would have it to George soon. He also really needed info on the hardened wines as there were quite a few of them and it was holding back his overall assessment of the collection. Finally, Kevin wrote that he was about to book a laboratory and technician for analysis of the bottles we had, and therefore really needed the remaining dozen to arrive. 'I will speak to God on Tamaz's behalf re the other bottles,' he wrote to George. 'In case I do not receive a response, could you please send the remaining twelve bottles as soon as possible. This is an expensive process and I would like to only do it once.'

That was ambitious, Kevin, I thought to myself. I never expected us to see the other dozen bottles. What? Was George, Tamaz or some other Tbilisi winery worker going to carefully package up the dozen antique bottles that they never wanted us to take in the first place, and just send them over? Not likely. But as I followed the email chain, instead of the bottles, we received a surprising answer.

'Thank you for your information you promise to send me,' George replied. 'Hardened wines are ported wines. Hardened in local wine language means strong. With regard to bottles, I faxed Neville results of previous testing of wine collection done years ago. Hope will be any useful.'

I rang Kevin. 'Did Neville ever mention to you that he had information from George about previous tests on the wines?'

'Not a word,' Kevin said. 'It seems like something he could have shared with us.'

'Maybe he forgot. Or maybe George only just sent it. We'll ask him.'

Inevitably, even if we knew we'd never see the other dozen, George would still dangle them in front of us, in emails, to remind us that they were there, along with all the others. Throughout these weeks, we were either emailing or phoning George to discuss the ownership of the cellar and how to get the bottles out of Georgia, while he was constantly discussing the impending 'takeover' of the winery, which would include the bottles.

During all this, I ran my fifty-fifty partnership idea past George, and he was agreeable, and quite quickly, actually. After I put the initial proposal to him, he didn't need much convincing. He immediately understood that this plan could see him receive more than US$1 million and I think he enjoyed the idea of being partners with these Australians he liked and maybe even felt he could trust. He also warmed to the concept of him being a partner in the marketing exercise and building his own relationship with London, if that's where we based the sale. I still didn't tell him any more than I had to as we hadn't finalised the deal and there were many elements that could still go wrong. But we began to draw up legal agreements in Sydney, while discussing potential lawyers that he may have access to, who could handle his legal documents and also confirm who owned the wine.

This question was killing me more than any of the others. We'd been home for well over a month, traded dozens of emails and phone calls, and still had no clear line on who owned the Savane Number One Winery and all of its assets, including the cellars. After one long phone call with George, running over the fine detail of our entire proposal, and repeatedly trying to pitch this one vital question, I was still left with one note at the bottom of my page, reading: 'Do you, George, have the legal position to agree to this?'

He certainly talked as though he was the man in charge, but then he always had, from before we went to Tbilisi, without feeling a need to mention the entire room full of other executives that we would discover upon arrival. When I pushed him again on the security and export procedure of moving the wine, he wrote back: 'The takeover plan includes that after the takeover, we appoint our supervisory board, our directors' board. Neville, Kevin and John definite members of both boards. My boys replace all security and present staff within weeks. Swiss bank style locks immediately.'

This was an eye-opening email for me. 'What it's saying,' I said to Kevin, 'is that George doesn't have control over the company at this stage, but if we can agree a deal to sell the collection and re-establish the Savane Number One as a going concern, he'd put himself in a position where he could take over the whole thing.'

'I think we stay focused on our deal, which is to buy a half share of the wine,' Kevin said. 'I'd love to get Neville's take on this.'

'Yeah. I've called him twice but he hasn't replied,' I said. 'There was another line in a George email that mentioned Neville. It said: "We should start takeover next week at the latest. Initially we need 140,000 dollars to complete all legal paperwork and make complete takeover. Balance of half payment after that and final balance after shipment of wines and all export procedures completed upon Neville's instructions."'

'On Neville's instructions,' Kevin said.

'I guess they talk about the mining. Maybe Neville just mentioned he would help with that export part if we needed it,' I said.

The legal emails and discussions continued for another week or so. I still hadn't heard from Neville or Harry, so I just ploughed on trying to agree to a deal with George, using KPMG's Sydney office to draft the paperwork. I did write a one-page summary to George, explaining that my plan would see the initial US$500,000 placed in a solicitor's trust account to be released when the wines crossed the Georgian border or left Georgian waters. It meant George wouldn't receive a cent unless the wines actually left Georgia, and he must have accepted it, because our lawyers continued to draft up the agreement.

My fax machine continued to run hot. One morning, I arrived to discover a fax from the Business Legal Bureau, Attorney of Law, Georgia.

The letter gave an official legal opinion from Tbilisi about what we were dealing with. It explained that the Georgian No. 1 winery (the Savane, as we called it) had been privatised in 1993 and listed the activities of the company. As of 1996, the letter said shareholders in the winery included Mr Tamaz (17 per cent) and Mr Revaz (11 per cent). But then further changes in 1998 had altered the shareholding again. Of course, that was only the year before our visit so it made sense that soon after that latest change of ownership, somebody had decided a way to raise much-needed capital could be to sell those old wines in the cellar. There was no mention anywhere of George's name or any business we understood to be George's. Where did George get his shares, or access to the company, to be making such major decisions?

I sat and thought about it. There was no doubt, when we were there, that George carried considerable weight at the Savane Number One and with the executives. He was certainly a major player in this, even if he hadn't apparently made his ownership move yet. Or was George a part of, or maybe a puppet for, the new owners?

One bright spot within the letter was that it outlined the stock and assets of the winery and stated clearly that: 'The enterprise has old traditions and unique collections samples of wine among them from collection of Stalin and Russian Tsar King Alexander III and Nikolai II.'

That was a nice piece of paper with a legal letterhead to take to an auction house as proof of our claim. In fact, once we received the other necessary documentation from George and his cohorts, we would be in a strong position to discuss a very attractive auction of this amazing collection. No matter how much ownership and legal tape I waded through, I kept one eye on those bottles.

While all of this was going on, I was trying to manage my usual workload. The Double Bay Cellars was busy. It was a great business and we had very good staff. With real estate prices soaring in that part of Sydney, along with pre-Olympic excitement and spring in the air, summer was around the corner and we struggled to keep up at times.

I was sitting at my desk doing paperwork, an hour or so after closing one night, when Kevin wandered in clutching a quiver of A4 paper and mentioned that he had some 'creative accounting' that I might be interested in.

I looked up and said, 'Aha! The Georgian cellar valuation?'

He nodded. 'You're the only person in the world that I know who would actually say "Aha!" but that was an entertaining one,' he said.

'Well, this calls for a drink, whatever the figure,' I said. 'Do I choose a good wine or a very good wine?'

'Make it rather good, I think,' he said.

I fetched a nice half bottle of a most respectable Bordeaux, a Château Pichon Baron, and poured us both a glass.

Kevin had taken his usual chair opposite me, inspecting his glass and sipping the Bordeaux. He was clearly in no hurry to get to the point.

'Ah, John,' he mused. 'How appropriate. A stablemate of our beloved Suduiraut. It's a great château, Pichon Baron, in the absolute dress circle position in Pauillac, with exceptional *terroir*, and one that I think it going to improve even more over the coming years.'

I had decided by now that he clearly didn't have bad news for me, and in fact was potentially even looking slightly smug.

'Okay, suspense king, stop playing,' I said. 'Let's hear it.'

He grinned and leaned forward.

'The key figure you're probably waiting to hear is eight,' he said in that deadpan Canadian way of his.

'Eight?' I said.

'Maybe seven,' he admitted.

'Can you expand on that, just a little?' I asked.

He said he could, if I'd allow him quite a few asterisks and side-notes. Could we get all 40,000 bottles out? How many racks would fall, destroying how many bottles, before or during the process? 'I concede this is unlikely,' he said, 'because the racks we saw actually seemed fairly secure, but I think we should factor in as a consideration that some might collapse as we unload the bottles.'

'Yes, fair enough,' I said.

Kevin had other concerns. 'Can we find a packaging company trustworthy and careful enough to nurse such fragile wines?' he asked. 'As well as the obvious age of the bottles, there are other dangers. During wars over the last century or so, for example, the best glass was in some cases diverted to the war effort, to make telescopic sights and other important optic equipment. Wine companies had to do their best to find other potential bottle materials and I even read that in some cases, second-hand bottles were used. How many of those are among the cellar's riches, just waiting to collapse when picked up?'

'Yes, fair enough, Kevin, I can see it's worth noting but every bottle we picked up seemed to be okay and certainly showed no sign of excessive fragility or possible deterioration, as long as they were to be carefully packed,' I said. 'But I like your thinking and yes, we need to be aware of all this.'

'Well, the good news,' Kevin said, 'is that even if you put all of those questions aside and assume that we would be able to lift the vast majority of the collection intact, my rough appraisal is that the cellar should fetch between seven and eight million US dollars under the hammer. It will probably piss Neville and Harry off, but I can't really get any more exact than that at this stage.'

I laughed and shrugged.

'Kevin, that's brilliant. We don't need it to be any more detailed at this stage. What you're telling me is that we would easily cover the overall cost of the purchase from George and the expenses of removal and carrying out the auction. We know those costs are going to be considerable, but this figure means there should still be a very handy profit even after all that, hey?'

'If we were to have any trouble getting George, Neville or Harry over the line on the fifty-fifty idea before, I think one look at these figures should convince them, in terms of the overall potential profit,' Kevin said. 'There's enough money to go around.'

He was right but the truth was that I wasn't necessarily even in this adventure just for the money anymore, much as I was not against the idea of doing well for our efforts. I was having a lot of fun, enjoying the closest thing to the *Raiders of the Lost Ark* that a wine buyer could ever hope to experience in his or her professional life. Besides delivering to George more than his initial US$1 million asking price, it would be rewarding if we could also help alert the world to the wonders of Georgia, its wine history and its potential as a tourism and wine destination. Kevin and I wanted to deliver the cellar, and deliver it well, using all of our expertise and skill. In other words, there was a lot of motivation to be successful, and here was Kevin's estimation to give us the financial certainty to charge on.

Buoyed by Kevin's news, I emailed Neville and Harry to tell them Kevin's estimate and then booked an appointment with the lawyers helping us at KPMG's Sydney office. We refined the official deal, which I was keen to at least send to George so that we could judge his commitment at this stage of the game. There's nothing like asking somebody to sign an agreement to make all the parties involved consolidate their thinking or flush out the elements they don't agree with. Once we had an agreement signed and we were confident that George and his crowd were definitely planning to go through with the deal, I would finally have something to take to Sotheby's, Christie's or another major auction house.

The agreement stated that we would pay a US$100,000 deposit on the wines upon signing and upon a valid legal opinion that George was entitled to agree to the deal as the owner of the wines.

We had a lot of provisions about who was in charge of various aspects of what was to come. The goods had to be packed under expert supervision, and the seller of the half share of the cellar (George) was responsible for having the wines delivered safely to the port or airport nominated by the buyer (us). As buyer, we were responsible for the freight and insurance of the goods being exported. However, it made it clear that George or the Savane Number One sellers were 'responsible for any government authority prior to export.'

'Delivery is executed when the wine leaves Georgia on exportation to the country we nominate,' it read. I was reasonably sure that the destination would be the United Kingdom. In fact, I was leaning towards Sotheby's as the auction house, given they had once staged a major sale of the Massandra Collection, from Russia's official winery. That auction had not included any antique French wines and that was one of the aspects we were pinning our valuation hopes on. My idea was that we would show them our sample bottles, by then authenticated, and Sotheby's would send an expert valuer to Tbilisi to authenticate the remaining bottles and to confirm the 'story' of the auction. Sotheby's would certify the wine and do the packaging, not unlike what they did for the Massandra Collection. Given they had already pulled off that monster, we would also remain open to their advice, and a better plan, if they had one. This part was their world more than ours.

The remaining US$400,000 would be put into the trust account, as explained to George. There would be provisions for 'an adjustment to the investment amount', depending on the condition of the bottles upon arrival in England. If there was major damage or bottles had gone missing along the way, those costs would be taken from the overall cost of the cellar and the US$400,000 balance would be adjusted accordingly.

Clause 9 specifically mentioned that the seller would need to indemnify and protect the buyer in the case of any breach of a warranty in the agreement. In simple language, if anybody came after us about the wine after shipping, claiming it belonged to the Georgian people or wasn't George's to sell, we would be covered.

'Dear Kevin,' George wrote on Tuesday 10 August. 'How are things from your end? Can we speed up the story?'

'Dear John,' George wrote to me, maybe another week later. 'When do you think takeover can take place? This week?'

I could feel the anxiety from George's end of things, as this deal actually began to sharpen. Or maybe it was excitement, because the sale might happen? We were talking about a lot of money in Georgian lari. We had George's full attention.

Until it seemed we didn't. After that flurry of hurry-up emails, everything went silent from the Tbilisi end for three full weeks. Eventually, Kevin wrote, asking George if everything was okay.

The next day, we received a reply.

'Everything is going to schedule under Neville's personal supervision,' George wrote. 'I just need one more week to complete papers from my end and after that, you can start your part of the work. We have legal office now. I can give you the email address if you are interested in the services. Kind regards, George.'

I put in a call to Neville but he didn't call back. I emailed, asking Neville to please give me a call. Was he currently in Tbilisi? What did George mean by Neville's personal supervision? Neville hadn't mentioned to us that he was guiding George to make sure the deal went through, but it was actually a smart idea, if he was, given their mining relationship. It could make the agreement sail through more easily.

A week later, George wrote again.

All takeover documents are completed and are currently sended to Sydney Neville for approval. Within 5 working days after it you can start up your activity dealing with new director and owner of Winery No. 1, Mr Neville Rhodes.

I was literally reading those words when my phone started ringing. I glanced at the email header and saw Kevin had been cc'ed in.

I picked up the phone and said, 'Hi, Kevin.'

'You're the business guy,' Kevin said down the line. 'Explain to me what is going on that our old mate Nev just became the director and owner of Savane Number One.'

I pursed my lips, thinking.

'All I can think,' I finally said, 'is that Neville and George have decided that that is the best way to make sure we can get the wine out, guaranteed. All along we've wondered who owns the Savane Number One and whether George had the right to agree to selling the collection. If it's Neville now in that chair, we're free to make it happen, aren't we?'

'I guess so,' said Kevin. 'It doesn't strike you as weird that Neville didn't think to explain that plan to us, though?'

'Definitely weird,' I agreed. 'Neville is super friendly but he only seems to communicate when he wants to. I'm going to chase him down now, to double-check that this is all above board, from our point of view.'

I sat at my desk, took a deep breath and stared into space, crafting letters to Neville in my head. We had a legal four-partner agreement in place, so I only needed to know how this development was designed to help our wine sale. In the end, I decided to approach from a less fraught angle. I wrote to Neville, explaining that I was heading to London the following week and would need some documentation from him, as official owner of the Savane Number One, stating that I had the right to discuss the cellar and the proposed sale with the relevant people while I was there.

'Neville, I'm sure you understand that I can't be discussing the cellar from simply a conceptual point of view. I would have to have documented access and irrevocable ability to deliver the cellar, to be able to really wind these people up and maximise our position,' I wrote.

I printed the letter and faxed it to Neville's personal fax number.

Two days of silence later, I emailed George, asking for a progress update.

'I send Neville paperwork to complete actual takeover,' George wrote back. 'I also try to contact him on daily basis without major success. Maybe you can do it more efficiently from that end. Steven Thrush is in Tbilisi these days, departing tomorrow to Sydney, so I will send some message to Neville via him too.'

I squinted at my screen, thinking: Who is Steven Thrush?

I was now two days away from flying to London, without the approval to raise the concept of the sale with Sotheby's. I did some research while I waited and discovered this Steven Thrush chap was involved in Alaniya Gold, so presumably he was a colleague of Neville's in the mining business.

I was not enjoying this vacuum we'd found ourselves in. I repeatedly rang Harry, who just shrugged and said he hadn't spoken to Neville and had no idea where things were at. I tried Paula, Neville's lawyer, but she didn't call me back. I had a mostly drafted international agreement to buy and sell museum wine worth millions of dollars and now my own partners had gone mute on me. I didn't understand it and I was starting to get a little nervous about how things were sitting.

Some people and deals get complicated, but my philosophy has always been that one has to stay focused on the main issue and not let the trash and shrapnel complicate things further. Very simply, George wanted US dollars for the wine and we were prepared to pay them, so all of this other talk and winery ownership and other complications were only noise, as long as they didn't actually torpedo the deal. Smart people condense a scenario down to the end goal and just punch on through, so I decided to take that road.

And anyway, I'm not one to give up easily, so I kept calling Neville. The day before I flew out to London, I almost fell off my chair when he actually answered.

'John,' he said, with nothing but happiness to hear from me, sunshine and warmth in his voice down the phone. 'How are you? Sorry I've been a bit hard to catch. Got a lot going on.'

'So I hear,' I said, 'which is why I rang. Neville, what is going on? I have a few questions, off the back of my correspondence with George. Am I correct in believing you now have control of the board of the Savane Number One Winery?'

'That's right,' Neville said. 'I am the director and owner of that business now.'

'The owner?' I asked.

'That's correct,' he said.

'Okay, so, Neville, if we turn up with a truck to move some stock out of that cellar, do you own and control it, or can somebody stop us?'

'No, I don't control that yet,' he said.

'Why not?'

'Because George has to get the legals drawn up in Georgia, to move any stock.'

'So George can do that on our behalf and your behalf?'

'Sure,' he said.

'Do I need to go to Tbilisi to deal with lawyers there, as George suggested, and have that documentation done?' I asked.

'That would be a way of doing it,' Neville said. 'However, I won't come. We don't need a football team there. Anyway, we're getting closer, hey, John? I really need to go. Have a great trip to London.'

After we'd hung up, I realised he had still not given me approval to officially approach Sotheby's.

I had an entire trip to London and France, buying wine for the shop, to ponder where things were at. With Neville now owning the winery, that took away the huge headache of who we were actually dealing with. No more Tamaz or Revaz, presumably, to stand in our way. But did this mean we were now paying Neville US$500,000 for a half share of the wine that he was supposedly trying to buy?

What also gnawed at me was that even Neville, from this new position of strength as the owner, hadn't been able to confirm that we could take the wine out of Tbilisi.

When I returned to Australia, I contacted Alan Bennett, a partner at KPMG's legal department, and explained where we were at. I was sick of the same old unknowns and decided to invest some money in legal work to know once and for all. Alan mentioned that KPMG had an office in Azerbaijan, the country south of Georgia, and we asked that office for help. Alan and I drew up terms of reference, relating to my same old chestnuts: who owned the wine, any and all government and licensing and approvals required for export, and the likelihood of any government claim on the wine as artefacts during or after export. Also, as a matter of interest, was anybody selling the wine also allowed to be part of the group buying the wine, as Neville now seemed to be.

Kevin, upon hearing that I was now waiting for this legal opinion, just snorted and said, 'I'm tipping that the lawyers say we have a snowflake's chance in hell of the Georgian government letting us sell them, but George and Neville say everything is A-OK, so hand over the money.'

I groaned. This was beginning to do my head in, so I did the only logical thing and left town, heading north to go visit a friend, Anne, in Noosa for a couple of nights of excellent wine, very good food and great company. Walking through the national park, watching logger-head turtles and dolphins in the ocean, was a good way to calm my whirring brain about the Georgian situation. What will be will be, I thought. You can't push it and shouldn't push it. This was about the adventure, not just the money. It's in the hands of experts now, so let them deal the cards and see how they fall.

That night, Anne organised a dinner with some local friends and announced we'd be playing a game called Jolene.

'You know the Dolly Parton song?' Anne asked. 'Well, one person is Jolene and everybody else has to role-play the part of a woman who is worried that Jolene is going to take their man. It's their job to argue succinctly and passionately why Jolene shouldn't take their man. Once everybody has stated their case, the person playing Jolene decides which man she will take, just because she can.'

'Wow,' I said. 'Is this a Noosa thing?'

'No, it's an Anne thing,' Anne said. 'And just for asking that question, Mr John Baker, my dear friend, *you* will be playing the role of Jolene.'

'Your happiness depends on me,' I said, pouring myself another wine.

This was going to be fun.

18

PUSH COMES TO SHOVE

Alan Bennett's Azerbaijan contacts took more than two months to report back. The year had clicked over to 2000, somehow without the dreaded and much hyped millennium bug destroying the world's computer systems. I hadn't heard from Harry or Neville but it had also been Christmas and New Year, then the summer break, so it didn't surprise me that correspondence was sluggish. George had exchanged cheery 'Happy New Year' emails with both Kevin and me, writing that the new millennium was when we would finally sell the wine and all be rich! But then had been quiet through the rest of the month.

I spent some time in Melbourne, watching and sort of helping a friend with a new restaurant. The manager and chief sommelier was a woman called Jane Thornton and I enjoyed seeing her team pull together the new restaurant. It was a world that I'd only briefly dabbled in, advising and investing once in a friend's restaurant in Sydney, but now I enjoyed watching a professional restaurant management team starting from scratch. As always, I was up for new experiences and opening up whole new worlds of knowledge. I was impressed with Jane, who was smart, missed nothing and yet was warm and funny with her team. She had an impressive CV, having managed or been sommelier of a couple of Melbourne's best restaurants. She certainly knew her wines and so of course I had to share some of my better

Georgian stories. I enjoyed my new colleague's reaction, especially to the visual picture of dozens of antique Yquem sitting in the wet darkness.

Once the restaurant was up and running, I headed north to my own business and got back to work in the shop.

A week or so later, Alan sent me a letter with the considered opinion of his experts. I asked Kevin to come over, and we sat on either side of my desk with a copy each and started to read.

'"The wines are very likely to be officially classified by the Georgian government as collection wines,"' Kevin read aloud. '"They would be required to be stored in a Vinotech." You know what that means. Proper, expensive temperature- and moisture-controlled atmosphere, and high security.'

'No more being covered in cobwebs in the Savane's wet cellar,' I agreed, frowning at my papers. 'What about this: "As collection wines, they could not be exported, however if they were collection wines but did not constitute museum property, they could be exported."'

'It gets better,' Kevin said. '"If the wines were classified as cultural values under the relevant Georgian heritage protection legislation, then a certificate permitting their exportation must be obtained from the Ministry of Culture. If they're over 100 years old or have any special cultural significance, they cannot be exported." Well, damn.'

I continued. '"If the wines are exported without obtaining the appropriate certificates or clearances, then it is possible that the Georgian authorities could apply overseas to have them returned, including instituting legal proceedings and invoking the UNESCO Convention on the Protection of Cultural Property."'

'There it is, straight off your whiteboard: Men in suits,' Kevin said, sighing.

'Potentially, yeah,' I answered. 'I still maintain that there's an argument against the French wines even being considered Georgian cultural heritage, given they were stolen from Russia and have nothing to do with Georgia apart from lying in that cellar for fifty years, and maybe the Stalin hometown connection. I'm not sure the people in Azerbaijan understand that whole story. Anyway, as we expected, it all comes down to title and rights of export. That's George's problem, under our deal. Let's send it on to him and Neville and see what they say.'

The response I received from Neville's office was from Paula, the lawyer, saying that after discussions with George, they didn't see any problems with getting the export permits. I wasn't totally convinced by this response and rang or wrote to Neville several times, without success. Any move from us now was going to start costing us money, so I didn't want to be casual about the potential risks identified by the report. But I also wasn't so impressed by the findings of the report, or whether they accurately applied to the wine, that it stopped me pressing on.

Harry contacted me and we ran through the possible complications and the fact neither of us could track down Neville. Harry was also concerned about potential costs from this point, including our paying a monthly fee to have a bank account in the venture's name while nothing was happening. He decided to close it.

'But Harry,' I said, 'we might be opening the account again in a week, if we hear back from Neville or George.'

'Then we have saved a week's fees, which is a good thing,' he said. 'Leave it with me.'

In fact, it was his wife, Eva, who contacted me a week later, to say she'd closed the account. We'd originally each contributed $10,000, to give ourselves $40,000 in operating capital. We'd spent $28,000 in expenses, more or less, and there was still $11,966 in the account when she closed it. I received a cheque for $2991.60.

I wrote to George, yet again pointing out that legally this was in his hands and Kevin and I would be guided by his judgement, as the local. 'We are ready and keen to proceed with the venture, George,' I wrote. 'As long as you are not concerned with KPMG's issues raised.

You understand the position in Georgia much better than we ever will, so it's over to you. Hope you are well, John.'

Time continued to drift, and silence prevailed. Written like this, it sounds strange to think another month and a half passed without resolving this issue, but in reality, I was crazy busy with the Double Bay Cellars, the early days of an olive-oil growing and manufacturing business I had somehow become involved with, and other aspects of work and life. I'm not one to dwell or stew when things aren't going quite as well as I like. Sure, I rang Neville and Harry, trying to find out where things were at, but I wasn't about to sit by my phone and computer, waiting for them to finally reappear.

George emailed me, once again raising the proposal that I might be interested in discussing becoming formally involved in investing in the Georgian wine industry in general, providing operation capital and expertise. As discussed during our visit, he wrote.

I responded, hopefully politely, that I had no intention of discussing any business venture other than the one I hadn't heard about from George, Neville or Paula for some time. Let us move and sell the bottles and then we can talk about future projects, I wrote.

The frustration built over time. 'We're one email away from victory,' I said to Kevin, as we pondered yet again what was happening across town in Neville's office and across the world in George's brain. 'We just need Neville, as chairman and owner of the Savane, to write to us saying they've confirmed the export details with the Georgian government and we are clear to proceed with the sale. One email.'

'Maybe Neville is writing that as we speak?' Kevin said. 'Perhaps he just can't choose the perfect font for such an exciting email.'

'I'd be happy with anything,' I said. 'I'd be happy with crayon on butcher's paper. Just give us the go-ahead and let's do this. You realise it's almost been a year since we were in Tbilisi?'

'I miss Nino's driving every single day,' Kevin said. 'Seriously, John, let's just get on with it, so we're ready to proceed as soon as Neville finally gives us the green light. You're heading to London again in a week or so, aren't you? Why not get a meeting with Sotheby's? Why not see if you can meet somebody from a château? Take one of the bottles and start that authentication process?'

'You're right,' I said. 'We've all come this far. It's time to push on.'

The very next day brought a letter in the mail from Neville's company, addressed to my company, Kevin's company and Harry's company. He wrote how the agreement made back in June 1999 charged us 'with arranging the purchase of the cellar', which had not occurred, and then followed the bombshell: ' I have had to purchase the cellar with my own resources. I also note that a joint venture bank account was closed on 30 June. Therefore, the venture is at an end.'

Three curt paragraphs had ended everything.

We'd been worried the whole time that the Georgians were playing us, that it was George who was trying to con us out of US$1 million. Actually, now I thought about it at 11 pm that evening, and nursing a heavy red wine which was not my first of the night, my imagination began to take flight. Had he always intended to buy the cellar? Maybe he had already done so before we got on the plane? With George in cahoots, Neville let Kevin and me fly over, establish the authenticity and value of the cellar, and then stage-managed the events since so that it looked as though we hadn't delivered, forcing him to end the joint venture. If so, I couldn't believe we'd fallen for it.

And had the street-smart Harry fallen for it? As I turned it all over in my head, I started to believe that probably he hadn't. I had thought it strange at the time that he and his wife had summarily closed the bank account, and now I speculated how this development had turned out to be a trigger for Neville's actions.

Maybe it was only Kevin and me who were not in on the game.

A couple of days later, I had a call from Neville's Paula Stanford. She told me that she wanted the twelve bottles of wine that I allegedly took from Georgia, which were the property of Mr Rhodes.

'Are you serious?' I asked the lawyer.

'Very serious, Mr Baker.'

'Well, I don't have any wine from Georgia,' I replied, 'and I didn't bring a single bottle from Georgia into Australia.'

Technically true as, of course, I did not, I thought as I hung up on Paula's spluttering response. I hoped she didn't have Kevin's number, given the dozen bottles were at his office.

Eventually the man himself, Neville Rhodes, wrote to say he'd paid US$100,000 as a deposit on the Savane winery and that meant any bottles, in the winery or in Australia, were his. He accused me of being hostile to Ms Stanford and told me to accept that our agreement was at an end, and to hand over his valuable wine.

There's no point detailing the whole who-said-what of the following exchanges. I told Neville the only reason we weren't still in business together was because he'd refused to answer our calls or emails. He claimed to have written to us explaining the situation back in April but never heard back from us. I said. He said. I said . . . it went on.

Finally, he wrote, 'The venture is over. Return my wine without further fuss to save the need for me to resort to lawyers.'

I read that line again and groaned. Why do people who refuse to talk reasonably, probably because they know they're being an arsehole, always threaten to resort to lawyers? It's so boring.

19

AMONG THE RUBBLE

'Why don't we just tell Pyotr and Nino that Neville kidnapped their mothers?'

For all of his inherent Canadian niceness, there's a deep-seated hard edge to Kevin that I find entertaining – even if on this particular morning he was probably joking.

'Georgian mafia revenge isn't our usual method of operation,' I pointed out.

'It would be satisfying, though,' he said.

'I look at it this way,' I said, leaning forward in my seat, 'There's one thing our old buddy Neville has forgotten.'

'That we Canadians inflicted Bryan Adams on the world and we're not afraid to do it again?'

'Even more alarming,' I said.

'Okay, what's that?' Kevin asked.

'He doesn't know a fucking thing about this wine,' I said, before leaning back and sipping from my glass of water. 'And we do.'

'It's a good point,' he nodded.

I continued, 'If we haven't been able to work out the customs issues, the heritage problems and the actual export logistics, with all of our knowledge and experience, I don't see how he's going to.

But then again, maybe the customs issues aren't of concern to him, like we think they probably are.'

'Maybe he's brazen enough to just ship it out now he's the owner,' Kevin said.

'Maybe, but even then, so what? How is he going to approach Sotheby's?'

Kevin stirred his coffee and nodded.

'A goldmine operator claiming he has 40,000 bottles of antique Yquem and so on. Unable to really give them any details. It's unlikely.'

'Exactly,' I said. 'The export logistics demand experts. The only way that cellar gets sold is with us involved. Or he has to start all over again with another version of us going there to do a new audit. As it stands, you and I know more about what's in that cellar than anybody else in the world, probably including the Georgians. Think about it. We have all of our notes cross-referencing the translated cellar list with the actual cellar, plus our notes authenticating what's on individual shelves, plus our tasting notes, *and* your valuation notes. They don't have any of that.'

'But Neville owns it, John. He's ended our agreement. We have no way to go in and get the wine, if he has cut ties with us.'

'He's going to need us, for marketing, for authentication and for exporting it out of Tbilisi, if that's what he wants to do,' I insisted.

'If we're willing to help,' Kevin said. 'Because there is the *other* road which is, pardon my Alaskan, "Fuck him".'

'Well, sure. We have that option. I just find it hard to let it go. Think of all those bottles. Dozens and dozens of antique Yquem, Margaux, Latour and Lafite! Most wine industry experts would be amazed to see one nineteenth-century Yquem in their life. We know where hundreds are stashed.'

'If we can't sell them, I don't care,' Kevin said simply. 'They may as well be on the moon. Sitting in the Savane Number One, whether owned by Neville or George or Pyotr or Natascha, they're of no value to us. It's time to move on.'

We sat silently for a while, alone in our thoughts, until finally I said, 'We may not be able to actually move on, as it stands. He may well be the sort of guy who will send waves of lawyers after us.'

'For what?' Kevin said. 'The dozen bottles? Then fine, let's sort that out.'

2 0

DIVIDING THE DOZEN

We met two days later, at Kevin's office, and stood in silence for a moment looking at the beautiful, sleek, dark necks of twelve antique bottles of wine. Still mostly covered in bubble wrap. Kevin and I delicately took them, one by one, out of the protective materials, wiped them gently and stood them on the large oak table that he used as a desk.

'We can't keep them all,' I said sadly. 'We need to remember that. We can't keep them all.'

'Or we do, but we need to take them to a new home in South America and change our names to Pedro and Juan,' said Kevin.

'I'm not that attached to them,' I smiled. 'The big question is how we divide these twelve bottles with incredibly different values between four parties?'

'There's good value in a number of the bottles individually,' Kevin said. 'We'll keep the ones that definitely cover our expenses. They can have the others.'

I nodded. 'But we need to divide them fairly and reasonably, so that we can walk away from this with our dignity, plus I don't want any bad blood or accusations of any kind. This partnership is ending unsatisfactorily enough as it is.'

'So we need to ensure that, while also ensuring we both end up with some kick-ass bottles of Stalin's wine,' Kevin added.

'Of course. Possession counts for a lot, while we have them,' I said. 'Which bottles do you want?'

We regarded the bottles. There was the 1870-something Yquem, the one for which we couldn't work out the fourth digit of the vintage. Kevin had noted when we chose it that the fill level was very, very high shoulder – an exceptional fill level for 100-plus years old.

Another Yquem was from 1858.

A Coutet was a rarity from the cellar in that it still retained quite a bit of its label and was from 1864. It was also filled to high shoulder; an extraordinarily valuable bottle of wine.

There was a 1919 Margaux.

The list went on. Now that we were not in the cellar, surrounded by thousands of impossibly old, valuable bottles, the uniqueness and value of the twelve here freshly dawned on us.

'One problem,' Kevin finally said, 'is that I don't particularly feel like sitting around a table with Neville and Harry, listening to which wines they'd like and why. Plus, Neville or his attack dog, Paula, would argue they're all his, which would not be helpful to the discussion.'

'No way am I doing that,' I agreed. 'Let's divide them fairly, so there can be no real argument. We collected them as part of the four-way partnership so they should be divided as such. Kevin, how would you divide them into quarter lots, according to value? Is it possible?'

Kevin stood and squinted and I watched that calculator brain of his consider the exercise.

He ran a finger over the top of one bottle, then drifted it to sit briefly on the cork of another. I was quiet, knowing how he works. I could almost hear his brain humming.

'Okay,' he finally said. 'The 1956 Salkhino – you know, the Georgian sweet wine? Neville gets that, plus the 1919 Château Margaux and the 1858 Château d'Yquem. I *really* hate to part with that one, but it's a genuine jewel. Owning that means he cannot argue whether he got 25 per cent, actually more than a quarter of the value of the dozen.'

'What about Harry?' I asked.

'Well, funnily enough, I actually discussed this with him once before,' Kevin said. 'Not long after we got back and I talked him through the dozen. Harry said he was most interested in that 1864 Coutet; the one with the part-label. On its own, because of the label, and the level of fill, it's straight-out worth a lot of money. He said he most wanted to own that bottle.'

In my head, I ran through recent sale prices I'd read about, and tried to remember how high the price of Coutets had been. This bottle was 130 years old.

'Do you think it's worth 25 per cent of the total value of the twelve, by itself?' I asked.

'I think you can definitely build an argument to say that,' Kevin nodded.

I shrugged. 'Great. So, what's left for us? You go first. I want you to be happy with your share.'

Kevin circled the remaining bottles, appraising. I wasn't remotely concerned about him taking advantage of choosing first. Kevin and I trust one another. He wasn't about to stooge me. And anyway, I was going to be happy with whatever bottles ended up in my cellar, sitting alongside my unique Lady Grange pair and other curios. There were no disappointments among this precious dozen.

'You know what?' Kevin finally said. 'I think I am most intrigued by the Yquem that we can't quite date. The 1870-something bottle. I'd like to have that authenticated, and I'd like to have that on my shelf. Or be able to sell it once we know for sure how old it is.'

'Just that bottle?' I said.

'It's enough,' he replied. 'Believe me, if it's real, it's worth plenty.'

That left seven bottles for me, which sounds a lot but they were definitely worth more for their curiosity value than their sheer market value. I had two Georgian cognacs, a Georgian Madeira, a Crimean Muscat, a Kardenakhi Port from 1953 and a 1929 Saamo, the Georgian sweet wine. Those six wines would definitely receive blank stares if I placed them on a sale shelf at the Double Bay Cellars. In an international auction? It was hard to say.

The seventh bottle had value. It was the 1874 Château Mouton Rothschild, although it was actually listed as a 'Buton', which is what Château Mouton Rothschild was called in the early part of the nineteenth century. That bottle had some serious credibility, as a genuine first growth wine aged for more than a century.

'Before we agree to this,' Kevin said, 'I have an idea. You retain half the right to my Yquem bottle, and I have half the right to your seven bottles. Even though we've divided the dozen by four, let's keep our mutual half as one entity in our heads. It means if the sales figures end up skewing one way or the other on our eight bottles, you or I won't feel badly done by. We've been in this together from the start.'

'Good idea,' I said, shaking his hand. 'Now, what do we do with Harry's and Neville's bottles?'

'I'll deliver them to Harry, along with a written appraisal of each wine, how I valued them and why, so there's no misunderstanding about the value they're receiving,' Kevin said. 'He can pass Neville's bottles on whenever they're next meeting to celebrate their mutual karma.'

As I've said, for a Canadian, Kevin can be pretty good at holding a grudge.

A couple of weeks after all this, and after Kevin had delivered the wine to Harry, I received a letter from Gadens Lawyers. The letter stated that Kevin and I had Neville Rhodes's wine and he demanded it. The letter said that there were twelve bottles of Château d'Yquem and we were to return them within seven days, or legal action would commence.

Where had Rhodes got the idea that we had a dozen bottles of Yquem with us? And why didn't he have the wine that Kevin had given to Harry to hand over to him?

I wrote back:

'Personally, I did not bring any wine to Australia and do not have twelve bottles of vintage Château d'Yquem. I suggest you direct your enquiries to the convener of the joint venture of which Mr Rhodes was a party and has the necessary information. You may glean more there. Yours truly, John Baker.'

I was licking the envelope to seal the letter when I had a call from an assistant to Jane Thornton, my friend who was setting up the new restaurant in Melbourne. They were having a post-launch celebration, to mark the fact that the restaurant was now operational and going well, and to thank everybody involved in making that happen. Jane's assistant said that Jane had asked to pass on that she'd like me to be there, and could I come? Sure, I said. I'm never one to miss a party, especially with a free wine list that I knew was very good, given Jane had selected it.

As we hung up, I found myself dwelling on the fact the assistant had said Jane would like me to come, rather than *they* would like me to come. I can have a tendency to overthink things. This was probably one of those times. Regardless, I decided I would definitely be heading south.

I walked to the post office, and was so busy being lost in the realisation that I was really looking forward to seeing Jane again that I almost missed recognising the potentially historic moment as I posted what would almost certainly be my last letter related to that unlikely cellar in Georgia.

I stared at the now closed mouth of the letterbox and almost laughed out loud as I headed back to the Double Bay Cellars. While I didn't personally have any Yquems from Georgia, I wasn't technically responsible for them, so I was pretty certain I was legally in the clear. The letter I was responding to seemed to suggest that Harry hadn't passed Neville's share of the dozen on, as requested. I enjoyed the prospect of the looming conversation between the pair of them after my response arrived.

Me? I was done with the whole thing. It had been a crazy adventure, I had been lucky enough to taste some of the most outstanding and unusual wines I knew I would ever sample – led by that 1899 Château Suduiraut, which will live forever in my wine memory. I had visited the country of Georgia and met some lively characters along the way. I had learned some lessons about business and trust and still somehow managed to have seven excellent bottles of historic wine in my personal collection. Look, I had always known it was a bit of a punt, but what an adventure we had had. What an experience.

And now? Well, for starters, there was a smart and beautiful woman in Melbourne who had invited me to a party. And I had my wine store to run. Life moves on.

Neville and Harry were welcome to continue bickering about their share of the dozen, and the cellar beyond.

If I was smart, I was out.

21

NEW BEGINNINGS

Sydney, Australia
2000–01

If I was smart . . .

The problem with a qualifier like that is that it doesn't embrace my natural inclination for adventure. Or, to be more practical, the fact that I had already invested so much time and effort in this crazy Georgian campaign.

But for a while, I didn't think much about Stalin or his mysterious wines. For a time, life got so busy that I was able to put the treasures of Tbilisi out of my mind.

The 2000 Olympics finally arrived, dragging the entire city into party mode, or at least that's how it felt. As I had hoped, the Games were good for me as the people of Double Bay loaded up on wine for the Olympic viewing parties happening in many houses.

I've never seen Sydney in such a happy collective headspace. The usual everyday atmosphere of people walking around, stony-faced, with headphones on, listening to Walkmans, or talking on mobile phones, melted away as strangers chatted and enthused about this gold medal that Australia just won, or that world record they saw in the pool, as they waited in the coffee queue or for public transport.

Canada managed to win three gold medals, in triathlon, wrestling and men's doubles tennis. Kevin was mildly interested, explaining that for Canadians, the Holy Grail was ice hockey gold at the Winter Olympics, probably followed by downhill skiing then curling, and only then anything Summer Olympics–related. Also, being Kevin, he was more interested in how much gold was actually in the gold medals than the achievements themselves. (It turns out under official Olympic rules, gold medals have to be at least 92.5 per cent silver, with a minimum of six grams of actual gold. So now you know.)

Kevin told me he had gone to the Olympic precinct at Homebush to watch the diving finals, which he described as 'maybe one-millionth the excitement of a really bad (ice) hockey game,' had found himself next to some Canadians and had talked about the recent death of Pierre Trudeau, long-serving Canadian prime minister, throughout the whole event. He had then headed to the boxing finals and between rounds talked Trudeau with yet more Canadians. He was shaken. Pierre Trudeau's body was lying in state in Ottawa, for Canadians to file past, paying their respects, at the same time that the Olympic closing ceremony took place half a world away. Kevin explained that that kind of national respect and viewing was usually only reserved for Canadian popular heroes like Montreal hockey legend Maurice 'Rocket' Richard.

For us non-Canadians, the Games continued to consume all of our attention. Like everybody else, we had a big-screen TV set up on the shop floor through the Olympics so customers could watch the big events while stocking up on bottles. Between sales, I found myself not only urging on Cathy Freeman and the other Australians at the Games, but also half looking out for Georgians and that familiar red flag with the black and white stripes in the corner.

Every now and then, my almost subconscious search paid off. As the Sydney Games unfolded, there were even a couple of Georgian Giorgis in competition, with Giorgi Vazagashvili winning a bronze medal in the judo, and then another, Giorgi Asanidze, taking bronze in the 85 kg section of the men's weightlifting competition.

A few months prior, I would have been on the phone to our Giorgi, or emailed, to share such news. One of the last emails I had was one in which I had been asking George if he had a preference for wine books in French language or English, and he'd replied saying either was fine. That had left me wondering if he or somebody there could read both languages, or if they didn't intend to actually read the books. Everything was a slight mystery when dealing with the Tbilisians.

But I never found out and now our lines of communication had gone silent. At home, the Olympics ended in a predictable prolonged riot of fireworks over and around the harbour bridge, and we all got back to our normal lives. Headphones and silent strangers resumed their places in the suburbs.

In late 2001, roughly a year after the Games, I was surprised to be asked to a meeting with one of the major liquor retailers. I had been somewhat of a pioneer of turning bottle shops into a genuinely inviting, attractive and knowledgeable space, a long way removed from corner liquor stores or a basic hotel drive-through, and now it seemed the ever-expanding major retail chains wanted a piece of the action.

Some executives from Vintage Cellars explained that their business growth vision demanded a strategic presence in the well-heeled eastern suburbs and they had targeted my humble store as the head start they needed, for location and credibility.

'I'm not sure I can see myself working for a retail chain,' I told them. 'No offence.'

'None taken,' their lead negotiator replied. 'We weren't inviting you to stay.'

Instead, they wrote me a large cheque and just like that we had an understanding and an agreement. The sale went through rather quickly and without a hitch. I found myself announcing to Kevin, Jillian, Frank and the more occasional staff that I was moving on.

It was the end of an era, but as I got used to the idea, I was also excited about the prospect of starting up a new venture. Just as I've always seen bottles of wine as objects to be enjoyed or sold, not worshipped, I have tended to be pragmatic about business. Even so, I remember those Double Bay years as some of the happiest of my working life, so it was hard to step away.

The sale was to have another major impact, however, as Vintage Cellars proved they were smart businesspeople by taking one look at the Double Bay operation and seeing where the true value lay. They asked Kevin and Frank to stay on, after I'd gone, so that the cellars wouldn't miss a beat. Kevin was paid well to continue being Kevin, hunting for antique wines, looking for hidden divorce stashes of wine, and other very Kevinish adventures.

I took some time off, drifting to Melbourne for a few weeks and happening to drop by that restaurant, to see Jane, before I returned north and threw myself into a series of new ventures. As a base source of reliable income, I set up a new cellar, in Epping, north-west of Sydney's CBD, not far from the big TV towers that dominate the landscape there. I teamed up with Tim Bourne, a manager from my original Newport Bottler store. Once again, I found myself deep in the challenge of starting from scratch, in terms of building a loyal customer base and creating events that would entice and empower the locals to try and buy excellent wines.

I also established a side business called Bordeaux Shippers, having realised that all my years of importing wines could be turned into something official. I had visited Bordeaux a couple of times for work – even once walking around the outside of Château d'Yquem, looking reverently at the walled château and the vines. But in this new role I would travel to Bordeaux once or twice a year, working out which wines to import that I could sell wholesale or retail in Australia. My first trip under this new corporate banner was to the famous Union des Grands Crus tasting, held over a weekend in May, as a way to further expand my knowledge of the wines being produced by many great houses of Bordeaux, by tasting as many wines from as many different châteaux as I could. While I was there, I organised visits to a number of the châteaux themselves, meeting with owners or winemakers, particularly from the classified growths.

And finally, buoyed by my dabbles in the restaurant trade, I started putting more time and effort into that world. As Sydney boomed, a new trend was for the promoter of a new eatery to take on investors in the restaurant, for start-up capital and potential expertise. Restaurants were like the new stock exchange, with investors putting their money into businesses that they thought boasted the right celebrity chef, location, menu or other tangible assets that would turn into a successful restaurant and profitable payday for the investors if the enterprise was sold at the height of its popularity. A great friend, José de la Vega, had invested in Maurice Terzini's Otto restaurant on Woolloomooloo's Finger Wharf and had done very well. When the same investors, including José, decided to go again, backing a new eatery called Nove, right next door to Otto, José brought me on board.

So, throughout 2002 and into 2003, I was busy, establishing and enjoying these new fields of commerce while learning more about the restaurant trade and travelling semi-regularly to Europe. Life was good.

Even though we were no longer workmates, Kevin and I caught up regularly. He enjoyed dropping by my wine night events in Epping, either to help out or just to say hello. We'd share a bottle after the customers had gone, and Kevin would tell me about some of his latest adventures, which often, to my well-trained ear, seemed to sail slightly out beyond the remit of his Vintage Cellars employment. Every now and then, a 'side project' would land a few bottles of one of the rarer Granges in his personal collection or would see Kevin chatting with independent wine collectors who might feel a need to pay him for his friendly advice. He started moving out of wine too, his natural sniffing-out-a-dollar entrepreneurial instincts just as much at play when examining the luxury watch industry or other fields.

'I'm assuming you didn't have any of these little side gigs running during the time you were technically working for me,' I said to him, raising an eyebrow.

'Never more than three at a time,' he said. 'Out of respect.'

Of course, Georgia came up in conversation more often than not.

'Those Yquems,' Kevin said. 'All those bottles of Yquem.'

'I wonder where they are now,' I mused. 'We never saw them or heard of them turning up in an English or American auction house. They were so rare and valuable that we definitely would have known if they did get to auction. I wonder what Neville did with them.'

'Probably sold them on eBay for twenty bucks each,' Kevin said.

I laughed. 'Make me an offer: old label-free bottles from abroad. Might be cider.'

'Ah, well' said Kevin, raising a glass. 'They were just bottles. Potentially very valuable bottles that could have been very good to us, sure. But only bottles.'

'Exactly,' I replied, meeting his toast. 'And didn't we have some fun?'

22

THE MAN IN BLACK

Sydney, Australia
July 2003

'That's him,' said José de la Vega, waving to the man who had just entered the room and was looking around the tables. He spotted us and started to weave between the diners.

'Hmm,' I said to José. 'Interesting-looking fellow.'

'He always dresses like that,' José said. 'Ever since I've known him.'

We were in the Icebergs Club Bistro, with its dazzling and sweeping view over Bondi Beach and the open-water pools directly below. It was the kind of warm, sunny day that makes your heart soar, especially as big waves crashed into the walls of the Icebergs pool, sending minor floods of sea water across the swimmers, while bronzed Sydneysiders basked on the concrete surrounds in bikinis or Speedos.

All of which made it even more jarring that the man approaching us was dressed head to toe in black – black pants, black shirt, black blazer – and was even sporting a rakish black hat that sat just above his eyes. He was Jesse James meets Johnny Cash, and looked to be about my age.

When he finally reached our table by the window, José said, 'John Baker, Terry Burke. Terry Burke, John Baker.'

We shook hands and I poured Terry a wine.

We exchanged pleasantries and some discussion of the exceptional location that we were in. Terry asked, 'Are you happy or sad you got out of your Icebergs investment, John? You and José were in on the development stage but decided to exit the opportunity, didn't you?'

'That's right,' I replied. 'We got our money back, more or less, but sitting here today, I must admit I wouldn't have minded retaining a piece of this place. Did you stay in?'

'I did,' Terry said. 'It has worked well for me.'

'Ah, well, I'm glad,' I said. 'You win some, you lose some.'

'Terry lives above here,' José said. 'He's the king of Bondi.'

The reason we were meeting was because José had a lead on a new restaurant opportunity being created by Maurice Terzini, the same restaurant entrepreneur that we had done well with, after he sold Nove, the Woolloomooloo eatery. This time, he was exploring the idea of a space that would eventually become North Bondi Italian Food. Terry was also a potential investor and José had wanted us to meet. José told me that he liked my non-industry feel for these ventures and had taken to using me as a kind of sounding board for restaurant pitches. If I was interested, José would explore the opportunity further, for both of us. But now, sitting with Terry, I had to admit I did have some reservations.

'Look, we have done well with Maurice, and this North Bondi idea might be another good one,' I said, 'but I also feel we're playing Russian roulette every time we get involved in one of these.'

'What do you mean, John?' José asked.

'Well, Maurice has had a very interesting career with a lot of success and no shortage of colour and action, but have you noticed that things have seemed to not work at some stage in one or maybe more of his previous operations? The way I see it, one of Maurice's new ventures is going to fail – the history of restaurants shows that– so the question is whether it will be North Bondi or another one? We're rolling the dice that it won't be ours.'

On reflection, my opinion only showed that I didn't have much of a nose for that world, because in fact Maurice proved to be a very good operator over many years and has been extremely successful in an industry that always has a share of misses. I guess I just didn't have the stomach for the ride.

Terry regarded me from under the brim of his black hat and his eyes gleamed with amusement. 'José, I can see why you like having John around as a second opinion,' he said.

'Do you agree, Terry?' I asked.

The man in black shrugged expansively. 'I agree that Maurice has had a few stumbles along the way but that's the restaurant game. I have done so well from his wins that I don't mind suffering the occasional damp squib.'

'Like the American entrepreneurs starting to show up in that new tech space in, what do they call it? Silicon Valley?' José said. 'Invest in twenty-five new tech start-ups and hope the one that works makes enough money to cover the twenty-four that didn't.'

'Well, I think I like playing better ratios than that,' Terry said. 'Especially given the tech bubble burst of the last couple of years. But yes, I wouldn't have minded having shares in AOL when Time Warner came calling.'

We finished our main course and sat back, finishing a glass of wine before coffee.

José said, 'You know, John, you and Terry have something else in common that I haven't told you about, but I thought you might get a kick out of.'

I feigned being wide-eyed as I looked at Terry. 'You also think the CIA might have brought down the Twin Towers?'

'Ha,' said Terry. 'No, almost but not quite that.'

'Terry has done quite a bit of work in the Republic of Georgia, formerly of the Soviet Union. A place you know well, John,' José said.

Now I was interested. 'Is that right? What kind of work, Terry?'

'It was in my capacity as a lawyer, a long way from restaurant investing,' he said. 'I spent some time there, establishing laws and statutes for private property ownership in the time after Georgia became independent and nobody really knew how to set laws like that up. There were a lot of wannabe property owners and business people asking, "But if the state doesn't own it, what happens then?" I stepped in and helped draft the guidelines.'

'Amazing,' I said. 'So you were in on the decision that, in Georgia, ownership of the property incorporates not just the buildings and land at ground level, but everything above and below the ground as well?'

He stared at me, open-mouthed.

'How could you possibly know that?' he asked.

'Believe me, I have had reason to ponder that ruling.'

It took the rest of the bottle of wine and a round of coffee for me to tell Terry the shorter version of the story, not just of the connection of the wine to tsars and Stalin, but of our fruitless attempts to safely and legally ship the wine out of the country. Terry was fascinated, stopping me every so often to ask a question or clarify a legal point that we'd run into. I told him about Nino and co all toting guns everywhere they went, and the mafia staff car. He laughed and said that sounded exactly how he'd expect Georgia to be, a few years after he'd left the embryonic republic.

'Have you heard the word "oligarch"?' he said to me. 'It's a rising, very wealthy, very influential class of Russian, which also extends to the former Soviet bloc countries. These guys are like mafia dons, running everything and with fingers in lots of pies. The word comes from the Ancient Greek *oligarkhia*, which roughly translates as "the rule of the few" and they grabbed the advantage of the post-Communist vacuum to build incredible wealth very quickly, and quietly. Some of these guys are ex-military or made their money by smuggling in western stuff like computers or jeans on the black market. They pretty much put down their roots in the Boris Yeltsin era, but the world's only really waking up to the fact they run everything over there now.'

'I heard that the current Russian president, Vladimir Putin, was one of them before he moved into politics,' José said.

'I'm pretty sure he was a career KGB agent, but he certainly seems to have some sources of independent wealth,' Terry nodded. 'Actually, Putin has done a good job of bringing the oligarchs into line with his government. They were a bit out of control under Yeltsin whereas Putin seems to have done a deal with the big ones that they can keep doing what they're doing – which is pretty much whatever the fuck they want – as long as they swear loyalty and alignment with Putin's government. A couple of them wouldn't, and had to leave Russia really fast, while another couple seem to have vanished without a trace.'

'It certainly wouldn't surprise me if some of the people we were dealing with are at least tied in with the Georgian equivalent of oligarchs,' I said. 'They seemed to have the run of that city, no questions asked.'

'So, where did you get to with the wine? Where is it now?' Terry asked.

'We have no idea,' I replied. 'We hit a dead end, because of the legalities, export issues and cultural heritage stuff. And the changing ownership of the winery to the Australian mining magnate. I didn't really know what to do from there.'

Terry looked at José. 'It's a shame John didn't have Wolfgang on board through all that.'

'Who's Wolfgang?' I asked.

'Wolfgang Babeck,' Terry said. 'Great guy. He's a lawyer here in Sydney, the European counsel at Dibbs Barker Gosling, which is a boutique but powerful law firm. He spent quite a lot of time in Georgia, back at the time it became a republic, even before I was there. I believe he actually drafted or was instrumental in the wording of the official constitution of Georgia, post freedom from Communist rule. If you ever need to know intricacies of Georgian law or how to get things done, Wolfgang is totally your guy.'

My head was spinning. All these lawyers wandering around Sydney who were experts on Georgian law. And who I had never previously heard of. I couldn't believe it.

We finished lunch and I headed back across town to my office in Epping; a long hack from Bondi. I had the salt in my nose from Bondi Beach and the sun on my arm as it rested on the open window as I drove. If only I had known about Wolfgang and Terry a couple of years before.

Crawling in traffic, my eye was unexpectedly drawn to flapping bunting along the road past Fox Studios. It was unmistakably a vertical Georgian flag, flying right over my head. I craned my neck to look at the next bunting, which had a Union Jack. They were advertising strips for the Rugby World Cup, due to start in Sydney that month. Georgia seemed to have a team competing. I had had no idea about that either.

Was that a sign? Meeting the Johnny Cash of lawyers, who told me about the Wolf Man of the Georgian Republic's constitution, and now the Georgian flag was waving at me from above my car.

What a day. I finally made it to my desk, cleared some pressing daily business, and then hovered over my email.

Do I or don't I?

As previously mentioned, if I was smart, I'd be out.

23

A NIGHT OF MYSTERY
AND ROMANCE

'Kevin Hopko,' I said, 'this is Jane Thornton. Jane, Kevin.'

'Well, well, well,' said Kevin, shaking Jane's hand. 'I have been looking forward to meeting you, Jane.'

'Likewise,' Jane said, smiling.

'And if you've been invited to an Options Dinner,' Kevin continued, 'our man here obviously has a high regard for your wine knowledge.'

Jane laughed, maybe nervously, and said, 'I hope so. I'm certainly chuffed to be here.'

'Well, let's not get carried away, you two,' I said. 'It's only a dinner.'

Wine Options Dinners were something a group of us ran for a decade or so in the late nineties and the first few years of the new millennium. It was a fun concept. A group of wine retailers or makers, people who worked in the industry but had a true love of the product, would come together for a dinner every three months or so. Occasionally, a consumer from one of our shops, who we rated for their knowledge and their cellar, would be invited along as well.

The night had rules. Only eight people were allowed to attend, with the cast changing depending on who was available that night.

Most importantly, you had to have a pretty good palate and know your wine, which is why it was so enjoyable for me to be able to bring my new partner, Jane, along as a genuine participant. I knew that her knowledge of wine, from her work, was at a level where she could contribute to the evening and fully enjoy it. In the hand not shaking Kevin's was a bottle of wine wrapped carefully in brown paper, with foil around the capsule so nobody could spy on the cork. Even I didn't know what it was.

Which was the major point of the evening. All eight attendees would bring a similarly disguised bottle of wine and then we would taste the wines in order, while enjoying the restaurant meal. For each wine, the person who had brought it would ask five questions and it was the other seven attendees' job, as the blind tasters, to see if they could correctly answer the questions and, by question five, actually identify the wine.

It was a genuine challenge, even for the most professional tasters, but of course the real joy of the evening was in tasting eight seriously good and diverse wines, because nobody brought an everyday wine from the local bottle shop. Well, if they did, it meant they didn't want to be invited again.

Tonight's dinner was at The Welcome Hotel in Rozelle, just west of the Sydney CBD in the backstreets of Balmain. It was a gastro-pub serving excellent food and one of our Options Dinner crew was a friend of the owner which meant they didn't mind us having BYO wine.

At most Options Dinners, the wine would be reasonably new, sometimes ageing back to ten years old, occasionally even twenty. The point was to showcase different styles and wine making regions. But you really didn't know what you were getting as corks were popped.

We settled into the evening and it didn't disappoint.

Frank Dangelico, my old cellar manager from Double Bay and my partner in setting up these Options Nights, stood first and poured us a white wine. Having been to almost all of these dinners, he didn't muck about. 'Question one,' he announced. 'Northern or Southern Hemisphere?'

We all swirled wine, squinted at it, put our noses to the glass. Frowned. Took a tiny sip.

'Wow, a lot of intensity,' said Kevin.

'Quite high acidity,' somebody else offered.

'Frankie, have you let it sit, decanted for a while?' I asked.

'I did, John. It's a wine that is better for it and I wanted you to taste it at its best. But stop avoiding the question! Come on, which hemisphere?' Frank asked.

We sniffed and tasted again. Most of us agreed Northern Hemisphere. A couple weren't sure. One guessed Southern.

'Northern Hemisphere,' Frank confirmed. 'In fact, I can tell you that it is French. Question two: the type of grape? Grenache Blanc, Roussanne or Picardan?'

So, that clue told most of us that this wine was almost certainly from the Rhône Valley because these are some of the main grape varieties of that region but, even so, it split the group. I was adamant Grenache Blanc was in there, but Jane was just as sure she could taste Roussanne. The rest of the table was equally unsure, naming several other grapes as well.

'Well it was a bit of a trick question,' Frank admitted. 'All three are in there, plus, yes, Bourboulenc, Clairette Blanche and a few others.'

We all complained that the question wasn't fair, but only in a good-natured way. This wine really was an excellent one to start with.

'Question three: more or less than five years old?'

Four were adamant it was a new wine, less than five years old. Three were equally sure it was at least that old.

'It's a 1996 vintage,' Frank confirmed. 'So, seven years old – which means, yes, you can still get hold of it. Okay, let's bring it home: which region of France?'

This was a classic Options Dinner question. As I said, Frank's earlier clue had pointed directly to the Rhône Valley which made me wonder if this was a trick. We had no way of knowing if Frank was trying to lead us down a false trail. Sometimes, the person producing the wine was only interested in seeing if the audience could tell a Bordeaux from a Burgundy but I knew Frank well enough to suspect there was more at play.

We all carefully agreed it was from the Rhône, waiting for an ambush, but no, Frank just smiled at us, before asking: 'is it from the northern Rhône, southern Rhône or elsewhere?'

The table began to be split. Several people opted for northern Rhône, especially because it was a white wine. A few of us went for the south. We all agreed 'elsewhere' was only an option to try and throw us off, and there was much friendly banter between Frank and the table. He gave as good as he got.

It was from the southern Rhone.

'All right, know-it-alls,' he said, 'would anybody like to take a stab at question five and name the wine?'

The table fell silent.

'I'll have a go,' I said. 'You've confirmed it's from the southern Rhône, where more than 90 per cent of the wine is red, which actually narrows down the options for an excellent white like this. I wonder if it could be a Château Beaucastel Châteauneuf-du-Pape Blanc?'

'Well played, John,' Frank said, bowing slightly. 'You are indeed correct.'

'Thanks, Frank,' I said. 'And it's an excellent choice for an Options Dinner. I've only tasted it twice before, I think, and not this vintage. What a magnificent white.'

Jane was looking at me incredulously and I leaned in to say quietly, 'Welcome to an Options Dinner, Jane, where it can be about playing the man and not the wine. We had that wine at Double Bay and Frank often recommended it to customers who wanted something a bit special, so it was an easier guess than it probably looked.'

She laughed. 'No kidding. Nobody could be that good!'

'Well, some probably can. There's a guy called Rudy Kurniawan in LA who apparently has an incredible nose and has started buying serious wines to build a cellar.'

'He's young, too,' said Kevin from across the table. 'You'd think it would take decades to learn.'

And so the night went on. We had a very fruity French Gewurztraminer, from the Alsace: the 1997 Wolfberger Altenberg de Bergheim. We enjoyed a 1995 Clonakilla Shiraz, which was more of a Shiraz Viognier. A 1991 Cape Mentelle Cabernet was correctly guessed by Kevin, understandably a regular at the dinners. Jane's bottle turned out to be a delicious 2000 Jasper Hill Nebbiolo, which segued beautifully into wholesaler Ian Hunt's 1980 Penfolds Bin 80A. Another industry friend, Melissa Parker, surprised us all with an NV Ste Genevieve Texas Red – several diners managed to narrow it down to North American origins, but nobody got the maker or the wine – and there was also a very fine 1992 Kenwood Artist Series Cabernet, from Sonoma.

Kevin produced what we all agreed was the wine of the night, a 1986 Château Cheval Blanc. This was a gorgeously seductive wine from one of the very great châteaux of Bordeaux, and Kevin's bottle was a brilliant example of the château's work. Even after six other stand-out mystery wines, we were all blown away.

Leaving me to stand up and say, 'Well, Kevin, my old friend and partner, as usual, you are a very tough act to follow. But I'll do my best.'

I had opened and checked my bottle earlier, then replaced the cork to be able to carry it without spilling. Now, on pulling the cork again, I hid it in my pocket immediately, so that nobody could inspect it. I poured the light amber liquid into the eight glasses.

Everybody took a glass and I almost laughed as I watched their faces. The diners peered at the wine, sniffed it, took another look at the glass. A couple were treating their glasses as though they might be combustible, a sense of something dangerous in their hands. I watched as their brains scrambled to process what they were smelling and tasting. All, except possibly for Jane, the only debutante, had registered this was not the usual Options Dinner wine.

I sniffed and tasted as well, just as curious as the diners who had no idea what it was.

'Northern or Southern Hemisphere?' I asked.

Northern, everybody agreed. This was not a wine from Australia, New Zealand, South Africa or South America.

I nodded. 'Correct.' And then I paused. 'Pre- or post–World War Two?'

That stopped them, as I knew it would. It is, of course, an absurdly wide time margin, and when would any of us see a wine anywhere near World War Two or possibly before?

The only person not looking astonished was Kevin. I had checked with him the day before whether he was okay with me pulling this stunt. He'd been all for it, and now sat quietly, enjoying the show.

The wine was narrowed down to 1945, and that meant I had everybody's attention because of course all of these people, some of my closest friends and colleagues in wine, knew where it must be from. They were all aware of the crazy Georgian adventure Kevin and I had tried to pull off a couple of years earlier.

'Oh, forget the five questions, John,' said Ian Hunt. 'For Christ's sake, just tell us about it!'

'Fair enough,' I laughed. 'It's a 1945 Crimean Muscat and, yes, it's one of the bottles that Kevin and I managed to carry out of Tbilisi and back to Australia. Records have it that Tsar Nicholas the Second founded the Massandra Winery in Crimea, just out of Yalta, in the year he was crowned, 1894. This Muscat is one of the winery's more famous drops, known as Red Stone White Muscat because it's grown in the vineyards surrounding an enormous limestone monolith known as Red Stone Rock.

'The fact it's a 1945 makes it interesting from the point of view that it is younger than when Stalin must have stashed the rest of the wines we saw in Tbilisi. That also makes it less valuable in a way, at least to me and my sense of romance about all those wines that saw so much history, because it would not have come from St Petersburg, like the others, but must have been bought after the war was over.'

'Do you think it still would have been one of Stalin's personal wines, John?' someone asked.

'Well, I don't think it can be, being a 1945, which is why I think out of the wines we have left between Kevin and I, it makes a nice candidate to pull the cork and actually share it with some friends,' I said.

We all toasted Tbilisi, and wine, and great dinners, and friends. The Muscat was fascinating for its origin and was an ideal accompaniment to have with our dessert.

Once the wines were finally finished, we all stood from the table and formed conversational huddles. Jane headed for the bathroom, meaning I found myself alone with Kevin for the first time that night.

'It goes without saying,' he said. 'Jane is wonderful.'

'Yeah, she really is.'

'Try not to screw that up,' he told me.

'Okay,' I nodded. 'Thanks for the sage-ish advice. I'll take that on board. What did you think of the Muscat? I thought it was surprisingly drinkable.'

'Yeah, those Crimean wine makers really know their stuff,' he nodded. 'I should keep an eye on that market. Even if Georgia was a bust, as the politics move around in Crimea and other ex-Russian states, other bottles might appear.'

'Well, funny you should mention that,' I said, keeping my voice low. 'Guess who I've been in touch with?'

Kevin stepped back slightly to look deeply into my face.

'Harry?' he finally said. 'He got back in touch to tell you he's no longer partners with Neville, is very, very sorry and now has a lead on a hidden cellar in Antarctica that used to belong to Robert Falcon Scott.'

'Close.' I said. 'Actually, surprisingly close. Yet far away.'

'Hit me,' Kevin said.

'I've been trading messages with our mate George.'

'Giorgi Aramhishvili?'

'The very same.'

Kevin guffawed loudly, a big barking laugh that had others swinging their heads in our direction. 'Okay,' he said, 'I cannot wait to hear this but it's a discussion for daylight hours. Why don't I drop by the shop?'

Winding back home to my place in a taxi, late in the night, Jane said to me, 'I still can't quite believe you just uncorked one of the dozen bottles you managed to get out of Georgia.'

'What do you mean?' I asked.

'You went through so much and had to give up those really valuable bottles, the Yquems and so forth, to Neville and that other guy.'

'Harry,' I smiled. 'He only has a giant Daimler. I thought he needed a good bottle to get by in this world.'

'Nevertheless,' she said, 'you were only left with a handful of precious bottles for all that endeavour, and then you just drink one of them with some mates! I can't believe Kevin agreed to it beforehand.'

'He gets it,' I shrugged.

'Gets what?' she asked. 'Seriously, I'm curious.'

I watched the dark streets of Sydney glide by as I thought about my answer. Hyde Park and the shrine.

'Jane, I guess from my point of view, it's just a bottle of wine. The fact it has that crazy history of how we got hold of it is fun, but I don't want it sitting in my cellar for the next thirty years. Or, sure, I could sell it for – actually, I don't know how much – and that would obviously be the smart thing to do, the financially responsible thing to do, but where's the fun in that? I'd much rather see what the wine tastes like and have some of my friends, who know enough to really and truly appreciate what they're tasting, enjoy it as well. Did you see their faces? It was a lovely moment. Didn't it make for a great finale to the evening?'

'Well, yes, absolutely. It was a fantastic wine to finish with, in every sense of the word.'

I smiled at her. 'Then there you go. The way I see it, wine is either an investment or to be enjoyed. This one, out of all the wines we brought home, was one to just enjoy. So, we did. Now it's gone but we have the memory and I suspect everyone there will never forget it. I'm very glad you were there.'

Jane snuggled back into my shoulder and put her hand across my chest. It felt good. 'You can be a bit strange but certainly very generous,' she muttered.

'*Merci*,' I said.

'Just don't pull a stunt like that with an 1870 bottle of Yquem, okay?' she said.

I laughed. 'I can't promise but I think that would be unlikely.'

24

I'M NOT OUT . . .

The next day, Kevin dropped by my cellars, as promised. I smiled as he put his feet up on the corner of my desk just like old times in Double Bay.

'I'm glad I opened the Muscat last night,' I said. 'The others liked it too, although Jane thinks I'm mad.'

'Well, that just means she's getting to know the real you,' Kevin said.

I made a face at him. 'What have you been up to, anyway?' I asked. 'I didn't really get to talk to you last night and you've been quiet lately, which always worries me. It means you're up to something.'

'I've been busy,' he said. 'I'm seriously costing how to start a luxury watch brand. I think I need to go to China. Oh, and I also, and you'll love this, just got back from southern Queensland, where I was dispatched to investigate one of those divorce cellars I know and love.'

'Let me guess,' I said. 'A giant cave full of old newspapers?'

'Oh, no, there was actually a lot of good wine there,' he said. 'A *lot*. A few decent seventies French wines, a lot of middle-of-the-road Australian wines, and then, hidden under some boxed slabs of beer, several large pillowcases stuffed with marijuana and a couple of smaller plastic bags full of mysterious white powder.'

'Jesus,' I said. 'What did you do?'

'I politely offered a decent but on the low side amount of cash for the good bottles, and promised that I had no real interest in purchasing the other goods on offer, just as I had no real interest in speaking to the local constabulary about what the woman's ex-husband might have been up to in that cellar,' he said.

'What a scene.'

'Oh, you have no idea,' he said. 'And yet you seem to have the even more dramatic story to tell. How's our Georgi? And who contacted who?'

'It was me,' I confessed. 'I saw Georgia was playing in the Rugby World Cup that's just started and I wrote on a whim. He promised to send me a Georgian rugby jumper.'

'As long as it arrives with the other dozen bottles we chose but never saw again, that sounds good,' Kevin said. 'One thing I have to hand to you, Johnny, you don't give up easily.'

I laughed and told him about Terry, the man in black, and Wolfgang, the other lawyer who knew his way around Georgian constitutional law.

'When you think about it, it was legal complications that derailed us, wasn't it? These guys might be able to help.'

'Except that Neville and maybe Harry stand in our way.'

'Well,' I said, and poured us both another glass of wine.

Kevin was staring at me with that unblinking look of his. 'That was what I believe the English would call a pregnant "well",' he said. 'A loaded "well".'

'I'm not sure that's a thing, but yes, it was a deliberate "well",' I said. 'I wrote to George and he wrote back the next day, I think as soon as he saw my email, if you factor in time zones. I printed it out.'

I read from the paper in front of me. 'Thank you for your email. I was very pleased to receive your message. Cellar is okay and in same condition you leave it.'

'The wine is still there,' said Kevin. 'That's interesting. What about our friends in Sydney?'

'Not so much,' I said. 'Neville's out. George says he let them down badly and is no longer involved. Didn't give much detail but George says they're very interested in picking up the conversation with us again. He also says, being George, that the harvest is coming on and they really need us or somebody to help bankroll the winery's operations.'

Kevin laughed. 'Talk about Groundhog Day.'

'I know. Amazing,' I said. 'George also has new phone and fax numbers, which he provided.'

'So, we don't know anything about what happened with Neville?'

'Yes, we do, because I have since traded three more emails with George.'

Kevin shook his head. 'Okay, fine. We're doing this the hard way, you bastard. Come on then, string it out . . .'

I laughed. 'I wanted you to enjoy it! I wrote back to George and asked about Neville and whether he was still involved with Alaniya Gold, or whether he was out of everything in Georgia, and George replied that he believed Neville was still involved in the goldmine. That made me ask George if he was still in gold and George wrote back, and I quote: "Good question, probably not. Neville had done some sort of trick with me two years ago and we've been involved with the Court."'

'So, what are you thinking?' Kevin asked. 'We have another go?'

'I have to confess I am tempted, but we will be on our own money this time, if we try. The wine is still in the cellar, Neville and Harry have exited stage left and, as far as I can tell, we're still the only ones who have done an audit. We have a couple of lawyers in Sydney who can potentially get us past the hurdles of last time. Why not try? Think of all those fabulous Yquems and friends, the likes of which we have never seen before in all our years in the industry and will certainly never get close to again.'

'Oh, you know I've thought about them for years now,' Kevin said. 'As you have. We just need to cover our butts on this. George has to agree to let us have some more bottles to cover expenses. And we need to do it properly, and fast.'

'Yes, I agree,' I said. 'We don't want this dragging on for years as we debate customs.'

Kevin thought for a while and then said, 'When are you due to head to France next?'

'For my Bordeaux Shippers business? In two weeks.'

He looked at me. 'You should take my Yquem. The 1870-something. Is there a chance you could get to visit the château and meet the winemakers? See if they'll confirm it's genuine? If we could truly authenticate that bottle, it would open a lot of doors at auction houses and the rest. Although we believe the wine to be genuine, Yquem is the cornerstone of the cellar and our potential investment. We've never actually done the work to prove it's real and that proof is still everything to us, to know that for sure.'

I nodded. 'Yes, you're right. It is essential. I'd love to see if I can visit Yquem and I may just know the right chap in Bordeaux to organise it.'

'You mean *tu connais un mec qui connaît un mec*,' Kevin said.

'Either way, I'll make some calls,' I said. 'My friend Jean-François is terrific and a good operator, lives in Bordeaux and knows Pierre Lurton, the president of Yquem. I wonder if he could organise a visit for them to look at the bottle. I'm happy to ask. So, we're back on?'

Kevin shrugged. 'What could possibly go wrong?' he asked, with exaggerated sarcasm. 'It's at least worth asking some questions, if the road is clear enough.'

25

GETTING THE BAND BACK TOGETHER

Almost immediately, I noticed a change in George, as we rebooted our email correspondence. It had been a few years and he had obviously taken some knocks, maybe from Neville and maybe others. There was an edge to him, in his negotiations, that felt different to the laughing, energetic George I remembered.

When I raised the old concern, that the wine would need to clear Georgian customs and not be held up for heritage reasons, he summarily waved me off, saying it was no problem and any value could be declared.

His take was that he would just low-ball the value of the wine stock, to minimise potential taxes, and then we'd all be clear to export and sell the stock.

I expressed concern about that as our official strategy, to which he wrote: 'That's the way it is, John. Stop worrying about it. What we want to know is what bottles and at what price? What is the timing of your exercise? How can we guarantee results and that the bottles would not disappear after export?'

I was a little affronted by that and told him so. We had always negotiated in good faith before.

George wrote back, sounding slightly a bit more like the old George, as he said, 'John, I hear you, but my partners are looking just for easy exercise like selling the bottles. I hope we will complete this project successfully.'

I wondered if these were the same partners, or different partners? Were Mr Tamaz and co still involved in the winery? It felt as though the ground had shifted in the time that we'd been apart.

One win was that George hadn't revisited the idea of us investing in the looming harvest, which was a relief, and he was also more or less receptive to the fact that we'd need some bottles as a guarantee for expenses we'd incur. But even then, he included a snide note: 'It could be that you have some still, yes?'

Nevertheless, by the end of this new exchange, he had agreed to put some bottles, nominated by us, into storage, as protection against our costs, even if he was worryingly elusive about where they'd be stored or how we would retrieve them if the deal didn't happen. I'd told him that either Kevin or I needed to visit Europe and I needed bottles to the value of $15,000 to $20,000 and he replied cryptically: 'Very interesting. Europe is good.'

But then he threw in again that, whereas I wanted protection against my potential costs, he had no protection at all. I asked what he meant and he raised again the concern that if the entire cellar was exported, it wouldn't just disappear. Not for the first time, he asked me, 'Can you guarantee an auction result?'

'George,' I wrote back, 'if you can't trust me, you shouldn't be doing this with me. In the end, we have to work together. Australia's not the wild west.'

There followed a two-day gap in correspondence, and I wondered if the whole thing was over as quickly as it had restarted, but then George emailed, 'No problem, which bottles at what price do you want for them? Maybe we could, say, sell $100,000 worth of bottles so we can have some operational capital both ends, not just $15,000 worth. If you want, you have your Sydney solicitor draw up an agreement.'

So, apparently, we were still in business. My response said it was a good idea and I'd get my lawyer onto it. But I also reminded him that I still didn't have a Georgian rugby jumper.

While I was involved in this curious dance with Tbilisi, Kevin had been more practical and had drawn up a progress schedule.

We met over lunch, with Jane, who happened to be in town. Kevin said he was comfortable with her sitting in on 'Georgian El Dorado', as he had taken to calling it.

Once we'd pushed back the plates, he handed us a printout of a spreadsheet.

'The progress schedule tells us where we are, where we are going and what we need to do to pull this whole thing off,' he explained. 'I've listed tasks, comments, rough costs, dates, timings and who is tasked with which actions. So, for example, you mentioned that George wants us to have a lawyer draft an agreement for us to access some bottles for costs, and also to draft a confidentiality agreement so you can represent the winery and us in front of Sotheby's or another auction house. They're both in there, tasked to you, and presumably Wolfgang, if he's going to be our guy.'

I cast my eye over the columns. 'This is great, Kevin. Thanks. You've even got a column for "Questions".'

'Yes,' he said. 'I feel like there are a few complications from the past that we need to at least note as things to keep an eye on. Our past partners, like Rhodes, what was agreed with whom and does it affect what happens from here?'

Jane said, 'It looks like quite a few legal fees are ahead, and a meeting with a big auction house is required pretty soon.'

'I wonder,' I said. 'I mean, I know we need to have that meeting, but are we at a point where we can draft that confidentiality agreement in time for the looming trip to Europe? Everything has been so slow with official documents, every time we've tried. I'm just not confident Wolfgang can draft something and then George will sign it – if he even has the legal right to sign it, something we still don't know after all these years – before Jane and I fly out next week.'

Kevin shrugged. 'We need to commit to some degree, right? Let's have Wolfgang draft it. If George miraculously signs, maybe you can have meetings with Christie's or Sotheby's while you're in London. If not, you just make the other visit we talked about and we leave it at that.'

Jane looked at Kevin and then at me. 'The other visit? What's the other visit? Are you two scheming again?'

I laughed. 'Only in a good way, I hope. It's time we went to Yquem and showed them Kevin's bottle. It doesn't matter how many legal agreements and partnership documents we draft if that bottle isn't authenticated as the genuine article. In other words, if a friend of mine over there can organise it, how do you feel about dropping by a famous château while we're in Bordeaux?'

Jane frowned and pretended to sigh. 'Well, I guess I've seen the Eiffel Tower before so okay, if we must. Let's go and hang out at Yquem.'

'Man, I wish I could be there if and when they see the bottle,' Kevin said.

'Can you come?' I asked. 'Do you have any reason to be in Europe that means you could drop by?'

'No,' Kevin said sadly. 'I really can't justify it and I need to head to China again. But that's okay. You know that part of the world and the right people and you'll take care of the bottle. I'll wait to hear how it goes. Once we get official authentication, we can get Wolfgang stuck into the paperwork and finally get this show on the road.'

'I promise to bring you back a souvenir snow dome with the Eiffel Tower,' I told him.

Kevin groaned and put his head in his hands. 'Do you really?' he said. 'That would be swell. But, look, just to humour me, on your list of things to do, before the snow dome, could you please make sure you write down, "Call Jean-François"?'

26

A LONDON LOVE LETTER

London, United Kingdom
August 2003

I have theories about a lot of things, having lived a varied and mostly fruitful life, and one of my theories concerns precious objects. It goes like this: the more you treat a precious object as fragile and delicate and in danger of being broken, the more likely it is to break. Call it Murphy's Law (when anything that can go wrong will go wrong) or just the universe's sense of humour.

So when Jane and I prepared to fly out to Europe on our trip, I took the almost certainly real century-old bottle of Château d'Yquem Sauternes, encased it in sturdy bubble wrap and cardboard to protect it, swaddled it in some shirts, and then packed it safely and tightly in with all my other luggage. It wasn't even alone. I also had some other bottles in there, including one for a London friend, Linden Wilkie, and some olive oil for Jean-François in Bordeaux. I'd told him about my early investment in Boundary Bend Olives (the owner of the Cobram Estate brand), and he was keen to have a bottle.

We flew out on a Tuesday, landing in London on a cold but sunny August morning. Of course, as soon as we arrived at our hotel, the first thing I did was check my precious cargo and was relieved to see that the bottle was fine. I placed it carefully back in my suitcase, with socks and a hotel towel around it.

I didn't have any meetings planned for three or four days and so we decided to shake off jet lag by walking the London streets. I'd been to the English capital many times but had mostly tended to see it as a work destination, like going to Melbourne or, lately, Bordeaux, while Jane hadn't been to London for years, so together we found a new magic in it and decided to savour the experience and enjoy the city with fresh eyes.

I had fun tracking down music icons that I'd never got around to visiting. As a former part-owner of one of Sydney's live rock'n'roll venues in the eighties, back in the heyday of INXS, Midnight Oil, Cold Chisel and other classic bands, I enjoyed making something of a pilgrimage to some of London's landmark nightlife venues.

Without telling Jane our destination, one morning I led her to the nearest underground station and we headed out to St John's Wood, emerging from the depths onto Finchley Road.

Knowing I had played some decent cricket in my youth, and my love of Test cricket, she thought she was onto me early. 'Are we going to Lord's?' she asked, looking at a sign for the home of cricket, apparently just nearby.

'We're not,' I replied, taking her hand and instead heading west downhill along Grove End Road for maybe half a kilometre, taking in London upper-middle-class suburbia, until we stopped at the point where Grove End Road meets Garden Road.

I looked at Jane, an eyebrow raised, and she looked around us.

'No,' she said. 'I have no idea why we're here. What is this?'

I took us a few steps north and indicated a street sign that read 'Abbey Road, NW8', although the sign was almost buried under the signatures of previous visitors.

'See that pedestrian crossing . . .' I said.

'Oh, you're kidding! *The* Abbey Road!' she said, recognition lighting up her face. 'So, if The Beatles had taken a few steps in this direction for the photo, one of the greatest albums ever could have been called *Grove End Road*.'

'That must be Abbey Road Studios just there,' I said, turning to a building just off to the left from maybe the most famous pedestrian crossing in the world.

We had several days like that, just having fun exploring London's random sites.

We wandered through the British Museum to see handwritten drafts of Beatles lyrics, and drifted past famous pubs or theatres, like the Tramshed on Woolwich New Road, east of the city and south of the Thames, where bands like Dire Straits and Radiohead played before they hit it big. We saw some theatre in the West End and visited Tate Britain and other galleries. We really were in tourist mode and I didn't want it to end.

Of course, we also ate and drank very well. For our pure pleasure and in the name of 'professional research' for Jane, we sampled an array of the city's interesting restaurants, often asking friends of hers or mine along for the meal.

We had a lovely lunch with Neil Beckett and Sarah Basra of *The World of Fine Wine* magazine, which had only recently been launched and became, in my mind, the greatest wine magazine there ever was. At the time, it was finding its feet but I told them over lunch that I might have a cracking article for them, if things went well over the rest of my trip. I stayed a little mysterious, building the tension and the story, even though they demanded I brief them on the potential feature.

'It involves wine,' I finally said, as though caving.

'John, you don't seem to understand how a magazine's editorial process works,' Neil said, giving me a friendly glare. 'You do get that we are a most reputable wine magazine, yes, trying to be the best in the world, and we could break your story if it is as good as you say.'

'I do appreciate that,' I said, 'except that it's fun to watch you fume because I won't tell you.'

'You haven't changed,' laughed Neil. 'Always taking the proverbial.'

I said, 'Okay, how about if I admit I have a bottle of Yquem stashed away that I'm about to take to the château itself, and when they pull the cork, I'm expecting them to be able to read the year on the cork and confirm that it's at least 120 years old.'

'Nice,' said Neil, nodding. 'Wow, that is rare, and in your retail world I'd imagine that would be worth a lot of money.'

'How much do you think?' Jane asked.

Neil thought. 'Prices aren't really what the magazine is about but if I had to guess, in pounds? I suppose it could be £3000, could be £10,000, which goes to show I'm not really on the pulse. I do know it would depend on a few things, like the condition, fill level and provenance.'

'The shoulder level is very high,' I said.

'Look, old bottles are fun,' said Sarah, 'but haven't we seen Yquems that old before, John?'

'Well, Sarah, all I'll say without giving away the game is that there are more where this came from – many more – and the provenance is where the story will lie.'

That stopped them. 'Many antique Yquems?' from Neil.

'And Lafite, and Mouton, and the other great crus,' I said.

Sarah: 'All one hundred years old or more?'

'Well, not all of them, but most. Some are newbies, only dating back to the 1930s and 40s,' I said.

'So, can you tell us the provenance?' Neil asked.

'Now, Neil, where would be the fun in that?' I teased. 'Look, on a serious note, if my Yquem turns out to be fake, then I don't have a thing, including a story for you or the costs of my trip. But if it's real, the article writes itself.'

Sarah laughed. 'You Aussies! Always living the big adventure. Fine, go hang out at Yquem. See if we care.'

'But if it turns out to be real, we get the story, yeah?' said Neil.

We shook hands. 'Of course. No other wine magazines have shouted us lunch while we've been here.'

'Wait, I never said I was paying,' Neil said.

We laughed and split the bill.

On the last day of our stay in London, I had a few meetings for the Bordeaux Shippers business, and also rang Jean-François.

'*Ça va?*' I said down the phone.

'*Oui, ça va bien*, John. *Et toi?*' he said.

I could picture him in his beautiful Bordeaux office, full of antiques and soft lamps, on the second floor of an old, squat three-storey yellow stone building in the old town, on Quais des Chartrons on the city side of the Garonne river. Jane was going to love it there.

'You have the bottle with you?' Jean-François asked me down the phone.

'Yes, safely tucked away. We're heading to Paris tomorrow and will be in Bordeaux in a few days,' I said.

'*Magnifique*,' he said. 'I have contacted my friend, Pierre, and he is prepared to grant you an audience, if you can give us twenty four hours or so notice. He is at the château for the next fortnight, with no plans for travel, so it should be fine.'

'Jean-François, I am going to owe you a very good bottle of wine for doing me this favour,' I said.

'Well, then it's nice that you'll have it with you on the day!' he said.

'Not quite that good,' I laughed. 'Anyway, technically, this one belongs to my friend Kevin.'

'A friend lent you a bottle of century-old Yquem to carry across the world?'

'More or less,' I said. 'We trust each other.'

'It would seem so,' Jean-François said. 'I look forward to seeing this amazing bottle, and to seeing you, John.'

'I'll call again when we are heading to Bordeaux next week, to confirm,' I said. '*Merci* again.'

'*De rien, mon ami,*' he rang off.

I had a few more minutes before Jane was due back from a shopping trip, so I dialled another long string of numbers and listened to the short buzzing sounds at the other end of the line, before the sound of connection.

'*Gamarjoba?*' said a male voice.

'George, it's John Baker,' I said.

'John! How good to hear from you,' George said. 'How go your day?'

'My day is fine. I'm in London, on a wine-buying trip.'

'You speak to auction houses?' he said.

'Well, I still haven't got the forms from you to authorise me to do so, so no, I don't think I can on this visit.'

'I told you it's okay,' he said. 'Why not just go?'

'They don't work like that, George. I can't turn up with a multi-million-dollar proposal, saying, "I know a guy who said it's cool."'

'Too much red tape in your world, John,' George said. 'You westerners need to be a bit more Georgian. Just make shit happen.'

'That's probably true,' I said. 'George, I'm planning on visiting Château d'Yquem next week, to have one of the bottles authenticated. Once we can prove it's genuine by their authentication, we can make progress, I believe.'

'It's real,' George said. 'One hundred per cent. No problem. Then we can get to sale price. My partners are getting impatient, John. They say you need to bring us the two million soon or they start talking to other interested parties.'

There was a lot to unpack in what George had just said. I breathed down the phone, digesting it.

'What other interested parties, George?'

'Oh, you know. There are others. You not the only person from world who has interest in Stalin and Tsar Nicholai and all these bottles, John.'

'You're talking to others, about doing a deal? You never mentioned that before, George.'

'I not, personally. But others here who are not me, yes? I can't guarantee you only negotiation.'

'Have these other parties visited the cellar? Done an audit?'

'Let's not worry about them,' he said. 'Let's just do our deal so we all good and we can make the money we always wanted.'

'Speaking of which, you just said two million. Where did that come from? We've always been talking an overall purchase price of one million dollars, US, which is now 500,000 initially with you retaining ownership of half the cellar,' I said.

'No, two million is price,' George said. 'Neville promised two million, minimum. That in deal with him.'

'Well, Neville is no longer involved and every piece of correspondence, every conversation, every draft deal you and I have ever shared had one million as the price.'

'John, I have partners who—'

'George, you need to sort out your end of this,' I said, my voice rising. 'You keep talking about these partners. Are you talking about Tamaz and company? The ones we met? Or do you have new partners? It's up to you to control your end. Our price was always one million dollars and I'm deeply disturbed you would try to double it over the phone. No silly buggers, George, or I walk away and you don't see any money at all.'

'I handle my end,' George said. 'You get bottle okayed. We talk soon about export of cellar.'

'I still don't have any proof that you have stored those new bottles to protect the costs of this current trip and other expenses, George.'

'It happening,' he said.

'And I still don't have a Georgian rugby jumper.'

George laughed down the phone. 'John, come up with money and finish deal and I buy you a whole rugby team.'

That night, Jane and I had dinner with Linden Wilkie and his wife, Aiko. Linden, who had become a great friend, had moved to London years before.

'Linden runs The Fine Wine Experience,' I explained to Jane as we waited for our entrées. 'It's a fantastic business. Linden really approaches the great French wines from the point of view that it is all about enjoying the bottle of wine and the experience of sharing it. He likes drinking great wines with a bit of laughter happening around the table at the same time.'

'I can see why you two get along,' she replied, smiling.

Linden nodded. 'It's true. I've never been one for caring about the investment of wine, or the labels. I love the aromas, and the living, breathing nature of wines, and how a group of people – even a foursome like us – can share a bottle, and debate it and taste different nuances and just have our senses so alive in the moment.'

'Speaking of which,' I said, and reached down behind my chair. I turned back to the table and handed Linden a bottle of 1990 Wendouree Shiraz, from Australia's Clare Valley. A beautiful wine.

'Oh, you found one!' Linden said, beaming with happiness. 'Did you have to search much?'

I laughed and wondered if I should confess and finally shrugged. 'You know, when we spoke and I asked you if I could bring some-thing over for you, and you mentioned that you were curious about Wendouree, I suddenly had a thought, went down to my own cellar and realised this bottle had been brought over by someone for lunch or dinner or whatnot, wasn't drunk on the night and ended up among my bottles. So now it's yours.'

'That's brilliant. Thanks, John,' Linden said. 'I have something for you too.'

He reached behind his chair and produced a bottle of Mas de Daumas Gassac, supposedly a particularly good and unusual wine from the Languedoc region in the south of France. Up until now, it hadn't been regarded as a region known for great wines, but I had heard Daumas Gassac was different.

'Oh wow, these aren't easy to get,' I said.

'No, it did take some work,' Linden admitted. 'It's a particularly good vintage, by the way.'

He spent a few minutes running through the Languedoc wine characteristics and why some vintages had been better than others over the past decade. Jane listened to it all, sipping her wine, and when he'd finished, said, 'Linden, you seem young to be so well-versed in all this, if you don't mind me saying so.'

'I did start pretty early,' Linden said. 'I was working as a sommelier when I was in my first year of uni, back in New Zealand, as well as hosting wine nights for fun, and I never really looked back.'

'He came to London to be in the thick of it,' I said. 'And it seems to have worked.'

'It has,' Linden said. 'Although it's a pretty crowded market over here. I'm toying with the idea of a change of scene, but not yet.'

'What are you thinking?' I asked.

'Asia,' he said. 'Although it means I'm going to have to step up my ability to be businesslike, rather than primarily an enthusiast with a business. There's a huge interest in collectable wines starting to build over there. I spent a year as an exchange student in Hong Kong, you know, when I was a kid, and I keep thinking about the money there, and the culture, and how well a genuine world-class shop and events company could fly in that part of the world.'

'Well, let's hope they keep getting interested in the antique wine market, because I might be holding an auction sooner rather than later, fingers crossed,' I said.

We drank to that, and to being reacquainted, and to Linden and Aiko meeting Jane, and to me meeting Jane, and to London, and to Dire Straits, and to anything else we could think of over the course of a long dinner with at least one too many bottles of wine. Especially given we had to be up early the next day to fly to Paris.

A PARISIAN PAVEMENT

Paris, France
August 2003

When the alarm sounded at 5.45 am, I felt every single glass of the night before pounding through my head, and even a shower alternated hot and cold a few times could only wake my body up enough to get moving. Jane and I blearily finished our packing and I realised that I had already collected too many bottles to try and put them all in my checked baggage.

I looked at the four bottles on the desk in our hotel room, including the Daumas Gassac from Linden, a Loire red I'd collected but hadn't tried yet, Jean-François's bottle of Cobram Estate olive oil and the Yquem, still swaddled in bubble wrap and housed in a rubber wine sleeve made out of wetsuit material. I had already closed my suitcase and I knew sealed bottles were allowed as hand luggage at that time between London and Paris. So I put all the bottles in a sturdy padded wine bag that we had brought along, knowing it could come in useful somewhere.

'Are you sure about this for the Yquem?' Jane asked.

'Jane, you know my theory,' I said. 'The more you worry about a bottle, the more you're inviting some kind of disaster. Pack it well but treat it like the others and it will be fine. The bottle has two layers of padding as well as the other bottles to keep the bag firm.'

We headed to the airport, drank enough coffee in the departure lounge to survive the short flight, made it out of Charles de Gaulle airport in one piece and took a taxi to our hotel in the centre of Paris. Jane had booked the hotel, having stayed there before, and it was in a brilliant location, right near the Marais and a short walk to the Centre Pompidou. It's my favourite part of the French capital, with the arty bohemian air of SoHo in New York but everything that's great about Paris, and within easy reach of all the main attractions as well as a lot of good restaurants and bars.

Arriving at our hotel and still feeling pretty ordinary from the previous night's indulgences, we clambered out of the taxi, with shopping bags, luggage and the bag of wine all carted onto the slightly uneven, ancient Parisian footpath. As I leaned back in to pay the driver, I thought Jane had the wine bag on her shoulder or in her hands as we had discussed so that we knew it was safe. But in the confusion of the busy pavement, and with the hotel staff taking suitcases from the taxi, the wine bag somehow ended up with our other bags and that's when, out of the corner of my eye, I saw a bag tip.

It was one of those fractions of a second where you just know, deep in your soul, that the bag that just toppled wasn't one of the many that could have fallen over without incident.

'Ooh' is all I remember thinking as my brain registered the horizontal wine bag, but even as I picked it up and reached for the wetsuit polyurethane of the protective sleeve, I was telling myself that the Yquem should be fine; it was well protected.

Right up until I realised the bag was slightly damp and a bottle must have broken.

And right up until I realised that the wetsuit sleeve in my hand was where the seeping wine was coming from.

'Oh shit,' I said. 'It's the Yquem.'

Jane was truly horrified, her face a white mask of shock.

Me? I felt numb, but I went to work. I prised open the wetsuit sleeve and the bubble wrap and felt where the hundred-year-old bottle had cracked across its bottom seal. The sleeve and wrapping had actually done their job and held the package together tightly, so not much of the wine had escaped. Now I knew where the break was, I turned the bottle upside down, managing to retain most of the liquid.

But now I was standing on a French pavement with an inverted, cracked bottle of probably genuine 1870-something Château d'Yquem and no idea what to do.

'John . . .' said Jane. 'I . . .'

'Jane, it's okay,' I said, looking her in the eye as she tried hard not to cry. 'Look, bottles break. It happens. Once they break, they're broken. We've still got most of the liquid. It was nobody's fault but mine for not packing it properly in my luggage, as I did from Australia.'

She didn't look convinced. In our travels, we'd fallen into the habit of me lugging suitcases and shouldering heavier bags, while Jane was in charge of the variety of smaller bags. But under the circumstances of our not feeling great, the uneven pavement, the bellboys taking bags without asking us which ones, it was simply a moment for Murphy's Law to play out. It certainly wasn't Jane's fault and I didn't want her to think so. I should have put the bottle in my luggage. I shouldn't have been lazy with a hangover that morning. I should have carried it at all times.

If I'd just . . .

If we could have . . .

If only . . .

It was done. Such thinking was pointless. The bottle had cracked and that was that.

Now we had to save what we could. Still holding the bottle, I raced into a corner store just down the street and bought two small bottles of Perrier water with screw caps.

I gave the bottles to Jane, who poured the water into the gutter. The doormen from the hotel carried all our bags in and helped us to our room, while I still nursed the broken bottle as steadily and gently as I could.

But I was now in some kind of post-traumatic shock. The wine would now become exposed to air and oxygen would be getting into the liquid, potentially deteriorating the wine. I had to get it into the screw-cap bottles as quickly as I could, and with ideally no oxygen, or certainly as little oxygen as possible in the top of the new bottles to try to preserve the ancient wine in the best possible condition.

We shook the Perrier bottles to get rid of almost every last drop of water and then I delicately lifted the broken Yquem from the wetsuit sleeve at last. Jane helped unwind the bubble wrap and I could finally see the poor bottle as it was. The bottom was broken off, I guess because such old glass was brittle. But by swinging the bottle upside down, I had managed to retain more than half of the liquid.

Now I carefully poured the remaining wine into the Perrier bottles and winced slightly as I deliberately let them overflow, wasting a little of the precious Yquem, to ensure Jane could put the caps on with no room for air.

I looked at the two now full bottles and saw that they were 250 ml bottles. The ancient Yquem bottle still had less than a cup of wine left, so I'd managed to retain more than 500 ml.

With what wine we had now safely screw-topped into the Perrier bottles, there was nothing for it but to strain the remaining wine into a wine glass, poured through a small towel to filter out any glass shards.

I gingerly put the remains of the century-old bottle down on another towel and Jane and I stared at one another, the shock starting to fade.

'What do we do now?' she asked.

'I feel like crying,' I said.

'Well, I could do with a drink,' she said, looking at the half glass of potential 1870 Yquem.

'Yeah, you're right,' I said. 'Why not?'

Jane tasted first and said nothing, lost in a haze of shock meeting exhilarating aroma and flavour. She handed me the glass and I swirled it, peered at the dark liquid, sniffed it and finally took a sip.

It was superb. Even with all my years of educating myself in wine, I wasn't really sure exactly what a 130-year-old Château d'Yquem was supposed to taste like, but if you'd asked me, I would have guessed something like this.

Oh my God.

Looking back, I only wished that when I had this once-in-a-lifetime experience of sampling such a wine, I hadn't been hungover or preoccupied with self-checking to see if I had had or was in the process of having a heart attack when I stood in our Parisian hotel room and tasted it.

What I should have done is an organoleptic analysis of this wine and written detailed tasting notes, then and there. But I just stood there, with my head pounding and slightly spinning.

But, honestly, the memory of that sip is a bit of a blur.

What is not a blur is Jane, having tasted it, looking at me quietly, and then coming over to me and wrapping her arms around me.

We stayed like that for some time until she pulled back to look at my face and said, 'John, I didn't miss that in the moments after that bottle broke, you were genuinely more concerned about me and my feelings than you were about your beloved Yquem. That was true love. Right there.'

She gently kissed me.

I didn't say anything. She was right. I had been more concerned about that look of death on her face than I was about the bottle. We'd managed to save the situation so that I was reasonably sure I'd preserved enough of the wine that the experts at Château d'Yquem would be able to look at it and have a fairly good idea of what it had been like a few days before, when we broke it. We had the original bottle with the cork still in it. We had the capsule and the glass. We had taken photos of it all, and while we were starting to become resigned to where we'd found ourselves, there was a way forward.

This latest setback was just another part of the saga of unearthing Stalin's wine.

But of course, none of this covered the unmistakable and unavoidable question that hung so heavily in the Parisian air that morning.

How on earth was I going to tell Kevin?

28

BROKE IN BORDEAUX

We shook off the disaster of the broken bottle to somehow enjoy several wonderful days in Paris. My goddaughter, Ana, was living there at the time, playing flute at the Conservatoire de Paris as part of her training to become a professional musician, so Jane and I enjoyed following along as Ana showed us her favourite parts of the city and we shared our own highlights with one another.

We had each been to Paris often enough that we didn't need to tick off all the tourist hotspots. We had more fun poking around some of the more obscure arrondissements. I took Jane to Belleville, with its artistic shops and great cheap restaurants. She took me to the Jardin du Luxembourg where we watched hip Parisians parade.

Secretly, in my head, a debate was raging. Should I tell Jean-François what had happened to the bottle? Would the heads of Château d'Yquem still deign to waste their time with a reckless Australian who had smashed an antique bottle of their wine? What if they wouldn't even bother to open the Perrier bottles? I thought back to the sip of wine I'd shared with Jane after the breakage. That liquid had looked like Yquem and, as best as I can remember given my discombobulated state, it certainly smelt and tasted like you would hope a century-old Yquem would. Surely that could only come from a wine that had started life, 130 years ago, as something quite superb?

Wouldn't the winemakers at Yquem be curious, even if it was now being presented in the ludicrous form of Perrier bottles?

We finally headed to Bordeaux, taking a high-speed train through glorious French countryside. I never tire of France, and it felt good with Jane's head on my shoulder, to watch the regions zoom by the window, signified by subtle differences such as the way slate roofs gave way to terracotta as we made our way towards the south-west.

The actual old city of Bordeaux is a port town and one of the most beautiful in Europe, I believe. It's on UNESCO's World Heritage List as a spectacular urban and architectural example of the eighteenth century, with what feels like hundreds of historic buildings, including at the port itself, and a huge town square, as well as two impressive cathedrals. The Saint-André Cathedral has sections dating back to before the year 1100, while Église Sainte-Croix is perched on the site of an abbey from the seventh century. It would be fair to say that Bordeaux is not lacking in history. Jane and I wandered the town and took in some works by Renoir, Picasso, Matisse and other masters at the city's museum of fine art, and of course I couldn't help but drag Jane into the Musée du Vin et du Négoce – a museum devoted to the history of the wine trade. It outlines wine production techniques in the area going back 2000 years, which is impressive unless you happen to be Georgian, with four times that much history among the grapes.

We eventually made our way to the office of Jean-François, who greeted us warmly. He and Jane hit it off, as I knew they would. We sat down for a suitably overblown dinner to reacquaint ourselves, and of course Jean-François said he couldn't wait to see the famous bottle. In fact, go and get it, he suggested, as he walked us past the enormous Corinthian pillars of the Grand Théâtre to our hotel.

'I'd love to see it right now,' he said.

'All in good time,' I replied. 'I don't want to spoil the surprise.'

Which was absolutely true, although probably not in the manner that he imagined.

As well as the next day's Union des Grands Crus tasting, which is always a highlight of my trips to Bordeaux and was an important day for my Bordeaux Shippers business, we visited Château Léoville Las Cases – a second growth Saint-Julien – which is a very highly regarded château and one of my favourite wines from the Saint-Julien appellation. As far as local château owners go, Jean-Hubert Delon is not known to be the most social. I wasn't even sure we would meet him, as we arrived, greeted the winemaking executives and began tasting several vintages.

I always made a point of dressing very well for these château visits. Some international buyers turn up in jeans, but I took the view that I was being granted entry to the centre of the wine making world, often by châteaux that carried hundreds of years of history, sometimes by generations of the same family. The least I could do was wear a jacket and look like I was a respectable wine merchant, rather than a tourist.

Maybe that's why, when Jean-Hubert did happen to drop by the tasting room about halfway through, he joined our tasting and seemed to warm to Jane and me. He already knew Jean-François quite well and became friendly and talkative as the tasting went on. I had been told by other buyers that Jean-Hubert only spoke French and so was mildly surprised when he chatted to us in passable English. But only mildly surprised. As happens with a lot of the Bordelais, when they want to speak English, they can! All in all, it was a worthwhile and enjoyable visit, I bought some stock for the business and we all parted as firm friends.

'An early night tonight,' Jean-François said as he dropped us back at our hotel. 'Tomorrow we visit Yquem! *À bientôt.*'

'You're sure you don't want one drink before you leave, Jean-François?' I asked.

'Well,' he said, hesitating in the driver's seat. 'It's been a big day, but it would be rude not to. We French do like to set an example in hospitality,' he explained to Jane, eyes twinkling.

'And we Southern Hemisphere interlopers genuinely appreciate it,' she said.

Jean-François laughed that easy laugh of his and said, '*Un moment. Je vais garer la voiture.*'

'You still haven't told him about the bottle,' Jane said as we watched my friend drive away, searching for a car park.

'I know. I feel very bad about it,' I said. 'I'm worried I'll humiliate him or disappoint him. He's been very good to me, but how do I tell him? I don't want him to be bundled out with me when I become the first Australian wine buyer physically ejected from Château d'Yquem.'

'At least Kevin would find that an acceptable end to the story,' Jane pointed out.

'True. Now that Jean-François is joining us, we have to make sure this remains an early dinner and only two glasses each! I am not showing up there with a smashed bottle *and* a hangover,' I said.

'I thought he was only joining us for one drink?' Jane asked.

In the end, we were good and only had three.

It was midway through the third glass, a lesser Sauternes than the château we were due to visit tomorrow, that I said to Jean-François, '*Mon ami*, there is one thing I need to tell you.'

And so I did. I didn't try to sugar-coat it. I told him I had been tired and not at my best after the dinner with Linden, and that I should have taken more care, but that the bottle had broken and I'd turned it upside down and eventually saved a lot of the wine in screw-top Perrier bottles. I felt pretty bad.

Jean-François listened intently, his eyes growing wider with each twist in the story. When I finally finished, and produced one of the Perrier bottles as proof, he looked at it, looked at me, stared at Jane, looked back at the bottle and then absolutely roared with laughter.

'I can picture the whole scene,' he said. 'John, we've all carted valuable wine when in a self-induced world of pain. You just drew the unluckiest card.' He started laughing again.

'You broke the bottle,' he said, waving his hands incredulously. 'You destroyed the oldest Yquem that I will – well, would have ever seen.'

'Jean-François, if you want to cancel the meeting, I will understand. I do not want to embarrass you or damage your reputation among your wine colleagues,' I said.

'Oh, no, there is no need for that,' he said, waving a hand dismissively. 'Look, we have a meeting already arranged with Sandrine Garbay. Of course we should go.'

'Who is Sandrine Garbay?' Jane asked.

'She's the chief winemaker at Yquem,' Jean-François said.

'The chief winemaker is a woman?' Jane said, genuinely surprised.

'Sure,' Jean-François shrugged. 'And the absolute top of her field. Pierre Lurton, the château president, might turn up as well.' My friend shot me a cruel grin. 'I'm sure he'll be interested to see the shattered remains of his ancestors' work.'

'*Mais arrête!*' I said, but I was smiling, relieved the meeting was still on.

Jean-François was savouring the last of his glass. He frowned and said to me, 'Explain again how you saved the wine? Did you say you turned the bottle upside down?'

I laughed and told him a few war stories of the long-time wine hunter. He shook his head.

'Well, tomorrow was always going to be an interesting day,' he said, rising from his seat. 'Now it's just become even more interesting.'

THE WINES OF BORDEAUX

Most histories of the Bordeaux region date the first vines to somewhere around AD 43–60, during the Roman army's occupation of Gaul. The idea was to provide the soldiers with a local supply of wine, but word about the quality of the produce didn't take long to spread. No less a historical figure than Pliny the Elder, who had been a Roman commander in Germany, wrote about wine from Bordeaux on his return to Rome (and only a few years before he was famously killed in the eruption of Mount Vesuvius, near Pompeii). The first-century incarnation of Britain also became aware that there was some decent wine emerging from what would later become known as Bordeaux.

The perfect vine-growing soil and climate, matched with easy access to the Garonne and Gironde rivers meant wine could be shipped to the ocean ports and then to the wider Roman empire, and really the recipe for Bordeaux's success hasn't changed much since, apart from the scale.

Fast forward to 1152 when a local, Eleanor of Aquitaine, married an English noble, Henry Plantagenet, soon to become King Henry II. Bordeaux wine featured at the royal wedding and Bordeaux was on its way, even becoming the second largest city, after London, under English control, with wine shipped regularly to Britain. King Richard the Lionheart made Bordeaux his centre of European operations, all the better to be closer to the grapes themselves.

Despite the region's popularity as a wine-growing precinct, it still had one problem as the 1600s rolled around. Most of Bordeaux along the river was flat, swampy and wet. The Dutch arrived and drained the swamplands, offering more useable land for vines and also allowing better roads to be built, for quick transport north.

The region's wine industry has ridden many bumps and highs, including the French Revolution–era confiscation of estates from royalty and aristocrats (though many were soon controlled by groups of shareholders to continue operating), and Napoléon III's marketing decision in 1855 to classify the region's wines into the famous five growths: first, second, etc. – along with appropriate price tags. Bordeaux's wine industry has survived two world wars, the Great Depression and numerous natural threats such as multiple devastating hailstorms and the vines being decimated by microscopic but lethal attacks of invasive fungi, oidium and later downy mildew, and then phylloxera, a tiny insect.

The phylloxera invasion had a lasting effect as future vines could not be planted so densely, meaning vineyards could only produce a reduced number of bottles each harvest. This limited produce, especially of signature years – such as 1982, the first vintage loudly lauded by renowned wine writer Robert Parker – coincided with an acceleration in the growth of new markets across Asia, and especially China, dramatically pushing up prices for the most sought-after wines from the top châteaux. It's the magic formula for any retailer, whether selling fine wine, fashion or cars: have a wildly desired product of which there is only a limited amount. The price tag will reflect that hunger.

29

CHÂTEAU D'YQUEM

Even without its famous grapes, the region of Bordeaux is a thriving business centre of France. The wider city of Bordeaux itself includes massive industrial centres building fighter jets, and there is some leading-edge medical and science technology in development there as well. In recent years, the city has had major refurbishment, with trams now running through the centre and along the riverbank, reborn from the tired warehouses that have traditionally housed the Bordeaux wine trade on the Quais des Chartrons.

But of course, the region is most famous for its wine production, worth something like €14 billion a year. No wonder people in Bordeaux drive nice cars.

Including Jean-François. After lunch, he drove us south-east of the city, the rolling landscape covered with more and more vines as we moved through the countryside. The motorway more or less followed the path of the Garrone River, occasionally visible in the distance to our left.

It was magnificent scenery.

'You know that a majority share in Yquem was sold five years ago to Louis Vuitton,' Jean-François said, as he drove.

'From the Comte, who actually ran the château and made the wine. Is that right?' I asked.

'Yes. He fought the sale for a while but then was kept on as manager, plus a nice cheque for his family's share. When he finally retired, they promoted Sandrine Garbay as *maître de chai*. She was barely thirty years old.'

'Have you spent much time with her?' I asked.

'Only a little,' Jean-François shrugged. 'She seems very down-to-earth, very unaffected by her status and her success. I like her.'

As we passed Cadillac, entered the Gironde department and headed into Sauternes, I felt my pulse quicken. We were in serious winemaking country now, probably the best on the planet, for sweet wines at least. Château Rieussec and Château Guiraud, Château Raymond-Lafon; there were so many world-renowned labels within minutes of one another. But here, on a small vine-covered hill, on the highest point in the region, stood the château we were aiming for. Distinctive sand-coloured walls and a sloping red-tiled roof, with darker tiles on the turrets of the main house and a small tower off to the right as we approached the property.

Originally a feudal castle, Château d'Yquem was extensively reno-vated and extended in the Renaissance. It started life as a royal estate, which seems fitting, belonging to the English Crown, and then, after 1453, to the French royal family. In 1593, it was acquired by the Sauvage d'Eyquem family – Ramon Felipe Eyquem had made his fortune as a herring and wine merchant – before segueing into owner-ship by the Lur-Saluces family, through the 1785 marriage of Sauvage heiress Françoise-Joséphine to Comte Louis Amédée de Lur-Saluces (who happened to be the godson of Louis XV, if you're keeping count of the royal connections). Apart from a brief spell as a military hospital in World War One, the château has been entirely dedicated to perfect-ing the art of creating the ultimate Sauternes for centuries.

On previous visits I had only ever stood outside the perimeter wall, gazing longingly past the gate, but today Jean-François matter-of-factly turned into the white-pebbled drive and cruised past the single white stone obelisk in the middle of the turn-off, which I noticed had a coat of arms carved into it, weathered from who knows how many decades or centuries in that place. The coat of arms had two lions, a crown and a crest, with vine leaves and grapes carved into the bottom, falling away from the shield.

I knew the crown on top of the design very well. It was on every bottle of Yquem. The crest itself was on the foil covering the cork.

We swept through the wide-open iron gates and Jean-François drove carefully past the famous vines until we reached the château and found a park among a dozen or so other cars, almost all Renaults or Citroëns, plus one expensive-looking Audi.

Jane was taking it all in, with a delighted smile on her face. I guess this was pretty heady stuff for a Melbourne sommelier a long way from home, and I was feeling the same way. I was an unashamed kid in a candy shop. Heading away from the drive were immaculate gardens full of brightly coloured rose bushes, lawns sloping down to meet the vines, while the château itself rose grandly for what was in essence a two-storey building with attics. It was joined by a lower, flatter, long building extending behind the iconic facade of a million wine labels.

'It looks as though we are not the only visitors today,' Jean-François said, raising his chin towards the other vehicles. 'Maybe we are only one of ten parties bringing century-old wine for Sandrine to have a little tasting party?'

'Oh, stop, please,' I said. 'I feel sick enough already about how we're delivering the wine, without having a wider audience.'

Jean-François gave me a wicked grin and told us to wait, while he went inside to check that we were expected.

Jane and I stood next to the car and she wrapped me in a hug. 'This must be an amazing moment for you,' she said.

'It really is,' I replied into her hair. 'I've dreamed of being officially received at Yquem. No matter what ends up happening with that Georgian cellar, the whole escapade has given me so many experiences, adventures and memories.'

Jane laughed and stood back to look at me. 'A potential multi-million-dollar profit in the air and you concentrate on the adventure,' she said. 'I like that about you.'

'Well, look where we are. You and I, standing in the sunshine at Château d'Yquem, about to mix with the makers of one of the world's greatest wines. Without Tbilisi, I wouldn't be here, so I'm grateful, come what may with the cellar and even with all the crap that's gone down with Neville and Harry and the rest of it. I think I saw an interview once with Sidney Nolan, the painter, who said that the feeling of happiness, of being truly happy, is something he treasured because nobody can take that moment away from you, no matter what unpleasant things are bound to follow that will interrupt that joy. Was it Nolan? I think it was. A retrospective archive interview, I think, when he died.'

Jane stepped away from me and raised an eyebrow. 'Well, it's wildly romantic, whoever it was. Enjoy this experience of being happy now because, as much of a dreamer as you are, life will definitely screw it up.'

'I think Nolan might have said it better,' I conceded. 'He had a better way with words and art than I do.'

Jean-François had emerged from the château with a young man, dressed in chinos, a crisp-looking business shirt and a blue blazer. Very shiny shoes and a smart haircut.

'John, Jane, this is Youenn, an assistant to the winemakers. He has offered to take us on a small visit of the vineyard before we head inside to discuss our business,' Jean-François said.

We shook hands and said hello to Youenn, who spoke immaculate English and seemed well-travelled, telling us he had visited both Sydney and Melbourne, as well as the Hunter Valley and other wine-growing regions of Australia.

As we talked, we strolled through the gardens and down to the vines themselves, where Youenn told us a little about Yquem's harvesting and processes.

'You can see the vines are not at their best just now,' he said, 'at least in terms of visual beauty, because we are unearthing the soil. This is something we do twice a year, earthing and unearthing, keeping the soil fresh.'

'There are hardly any weeds,' Jane said. 'Do you use weed killers?'

'Never a chemical weed killer,' Youenn said. 'The only addition to the soil is fertiliser but that is organic only and used very sparingly.'

'What do you mean?' I asked.

'The entire estate has 126 hectares, although only 100 hectares is ever used for production at a time, so that the vines and soil can have some rest,' Youenn explained. 'Even then, only 20 hectares receive fertiliser each year. We do not want the soil to become too rich or fertile, as it would start to detract from or fight the character of the grapes, if you will. So we give it just enough natural compost to be healthy without becoming overpowering.'

'What is your pruning regime?' I asked.

'Early winter, and quite severely,' he said. 'We spur-prune most of the vines, with the Sauvignon 90 per cent pruned, but the Sémillon and the single Guyot vines less so.'

We were walking among the vines themselves, and I couldn't stop thinking about the centuries of great vintages that had come from these sloping hills.

'Tell John and Jane about the vineyard workforce,' Jean-François said. 'The women of the vines.'

Youenn laughed. 'Ah yes, *les femmes*.'

'Hmm, I'm interested,' said Jane.

Youenn pointed to a worker further down the hill. 'We have twenty female vineyard workers, and each is assigned a specific plot within the vineyard. It means they are personally acquainted with every vine in their plot, nurturing and controlling the vines.'

'What do they actually do during the year?' Jane asked.

'They green-prune their vines, like bud pruning,' Youenn said. 'They are responsible for tying the vines and eliminating side shoots.

Obviously also as the Botrytis mould takes hold of the grape, they must carefully monitor and judge its progress. Nothing is left to chance. We love nature and work with nature, but nature must also work with us to create exactly the right Yquem grapes. Our workers also thin the leaves on the eastern side of the vines as we approach harvest so that any dew on the grapes can dry more quickly in the morning.'

'Why only the eastern side?' Jane asked.

'Because the rain, if it comes, will come from the west and the leaves left on the west can protect the grapes,' he explained.

'What happens if the Botrytis grapes are not to your satisfaction, when you come to the actual harvest?' Jane asked.

Youenn shrugged expansively. 'There have been years where Yquem simply does not produce a vintage. If it is not to our standards, we call it and sell the juice to other producers.'

'So, you'll write off an entire year's work?' Jane said, incredulous.

'Quality is everything, *madame*. The last year without a vintage was 1992. Before that, 1974, 1972 and 1964. Nine times in all. Le Comte Alexandre set our very exacting standards and we maintain them to this day. It is why Yquem is regarded with the esteem it enjoys. Now, should we return to the château?'

We picked our way back through the vines, taking in the magnificent facade of the château, before Youenn led us inside. There was the famous winding stone staircase, the mirrors and tapestries. We definitely knew we were in a French castle.

But Youenn walked past all of that and took us to the tasting room, where we found a small group of mostly men already gathered, sniffing and swirling glasses of nectar-coloured wine.

'Ah, Youenn, well timed,' said a slightly older man, also immaculately dressed. '*Bonjour*, my name is Serge, and I am the marketing manager at Yquem.'

We all shook hands as Jean-François introduced us and then escorted us over to the larger group.

'We are very lucky to have with us today some senior executives from our very good friends Château Lafite, from north of Bordeaux,' Serge explained. 'We like to compare notes and discuss how our harvests are progressing. As well as our individual success, we like to know that all of the Bordeaux premiers crus are healthy and successful.'

One of the Lafite group, an export consultant called Amélie, I had met before on an earlier buying trip, which helped our credibility with this new group. We all said hello and then got down to the business of tasting some Yquem. Serge and Youenn poured us tasting glasses of the latest vintage. It was divine, never in doubt of being a cancelled vintage.

'I'm getting gorgeous apricot and mandarin, and a melange of flowers,' Jane said, sniffing.

'A hint of vanilla,' Jean-François ventured.

'Almost tropical fruits on the bouquet,' I said. 'You can tell it's a young vintage.'

'But amazing,' Jane said. 'The flavour just stays with you with such delicious viscosity. I've never experienced such a long, exotic finish.'

Jean-François smiled. 'At Yquem, they use a French expression for that aftertaste: *il fait la queue du paon*. It's difficult to translate but basically it means that the taste spreads out like a peacock's tail.'

Jane laughed. 'That's perfect.'

Serge and Youenn now invited us to take a second glass but from a different bottle, and I couldn't believe my eyes when I read the year on the new one. It was 2001, considered one of the greatest modern vintages of Yquem. I had not had a chance to taste it and now I was being handed a glass.

Jean-François leaned in and said quietly, 'We should be very glad the Lafite group is here. I'm not sure they would have opened a 2001 just for us. No offence.'

'None taken. I like Lafite more than ever now,' I said.

We sniffed, we swirled glasses. We tasted. The wine was simply exceptional.

To Jean-François, Jane, Amélie and two other Lafite executives who happened to be standing with us, I said, 'Now, we all know that this 2001 Yquem has been voted a 100-point wine by Robert Parker and other good judges. I don't normally score wines of this level but looking at this wine, can you find a reason to take away even a point? If you don't think this is a 100-point wine, please, I would love to know why. Can a wine be perfect?'

I think we all agreed that a wine certainly can, with an enthusiasm of knowing there was something very special in our glasses. I remembered how Kevin has a theory that wine always tastes better at a vineyard because your senses get caught up in the location and the vines and the fact you're probably having a nice day if you're touring wineries, and so on. Maybe he's right and that's why I was almost swooning as I tasted that 2001 Yquem but even now, looking back from a distance of some time, I can clearly remember how perfect that wine was. Its aroma, its length, its structure, its personality were everything you could ever want in a wine. I felt like I was looking at the view from the top of Mount Everest.

We all chatted for a while but then Jean-François gently took mine and Jane's elbows and said, 'Sandrine is ready to see us now. She's in her laboratory if we would care to go over.'

My heart was beating fast as we bid goodbye to the Lafite party and left the château, walking to a low, long building that could once have been a stable but now was revealed to be a state-of-the-art wine laboratory, adjacent to the strictly temperature-controlled cellar for the fermenting barrels, all new every year and made from a particular oak found in a forest in eastern central France. Again, at Yquem, every detail was managed and in keeping with what nature provides for each vintage. Nothing left to chance.

Sandrine Garbay met us with a friendly smile. She greeted us warmly with the traditional kiss to each cheek and said, 'Ah, the mysterious Australians with the hitherto undiscovered wine treasure of the Georgian Republic. It is quite a story, Mr Baker, from what I understand.'

'Oh, yes, it is quite a story,' I agreed. 'I suspect it's not over yet, either.'

'One moment, before we go on,' she said, picking up a phone. She murmured in French and then replaced the receiver. 'Pierre Lurton, our president, is very interested to see this wine as well.'

Jean-François and I exchanged glances. 'I think it will certainly surprise him,' I said.

As we waited for his arrival, I looked around Sandrine's laboratory. It had timber panelling on all the walls and a large marble table, where she worked. The room was very neat, very ordered and clean.

Pierre had a busy manner, bustling into the laboratory and shaking hands with us all and exchanging pleasantries with Jean-François, who he obviously knew pretty well. Sandrine had apparently briefed him about why we were here because he clasped his hands and said, 'A lost 1870 vintage? Let's have a look at this famous bottle then.'

I reached into my carry bag and carefully pulled out the double plastic bag with the remnants of the original bottle. Placing it on Sandrine's marble top, I then reached back into my bag and produced the two bottles of Perrier.

It was only then that I dared to look at their faces. Sandrine's was somewhere between astonishment and hilarity, while Pierre was magnificently poker-faced.

'What is going on here, please, Mr Baker?' he said.

There was no way around it. I told them the story of what had happened, starting with a brief explanation of how we discovered the cellar in Tbilisi, and of our visit, and of getting some wine out for authentication, and feeling sick all over again as I had to recount the events of Paris and why the precious bottle was in pieces on their table. I half expected Pierre to storm from the room, and for Sandrine to banish us from her laboratory forever, but instead her eyes lit up as the story unfolded and she laughed out loud as I got to the final stanza where we desperately ran to buy the Perrier.

When I had finished, Pierre shook his head very slowly, gave Sandrine a look of pure astonishment, and then turned back and said to us, very earnestly, 'Only you Australians would do something like this!'

I'm still not sure if he was referring to the broken bottle or the whole crazy Georgian venture. I suspect it was the former, but luckily he also found the story entertaining and fascinating.

'How many more Yquems – possibly even intact – do you think might be in that cellar if this one is real?' Pierre asked me, amusement mixing with business in his eyes.

'We believe there are 217, less the two that we carried home with us – this unfortunate bottle and one other that is no longer in our possession.'

'More than 200 Yquems?' he said. 'One hundred or more years old?'

'Mostly,' I said. 'It appears Josef Stalin or somebody in his circle was a fan of the château as well, because some bottles are younger than the Revolution and the Tsar's demise. But the majority are from the 1800s.'

'Sandrine,' Pierre said. 'What do you make of the bottle?'

Sandrine opened the door and called to somebody in the next room. A tall middle-aged man arrived and was introduced as Henri, her laboratory assistant. Sandrine and Henri had a brief but earnest conversation and, as she had, he put on gloves, the thin rubber ones favoured by forensic scientists, and now opened the plastic bag and carefully removed the broken, ancient bottle. After examination, he laid it out on the table so Sandrine could then inspect it.

The bottle was mostly intact, apart from the bottom, and so she lifted it gently, and peered at the shape, before turning her attention to the neck of the bottle where the cork and capsule were still intact.

'I can definitely see the Yquem stamp on the cork, and it looks correct,' she said. 'The capsule too appears to be authentic as one of ours from back then.'

She looked up at us and said, 'I've actually had some experience of examining Yquems this old before; we have a number of bottles in the château library and all these materials do look very similar.'

Sandrine carefully removed the capsule, trying to retain as much of the Yquem logo as possible. She took the capsule aside to spread it out, to exhibit the logo. '*Oui*,' she said, almost to herself, nodding.

She turned to her assistant and said, '*Henri, pouvons-nous s'il vous plaît retirer le bouchon?*'

Henri nodded and produced a corkscrew, gently picked up the bottle and started screwing into the cork to remove it. Jane shifted on her feet next to me and placed a hand on my arm, saying, 'John,' but I was transfixed at seeing the cork emerge so Kevin and I could finally discover the exact year of this mysterious 1870-something bottle.

But as we watched, Henri struggled a little to get the cork to budge. The 130-year-old cork was in good shape and he was expertly exerting just enough pressure to make it move. But then Sandrine, watching intently, let out a slight cry of frustration as the ancient cork broke under the struggle of the corkscrew.

'*Merde*, these old wines' is all Sandrine said, waving a hand at Henri's corkscrew with a large chunk of broken cork now impaled on it. 'It's not your fault, Henri,' she said to her assistant, who looked horrified by what had just happened.

Sandrine stepped in to fish out the remaining piece of cork and, of course, the break was exactly across where that fourth digit lay. I couldn't believe it. The last piece of evidence to ascertain the exact year had probably been destroyed.

We double-checked, huddling around to look more closely at the cork. Most of it was intact, reading '187', the first three digits, but in adding the end piece to complete the jigsaw of the date, between the break and the age of the cork and the imperfection of the digits after all these years, it was unreadable.

There was an uncomfortable silence in the room.

'I'm sorry. That was unfortunate,' Sandrine said. 'Let's see what the wine is like.'

She opened one of the Perrier bottles and poured the wine into a glass.

'So, it was one week ago that the wine was exposed to air?' she asked.

'No, actually, five days,' I said. 'For probably ten minutes or so, by the time I was able to pour it into these bottles, and I let them overflow a little before I screwed the caps on, to remove any air.'

We all tasted the wine. It was still amazing, as it had been five days ago when Jane and I tried it in our dazed state, after the breakage, but it now definitely had a slightly oxidised edge.

Henri, Sandrine and Pierre all compared notes, speaking rapid French, as they sniffed and tasted. Sandrine raised an eyebrow and nodded twice. Henri, having given his opinion, left us to it, heading back to the other room.

'How does the wine taste to you, compared to last week?' Sandrine asked.

'It is different,' I said, 'even beyond the slight oxidisation. The wine is heavier, almost caramel-flavoured. Last week, the acidity of the wine was fresher, a little brighter.'

Sandrine and Pierre were both sipping again from their glasses.

I waited, barely breathing, as Sandrine took one more sip, frowned, thought for a moment and then nodded.

'I believe this is definitely Yquem,' she said.

I finally breathed out. It was real.

'Having tasted it, this is what an Yquem of that age should probably taste like, even with the recent exposure,' she said. 'Add to that the cork, the bottle, the capsule. It is all correct and as it should be. I do believe that this is a genuine Yquem from the 1870s.'

'This means a great deal to me,' I said, 'and I don't just mean in terms of helping validate the plan to organise the sale. I appreciate you taking the time to test this wine and provide your expert opinion.'

'My pleasure,' Sandrine said. 'This is a fun day for me as well.'

'Actually, John, if it makes you feel better, it's very lucky that you broke the bottle,' the Yquem president, Pierre, said, smiling.

'How so?' I asked, genuinely surprised.

'We have a policy here at Yquem that we will not open any bottle older than 1945. If somebody brings us a bottle for authentication, we will look at the bottle, the cork, the capsule, but we will not actually open it. So, the only way for you to receive a true, unambiguous authentication from Sandrine was for her to be able to taste it, and *voilà*, your broken bottle gave her the opportunity to do so.'

I laughed with relief, happy that the wine was real. 'See, Jane, we're geniuses,' I said, although sounding almost ashamed.

Before Pierre left, he grilled me about the fine details of the Georgian cellar. I think now that he knew the wine was genuine, he had a sharpened interest in what exactly we had stumbled onto.

I explained the ongoing customs issues and the wine maybe being a cultural icon more than merely a bottle to be sold. Jean-François was the one who came up with an idea, suggesting I just try to do a deal to buy the Yquems and the other valuable French wines. 'Leave the Georgian wines and Stalin's personal collection behind, and try to export the French classics that customs or other Georgian authorities might not care so much about,' he proposed.

'They are not Georgian, and belonged to the Russian Tsar, so of what interest are those particular wines to the Georgian authorities?' he asked.

It was an interesting idea that had never occurred to me.

Pierre said, 'John, if you can get the Yquem to Paris, we will send somebody there to inspect the bottles. We would authenticate them if we believed they were genuine, and it looks like they probably will be, going by the one you brought us today. Then you could go to your auction house with the full backing of the château.'

'Pierre, that would be amazing,' I said. 'I can't thank you enough. I would love to work with you on bringing these amazing wines back to the surface. Sandrine, is it possible you could write me a letter or some piece of documentation, saying that you confirm the bottle today is the real thing? It would be great to have for my meetings with Christie's or Sotheby's.'

She frowned. 'John, I'm sorry but I don't think I can. I would have needed that fourth digit on the cork, to say the exact year. Without an exact vintage, we really can't put our name to an official certificate. I'm very sorry. I would like to help.'

I guess it was fair enough. She'd be authenticating a wine from a particular decade, a ten-year spread, from bits of a bottle and some wine in a mineral water container. It's not the same as a scientifically tested bottle from a specific vintage, no matter how real all the individual parts appeared.

We said goodbye and another round of heartfelt thanks and headed back to the car. I took with me the broken bottle and the remnants of the wine, now poured into an unlabelled Yquem half bottle and sealed with a cork.

'What an amazing afternoon,' I said as Jean-François drove back down the pebbled drive, away from the château. 'Everything I could have hoped for.'

'There's only one thing I don't get,' said Jane.

'What's that?'

'Why did Sandrine's assistant try to use a corkscrew? The bottle was broken. Why didn't Henri just push the cork from the inside with a piece of rod or dowel or something? He could have pushed the cork out intact.'

That completely stopped me. 'Oh, of course, you're right. It didn't need a corkscrew. Why didn't that occur to me? You should have said something.'

'I tried to get your attention,' Jane said. 'But I felt kind of awkward, potentially telling an expert like him, or Sandrine, how to do their business.'

'He must have successfully pulled corks like that so many times,' said Jean-François. 'It was clear from his actions that this is just what they would normally do. John, you and this bottle were not a lucky match.'

'Well, in a way we were, Jean-François. Our unfortunate struggle meant we know it was definitely a real Yquem. That's been the biggest question of this whole operation now for years. I can't believe that I finally know the answer. Wait until I tell Kevin.'

'And that we broke his bottle,' Jane said.

'Hmm,' I said. 'Actually, now I think about it, there's no need to call him immediately. That can wait.'

THAT OLD CHESTNUT

Sydney, Australia
September 2003

Kevin was remarkably decent about the bottle, in a typically Kevin way. Of course, the entire conversation was about the broken Yquem.

We sat at a cafe near his house with morning coffees, enjoying the springtime sun. He wasn't going to let me off the hook straight away.

'It's not like the bottle was worth anything,' he said, fixing me with a look. 'It's not like it was the most valuable bottle I've ever had in my collection or probably ever will again.'

'I'm sensing sarcasm,' I said. 'Which I probably deserve. I did bring you back some very fine Perrier mineral water.'

'But of a strange hue.'

'There's that,' I admitted. 'Still, quite the souvenir. Better than a snow dome.'

Once he'd run out of ways to good-naturedly insult me for the broken bottle debacle, we considered where we were at.

'You know that old saying: every war has victims?' he said. 'I guess the bottle is that for us. We lost a soldier but progressed in the battle. It's actually a pretty amazing turn of the universe that Pierre said they couldn't have tasted it if you hadn't broken it, and then we wouldn't have known for sure that it was real. But they did, and we do, which is cool. We now not only know pretty much for certain that the Yquem was real but that probably all the others in that cellar are also genuine. It's taken us years to know that and it's a huge piece of information. Now we can try to make this whole thing happen.'

He was right. To this day I still wince at the thought of seeing that bottle break on a Parisian footpath. What would it be worth, intact and authenticated? Probably at least A$20,000, which would have given Kevin and I A$10,000 each if we had sold it. No, actually, it would probably be worth more than that, but *would* we have sold it? It was such an important part of the jigsaw puzzle and, despite all of my somewhat dismissive beliefs that objects are only objects and an expensive or rare bottle of wine is nothing more than that, I had been quite attached to our mysterious, undated relic. The chances are it would still be sitting in one of our cellars, gathering more dust.

Kevin was a fan of Jean-François's plan that we should consider trying to alter the overall deal with George to only target the Yquem.

'We were talking one million US for the whole cellar,' Kevin said.

'Or two million, last time George and I spoke. I told you he was trying that on,' I said.

'Yes, very strange. He'd always been straight-up about the money before that, but even so, if we assume our original one million price tag, we could potentially offer half of that for only the Yquem and the other French classics, and probably still sell for not much less than we would for the whole cellar.'

I thought about it. 'Would that be enough to get us past the potential customs and heritage issues that have plagued this thing from the start?'

'No idea,' Kevin shrugged. 'Definitely a question for the Wolf Man.'

Late that night, my phone rang, and it was George.

'John,' he said. 'It is time for us to bring this to bed.'

'What do you mean, George?'

'There is concern over here, we waited so long for you to make us offer, to actually show us money for sale. It is time for you to pay us if you want the bottles.'

'George, where is this coming from?' I asked. 'You know exactly where things are at. I need paperwork from you about the customs matters and I need a signed agreement giving me permission to speak to auct—'

'John, we talk about these things for years,' he snapped. 'We have told you not to worry. Here, we like to see you do actually have money. That you serious about buying these wines.'

'George, I'm not just going to transfer half a million dollars on a promise. You know that.'

'John, this is becoming difficult for me, at this end. There are expectations and you need to fulfil your end of the agreement.'

'This is very unlike you, George. I'm concerned,' I said. 'Can you please send me the paperwork I've asked for? I'll try to finalise the legal agreements at this end. I would also love to make the deal happen sooner rather than later.'

'It needs to happen soon, John. Very soon.'

He said goodbye and hung up and I stood there, in my dark lounge room, holding the phone and wondering what that had all been about. I hadn't even had a chance to run the new idea past him.

Since my lunch with Terry Burke, the man in black, and my subsequent meetings with Wolfgang Babeck, the lawyer who had actually helped draft the Georgian constitution, I had spent some money and gained quite a lot of insight into my perennial issue of whether we could hope to export the wines to London – or maybe now Paris for the Yquems – without Georgian authorities stopping us.

Armed with my new knowledge from Bordeaux, I sat with

Wolfgang in his plush Clarence Street office and pondered our chances.

'On the one hand I still have George in Tbilisi waving off the issue and saying he'll "take care of it",' I said, 'with no more visibility of how he'll "take care of it" than when we visited, now some years ago.'

Wolfgang nodded. 'Whereas I feel compelled to point out that Georgia is a signatory to the *World Heritage Act*, signed at The Hague, which could expose you to legal action if you were found to be in possession of Georgian antiquities with a cultural significance.'

'Even if we had legally bought them?' I asked. 'Had paperwork and official documents proving George and his mates had sold them to us in good faith? Or better still, that George had retained ownership and we were only acting as his agent, and only for the French classics, not Georgian wines or Stalin's private wines?'

I found myself admiring Wolfgang's cufflink on a perfectly ironed shirt, as his suit sleeve rode up when he reached for his cup. He sipped coffee and I realised that the cufflink was a golden embossed version of the Georgian flag.

He said, 'I think we both have been around enough blocks to understand that if you found yourself at The Hague on charges of cultural piracy, waving a piece of paper from Giorgi, who now has gotten away clean with half a million or one million US dollars from you, there's a strong chance we can't trust Giorgi to turn up in court to faithfully corroborate your story.'

I had to stand up and pace the room. This same old question had never been resolved.

'There is one thing I could do,' I suggested. 'I could go back to Georgia and have these discussions face to face with George and his partners. Maybe it's time we sat and tried to do the deal. What do you think?'

Wolfgang shifted in his seat. 'I can see the logic, but I would be concerned.'

'Why?' I asked.

'Georgia has changed since you were there, John. I'm not saying this is who you're dealing with, but you might find that characters who were reasonably harmless cowboy criminals a few years ago have stepped up their game and moved into slightly more dangerous fields.'

'You mean oligarchs?'

'There are certainly a few of them pulling strings in Tbilisi, yes,' he said. 'But even some of the minor players, the ones who after the formation of the Republic cut their teeth on mining or, say, wine, might have stepped it up to large-scale government defrauding, funding the military for Chechnyan rebels, drugs and more.'

I pondered what Wolfgang was saying. 'Do you know if George has been mentioned regarding any of these activities?'

Wolfgang's face was intent but friendly. 'Not specifically, no. But he moves in circles where it would almost be a surprise if he had managed to stay completely clear of such people. That's all I'll say.'

31

HOW BADLY DO YOU WANT IT?

I rang George's number repeatedly over the next five days. It rang out every time; not even an answering machine.

After our strange late-night phone call, I had emailed him, confirming the Yquem authentication and explaining again that we should now talk about the next step, such as my long-awaited letter of confirmation for an auction house. I hadn't raised the only-Yquem idea, because I wanted to talk to him about it and feel him out.

But there was only silence.

I finally wrote another email, laying out where I was at and what the deal would need in order to go through.

'George,' I wrote, 'I understand that you are feeling pressure at your end, but so are we. Kevin, I and yourself have always corresponded in good faith, and with respect.'

I laid it all out yet again, for what felt like the hundredth time. The need for certainty about customs, the need for paperwork about the deal, and our station as agents. I could almost write the legals in my sleep.

But I felt, right now, I needed to clearly state it all one more time.

'Do you legally have the right to sell the wine, George?' I asked.

As I said, Groundhog Day.

I finished with:

In short, George, I agree completely with what you said the other night, that it's time for us to do the deal. But if we are going to come up with the money, to actually purchase your amazing cellar, you need to clear our way, without a single potential legal, government or potential delivery hurdle.

I sent the email and heard nothing.

I rang a couple more times and heard nothing.

I wasn't sure what else to do.

And so I got back to work. My Epping store was busy and my Bordeaux importing business was really starting to make strides. I had created a retail website for it and had been warned that this would be a lot of work: to make an online store work properly, you needed to approach it as though you now had an entirely separate, different business. I had laughed at that warning, thinking it melodramatic, right up until I started the project and realised such advice was absolutely correct.

But the website was selling wine, so in my usual way I enjoyed diving in and trying to learn how internet sales worked best and how to wrangle this new world. Happily, we were still some years away from social media rising to take over everything. I'm not sure I could have coped with that as well.

I decided it was time to have another clear-the-shop tasting night for my most loyal and enthusiastic customers. Because I now had good stories to tell, I made a 1985 Château Margaux the final highlight of the eight wines being offered.

Kevin had just returned from a trip to China, where his watch manufacturing business was starting to build up a head of steam, and so he dropped by to assist in preparing the shop floor, setting up the tasting tables, the cheese and other nibbles, and then to play his traditional role of bouncer to anybody who tried to jump the queue and make a beeline for the head table and the Margaux. I loved that years after he had technically worked for me, he still unquestioningly and happily volunteered for that role. Secretly, I think he enjoyed playing the polite hard man.

We held the event on a Thursday night, starting at 7 pm, roughly a month after my last contact with George. I had limited the number to fifty people, with an entry fee of $50. We would close the shop for these events and I would only have to open three bottles of each wine, as we tended to get sixteen pours from a bottle when we were in control of a managed tasting. Some people did not taste all the wines, while the keen tasters would hang around to see what was left over for a little more.

The night went pretty well, with happy and enthusiastic customers and some strong sales. Towards the end of the evening, the door swung open and a man stepped into the shop and stood in the doorway, taking in the scene. He looked familiar but I couldn't immediately place him. He definitely wasn't one of my usual customers, who were the only ones invited to this event, so I noticed him the moment he arrived.

He had closely cropped dark hair, and a stubble beard. He was wearing dark denim jeans and a leather jacket over a polo shirt. He had a gold chain around his neck and a slightly dangerous yet calm air about him.

Then I realised who I was looking at.

I caught Kevin's eye and I think we both clocked who it was at exactly the same moment. Maybe it was the fact he was a few years older and plumper, or maybe it was the lack of a handgun in his waistband that had confused us. Or just that he was so out of context.

I excused myself from the customers I had been chatting with and walked to the door, where he regarded me with a subtle smile.

'Hello, Mr John. Surprise.'

'Hello, Pyotr. You're a long way from home.'

Pyotr smiled more now. 'Is nice to visit Sydney. Anyway, Georgia is not much fun right now, as winter approaches. I like to visit your country and also see your business.'

'How did you find us?' I asked. 'We were at Double Bay when we visited you in Tbilisi, and this shop didn't yet exist.'

'Yes, but you gave me your business card the day you left, remember? I called in to the address on that card and they sent me to here.'

My spider senses were going crazy but I tried my best to appear calm and happy to see him. 'Well, you timed it well,' I said. 'We've been tasting some very good wines this evening and you're welcome to join us as I'm sure there are some nice wines left over.'

Kevin had by now tidied up his post, placing the remaining Margaux under the table for 'afters'. He approached now and shook Pyotr's hand.

'*Gamarjoba*, Pyotr,' Kevin said.

'Victory!' replied Pyotr.

'It's been a while,' Kevin smiled.

'Good evening, Mr Kevin. You are looking well and healthy.'

'Some days more than others.'

I said, 'Pyotr, let me finish up with my customers for a few minutes and then we can have a quiet drink together. Is that okay?'

'Of course, John. I enjoy looking around.'

For the next little while, I continued to work the room, talking to my regular customers and selling some Bordeaux wines at decent prices. All the time I kept an eye on Pyotr, who seemed to be enjoying himself, wandering the tables with Kevin, sampling some wines, and even occasionally attempting small talk with the Sydney North Shore locals.

Eventually, the last customers left and the two casual staff assisting me that night took over the cleaning up and rearranging of the store back to its usual format. I quietly told them that Kevin and I had to take care of some unexpected business and left them to it. The staff gazed in open curiosity at this stranger who had effortlessly drawn all the attention of the room, just by his presence. I remembered how the Tbilisi hotel security used to snap to attention every time Pyotr entered the foyer. He still had that effect on people.

By now, Pyotr was with Kevin at the Margaux table – the bottles having magically reappeared, as only Kevin can make them – and so I wandered over and said, 'Well, that's done, Kevin. Why don't we grab a quiet drink with our friend here?'

I led the way to my office, taking the open Margaux with us. I poured us all a glass as Pyotr took in my books and bottles, the artwork on the walls. He took off his leather jacket, which looked expensive, and hung it over the back of a chair, accepted a glass, raised it to us and then smiled that guarded smile of his.

'Oh, a very fine wine, Mr John. Thank you. Your expectations of seeing me tonight were low, I suspect,' he said.

'You could definitely say that,' I said. 'I have to admit, it took me a second to process that it was you walking through the door.'

'Process? What process?' He looked confused.

'No, to realise it was you,' I said.

'Oh, yes, I'm sure.'

'So, why are you in Sydney, Pyotr?' Kevin asked.

Our visitor shrugged. 'Over the last few years, we Georgians have started to move further into the world, instead of living always in Tbilisi. We like to move around and experience new culture, new western ways.'

'So, you're on holiday?' I asked.

'In a way,' he said. 'And for meetings.'

Meetings like this, I thought. This was no casual drop-in.

Kevin had a look on his face that appeared to be completely relaxed yet I knew calculations of every comment and moment were whirring underneath.

'I've been trying to raise Giorgi on the phone or email for some time, Pyotr,' I said. 'How are things with him?'

'Events move fast in Georgia, John,' he said. 'It might be best if you no longer try to contact George.'

'What do you mean? Is he no longer in charge at the Savane Number One, or this business deal we're trying to finalise?'

'There is no deal, John,' Pyotr said flatly. 'There is no sale of wine.' He sipped his 85 Margaux and gazed evenly at me.

'Pyotr, I don't think I quite understand. Kevin and I have been working on this, off and on, for several years now. George has always indicated that he was open to us buying the wine. What has changed?'

'A great deal has changed, John. This is what I tell you.'

Kevin leaned forward and said, 'Is George all right, Pyotr?'

Pyotr thought about that and moved his shoulders. 'Yes, I think so.'

'But he's not part of the winery anymore,' Kevin said.

'As far as you and John are concerned, he is no longer somebody to talk to.'

'Then who should we talk to, Pyotr?' I asked. 'Who's now in charge?'

Pyotr gave me a look that was completely calm and yet made my stomach flutter. 'This is what I say, John. You hear but you not listening. There is nobody for you to talk to anymore. There is no talk.'

I pushed on. 'The last email I sent to George, almost a week ago, I suggested I come to Tbilisi to try and finalise the sale of the bottles face to face, with George and whatever partners he needed to bring to the table.'

Pyotr sighed and sipped his wine. 'John, that would not be a good idea.'

'Is the wine still there, Pyotr?' Kevin asked.

Pyotr looked at him in surprise. 'Yes, of course. There are many, many bottles. Where would they go?'

'Well, that's what we would like to discuss,' Kevin said. 'They could go to Europe and make you, and us, a great deal of money.'

'That's right,' I said. 'Pyotr, you know we have great connections into Europe. We even visited the winemakers at Château d'Yquem – remember all those Yquems in the cellar? – and they are ready to examine all their bottles to see if they are genuine. We just have to take them to Paris. With the audit that Kevin and I have done, and with your help, we are ready to move the cellar to go to auction.'

'John, I am truly sorry but that is not going to happen. The people I work for, and that is not George all the time, they would like you to know that it is time for you to walk away from Tbilisi.'

Kevin and I processed this.

'But we're so close,' I said. 'So close to the deal.'

'No, you are not,' he said flatly.

'And if I was to get on a plane with you, to Tbilisi, to try and discuss this with your people, Mr Tamaz or whoever they are . . .?' I asked.

Pyotr looked at me for a long time and then slowly spread his hands. 'John, please listen to me carefully. We are at a point where you need to ask yourself right now what you are prepared to pay for the chance to see those bottles again.'

We looked at one another for a long moment, until he said, 'To be clear, I am not talking about American currency.'

There was silence. Finally, I nodded and said, 'Okay, Pyotr. I see.'

'Can I ask who you do work for, Pyotr?' Kevin asked. 'Who has decided that we are not part of the picture?'

'It may be better you don't know,' Pyotr said. 'Not everybody is nice like me and George and Nino, Kevin. Some people now, in Russia, in Georgia, in the world, are dangerous people to know their name. I protect you here. Just need you to understand what maybe happens if you come back.'

'Are we in danger from you, Pyotr?' Kevin asked.

I caught my breath yet marvelled at the question. Kevin, forever the master of cutting to the chase.

But the Chechen only laughed, an unexpected snort and chuckle. 'No, Kevin, no. I like you. I happy to be here, drink your good wine, help you be safe.'

'But if we turned up in Tbilisi, with a large cheque, trying to buy all the antique wine . . .' I ventured.

'Maybe different ending,' Pyotr said. All mirth gone.

'Wow,' I said. 'Okay, Pyotr. We understand. But . . . wow.'

We all drank some more, the silence heavy.

Finally, I said, 'Pyotr, this is unrelated to me trying to do a deal or find a way forward, all right? So, please understand I'm not pushing any game here. I understand the message you're telling us, I promise. However, I do want to know, just because I like him and have always felt a connection with George: is he safe? Is he in trouble?'

Pyotr shrugged again. 'George not in Tbilisi right now. He difficult for everybody to get hold of for a time. It is good move for him, I think.'

'He has a new phone? A new email?'

'John,' Pyotr said, the slightest of edges entering his voice. 'There is no phone. There is no email. But if there was, you have no need of them. I say this again, and you are a smart man.'

So that was that. Pyotr finished his wine and stood to leave.

'It was pleasant to see you both,' he said. 'I'm sorry to end your plans for bottles. We like you a lot. We sad, too, we cannot make money together.'

We walked him to the door of the now empty store, the empty bottles from the night's event packed in boxes and the tables wiped down.

Pyotr put his leather jacket back on and prepared to leave.

Kevin said, 'Pyotr, can I ask, did you come all the way to Sydney just to deliver this message?'

Pyotr laughed and shook his head. 'No, I meet girl and she come here for Rugby World Cup. It starts soon, yes? I come to see her. Watch some games. You just happily here also so we can talk for real and say what needs to be said.'

'So, you're in town for a while?' I said.

'It doesn't matter, John,' he said and smiled at me, almost sadly. 'I see your brain work and work. It is time it didn't, on this. I am now like all of the Tbilisi people at the winery to you, part of your past. A ghost. Goodbye, my friends. Please, for me, decide you'd like to be safe and live long.'

He put out a hand and I shook it. What else was there to do? Kevin shook too and then Pyotr disappeared into the night. As he'd said, like a ghost. We closed the door and my knees felt suddenly shaky.

Kevin and I sank into two of the chairs in the deserted shop and looked at one another, wide-eyed.

'Did that just happen?' I said.

'I'm very certain it did,' he replied. 'I believe we were just told we may be killed if we attempt to visit the Savane Number One again.'

I asked, 'Do you think George is dead?'

Kevin shrugged. 'I have no idea. Maybe. I hope not.'

'But we would be, right? If we tried again. By whoever Pyotr works for.'

'Or by Pyotr,' Kevin said. 'John, I don't think we should misunderstand what he told us, or think it was a negotiating tactic. We've been told very clearly: we are done, as of now.'

I sat there, anger meeting my surprise and fear. 'I don't think I like being told to go away, or else,' I said.

'Neither do I,' said my Canadian friend. 'But I am also quite fond of breathing.'

32

THE VIEW FROM BRONTE

I've always loved the Sculpture by the Sea exhibition that takes place on the Sydney eastern suburbs' coastline. Jane was in town and so we headed to Bondi to walk the astonishingly beautiful track along the cliffs past Tamarama and towards Clovelly, admiring the large-scale sculptures and installations scattered along the way.

There was a breeze and a decent swell, so the waves crashed beneath us as we came down the path into Bronte, hot from walking in the sun, and stopped for a coffee at one of the cafes that overlooked that narrow beach. Life felt pretty good.

'Can I ask you something, Johnny?' Jane asked, taking my hand across the table.

'Of course,' I said.

'How are you feeling about the Georgian bottles? Are you comfortable with letting them go?'

It had been almost a month since Pyotr's unexpected visit. I'd told Jane all of it over the phone the night it happened but she was right, I had spent a lot of the intervening weeks mulling on the conversation, turning it over in my head and trying to reconcile the fact that all our work and expense and anticipation relating to Stalin's wine were lost.

Now, I could only say, 'Yes, it is what it is. There's no point wasting any more thought on it. It's done.'

'Would you put your safety at risk to go and get all those century-old Yquems?' she asked.

'No,' I said. 'Definitely not. You know how I feel: a bottle of wine is a bottle of wine. Even if it's historic and has that amazing heritage and is worth a lot of money, it's still a bottle of wine. Am I going to risk being "disappeared" for it? No way.'

'Still, it's hard to contemplate,' she said, serious eyes watching my face. 'Those thousands of bottles. Was it 217 Yquems? Just gathering dust.'

I laughed. 'Dust that lies under potentially armed, ruthless mafia figures or, at best, rogue businessmen. They can lie there. It's over.'

'It's good that you can be so definite in walking away,' she said. 'I'm not sure I could let it go so readily, if it was me.'

'As I said, what choice do I have?' I took her hand. 'You know I'm not one to get mushy but I have a lot to live for, right here in Sydney. There's you, there's my business, my friends. I've still got the remaining bottles from Tbilisi in my cellar and I still have all the stories that I'll be telling at dinner parties forever. It's been a wildly entertaining and fun adventure, and that doesn't change.'

'I guess not,' she said. 'So, you're done with it?'

'I'm done with it,' I said. 'And to prove it: earlier this week out of nowhere, I even had a call from a friend in New York, a singer who I had told the story to one time, and he called to say he knows a guy who is a documentary maker and is also connected to a super-rich American businessman and wine lover who has connections in Russia. This doco maker and the businessman heard the story and got all fired up, ready to come up with one or two million dollars, no problem, and film the whole thing as they do the deal and grab the wine. I said, well, good luck, if you fellas want to try.'

'Do you think they will?' she asked.

'I have no idea. I wasn't about to give them a lot of the details they'd need and I'm not about to wade back in to find out.'

She smiled. 'My smart, sensitive, pragmatic man,' she said.

'And alive,' I grinned.

We finished our coffees. Jane adjusted her baseball cap. I watched as she tucked stray strands of hair under the cap and reapplied sunscreen. Kevin had said, after Pyotr left, that he was fond of breathing. I was fond of lots of things about life.

It was worth keeping it that way.

I took a deep breath, exhaled and then stood up.

'Come on,' I said. 'Let's keep walking. There's so much more to go and see.'

EPILOGUE

London, UK
February 2019

There was a low mist hanging over Kensington Gardens and a chill in the air. It was mid afternoon but felt later, as London winter does. I had walked up from Westminster, through Sloane Square and Knightsbridge until I entered the gardens. Now, I was sitting on a park bench overlooking the Round Pond, with Kensington Palace behind me.

It was definitely him. I watched as he walked towards me, even though he was still a couple of hundred metres away. The same girth, although a bit more spread now under an overcoat, wearing glasses and his hair with streaks of grey, shorter and with a neat side part instead of the dark mop it had been when we met.

Finding him had been easier than I'd expected. In the intervening years since my Tbilisi adventure and subsequent warning-off, the internet had evolved, sprouted social media, its tentacles reaching into every corner and nook and cranny of the world. Even so, I hadn't expected to find Nino so quickly on a basic Facebook search: now apparently the father of at least one child and with a pretty wife, but not the same girl he'd been driving around when we visited all those years ago. Nino with a Facebook profile that featured a lot of friends with massive, bulging muscles, shaved heads and sleeve tattoos. Pyotr had zero social media presence and I was unable to decide whether the Revaz Rustaveli that I found was the one I'd met. He certainly looked older, if it was. I found an article discussing several Tamaz brothers who had been asked to answer some pointed questions relating to missing gold from the Georgian government. Could that be the same Tamaz?

And now here was George, walking towards me.

Most surprisingly of all, I never would have found him without a throwaway remark from none other than Neville Rhodes. We had found ourselves at the same party at Quay Restaurant in Circular Quay, and it seemed churlish not to go over and say hello. In fact, years after the events, Neville clearly had moved on as well because he seemed genuinely happy to see me and readily laughed as he reminisced about his own adventures, or misadventures, in Tbilisi, on the goldmining front as well as his wine ambitions.

'I wonder where George is now?' I had said, more rhetorically than anything.

'Giorgi Aramhishvili?' Neville said. 'That rogue. He is now, will you believe, Mr George Kensington Esquire, living large in one of the better pockets of London. In fact, get ready for it, in Kensington. He is Mr George Harrison Kensington, of Kensington.'

'Giorgi from Georgia is now Mr Kensington from Kensington?' I said. 'Are you serious?'

'Absolutely. He has been a director of several mining companies, the occasional one of which has even been semi-legitimate,' Neville said. 'He's had a few adventures along the way, in Singapore and Hong Kong, going by some of the juicier articles or legal transcripts, but mostly, I think life is pretty calm for Mr Kensington.'

I couldn't believe it, and armed with this new information I found myself Google searching after I returned home from the party. Sure enough, there was George Harrison Kensington on everything from

LinkedIn to, yes, company warnings. It would seem George had dabbled in petroleum companies, all kinds of mining, and even as a consultant to 3G phone network rollouts across the former Soviet Union.

I had spent more than a decade wondering if he was even alive. He had been living and working under his new name all this time. And so, on a whim, I had reached out and mentioned I'd be in London soon . . .

He approached me now and smiled as he held out a leather-gloved hand.

'John Baker. What a lovely treat,' he said, his English flawless.

'Hello, George. It's been a long time.'

'It certainly has. How are you, old friend? How is your life?'

George sat on the bench, creaking down as though he had bad knees. He was younger than me and had seemed considerably younger in the Tbilisi days but now I felt he was a bit of an old man. Maybe it was just the cold English weather.

'When did you leave Tbilisi, George? Was it then? I'm sad to think you're not there anymore. You were always so passionate about your country and your city. I remember you toasting the Mother of Georgia statue. It meant so much to you.'

He shrugged, resigned. 'Sometimes life takes you away from the things or the ones you love, John. Sometimes you have to begin again. It was time for me to leave, to remove my family from that place. It was definitely the right choice, if I even had a choice. I am not sure you could understand. Anyway, Tbilisi was no longer what it had been in my youth. Nowadays, it is all fucking infinity pools, tourists and American chain stores.'

I didn't know what to say to that. But George just chuckled.

'So now I'm a geezer,' he said in a fair approximation of an East End accent. 'London is not so bad. It has good football games – go, Chelsea – and there is a shop specialising in Georgian wine not far from this park.'

We chatted for a while about my life and his, catching up on the years. He was predictably a little evasive about the fine detail of his work, what he did now and what he had done. He volunteered that he had children now, and they were UK citizens. He had no plans to return to Tbilisi to live, he said.

'I'm sorry things worked out the way they did, John,' he finally said, after we'd chatted for twenty minutes or so. 'I know how much work you put into the cellar and I would have loved to have completed the sale with you.'

'I never knew why it all got shut down, George,' I said. 'I didn't even know if you were alive. Pyotr dropped by my shop in Sydney and warned us off. Were you behind that?'

George grimaced. 'John, these are unpleasant things to revisit after all this time. I think Pyotr was doing you a favour but no, I was otherwise engaged at the time. I'm glad you had the sense to heed the message.'

We sat and looked at a squirrel darting out from behind a tree, regarding us and then not bothering to hide, deciding we were both harmless. I wondered if that was true.

'George,' I said. 'Can I ask: what happened to the wine? In all these years, I've never been able to stop wondering. Those three bottles of 1847 Yquem, they'd be worth a million dollars on their own. And all the other Yquems! Plus, the dozens of Margaux, the Mouton, the Lafite, all the rest. So many treasures and with all that astonishing history attached. What happened to them? Where are they now? Are they still there?'

George looked out over the park and smiled, then turned his head to me, still grinning broadly.

'John, that is Georgian business. How could I know? I'm a Londoner.'

I shook my head but had to smile as well.

'Fair enough, George. I'll just keep on wondering. I have one last question.'

'If you must,' he said.

'Can I buy you a drink, George? For old times' sake? We can talk about Josef Stalin, Nicholas the Second, French wine and sulphur baths.'

George smiled broadly and carefully stood up from the bench.

'Absolutely, John, my friend. I would like that very much. Should you be the *tamada*, or should I?'

'Maybe we can take turns,' I said. 'The only thing, George, and I'll be honest, is that after we've had a couple of drinks, there's a strong chance I might ask you where the wine is.'

George laughed and put a big hand gently on my back.

'Well, that remains the question, John,' he said as we started to walk. 'That is the question.'

GLOSSARY

badridzhnis khizilala – a kind of eggplant caviar.

Cape Mentelle Cabernet – a robust, predominantly Cabernet Sauvignon wine from one of the first vineyards established in the Margaret River region of Western Australia.

Chacha – a brand of vodka made from Rkatsiteli grapes which are also used to make white wine.

charkhlis mkhali – Georgian beetroot salad (aka *pkhali*).

Château Beaucastel Châteauneuf-du-Pape Blanc – one of the great estates of Châteauneuf in the Southern Rhône of France. Long-lasting wines with a particularly wonderful blanc made predominantly of Roussanne.

Château Cheval Blanc – one of the great estates of Saint-Émilion, on the right bank of Bordeaux. Unusually for Bordeaux, the estate has a high percentage of Cabernet Franc vines, giving it rich, fragrant wines.

Château Cos d'Estournel – arguably the great estate of the appellation of Saint-Estèphe, on the left bank of Bordeaux.

Château Coutet – elegant, fine, zesty style of Sauternes.

Château Guiraud – high-class, more robust style of Sauternes with more Sauvignon in the blend than most Sauternes.

Château Haut-Brion – a superb first growth (there are only five first growths) of Bordeaux. The first wine in the world to have its own label, in 1660. Refined, harmonious wine that can live . . . almost forever if well cellared.

Château Lafite Rothschild – first growth of the major appellation of Pauillac (three of the five first growths are in Pauillac). Some will say it is the greatest red wine of Bordeaux. Particularly engaging for its perfume of roasted herbs and spices. Refined and seductive, rather than weighty.

Château Larose (Gruaud-Larose) – large second growth estate (château) in the appellation of Saint-Julien on the left bank of Bordeaux.

Château Latour – the monumental, aristocratic first growth commanding the prime position of the riverfront at Pauillac on the Gironde. Can be the most imposing, structured wine of the five first growths.

Château Margaux – maybe my favourite Bordeaux wine. The charming, supple, refined first growth of the appellation of Margaux in Bordeaux.

Château Mouton Rothschild – first growth estate of Pauillac on the left bank of Bordeaux. Can be quite voluptuous and concentrated.

Famous also for commissioning some of the great artists of the twentieth century to paint its labels.

Château Pichon Baron – brilliant second growth of Pauillac, on the left bank of Bordeaux. Exceptionally located next to Latour and other great estates. Arguably the most photographed château in the entire region.

Château Raymond-Lafon – rich, very good Sauternes neighbouring the monumental Château d'Yquem.

Château Rieussec – very good Sauternes also neighbouring Château d'Yquem. Now owned by Château Lafite Rothschild, and the quality of the wine has improved accordingly.

Château Suduiraut – superb Sauternes estate in the same ownership as one of my favourite Bordeaux, Château Pichon Baron. Luscious Sauternes with good vitality and energy.

Château d'Yquem – please refer to page 14.

classified growths (*crus classés*) – Emperor Napoléon III had the best wines of Bordeaux classified into five levels (first, second, etc.) for the 1855 Exposition Universelle de Paris. The wines included became known as classified growths.

Clonakilla Shiraz – the most prominent and probably the best winery in the Canberra region.

deda-khelada – a big Georgian wine jug, aka mother-jug.

Dom Pérignon – the luxury cuvée (wine) of the Moët & Chandon group (owned by LVMH) and named after the legendary cellarmaster who first blended Champagne.

dry red – a wine that is fermented to the point where there is no apparent sweetness. Most red wines would be considered dry reds.

fill level – the question of how full a bottle is. As a wine ages, some wine may evaporate through the cork. Ideally a wine will have a high fill level relative to its age.

green pruning – the removal, between spring and summer, of excessive vegetation from very lush vines.

Guyot – a pruning technique for grape vines. The system trains one or two fruiting arms along a main trellis wire.

Hennessy Jubilee Cognac – a rare cognac produced by the esteemed cognac house of Hennessy to coincide with reigns of monarchs.

ikhvis chakhokhbili – Georgian duck stew.

2000 Jasper Hill Nebbiolo – one of the first vintages of Nebbiolo for the Heathcote, Victoria, winery Jasper Hill.

kantsi – a Georgian wine horn.

Kardenakhi Port – fortified wine (like port) from the Georgian region of Kardenakhi.

khachapuri –Georgian cheese bread.

Khikhvi – a Georgian wine that can be produced in light dry, semi sweet, sweet, and, as we tasted at Savane Number One, fortified styles.

khinkali – dumplings.

Kvareli – a Georgian wine from the fertile Alazani river valley north-east of Tbilisi.

kvevri – large earthenware vessels used to make wine in the traditional Georgian method, and now fashionable with some modern winemakers.

lobio – kidney bean salad.

machari – new wine ready for fermentation in *kvevri*.

marani – where *kvevri* are stored.

Mas de Daumas Gassac – high-class pioneering winery in the Languedoc region of France.

Massandra Winery – the official Imperial Russian winery, still based in the Crimea.

museum wine – a term that I use with 'rare' to title our exceptional tastings and sales of 'rare and museum wines' which include wines that are old, rare and one might consider belong in a museum rather than a wine cellar.

Napareuli – a Georgian wine variety.

Palmer – a significant neighbour of the sublime Château Margaux and probably the second best wine of the Margaux appellation in Bordeaux. There is 40 per cent Merlot in the blend, which is unusual in Margaux.

1980 Penfolds Bin 80A – a special release of Penfolds, being a blend of approximately two-thirds Cabernet from Coonawarra and one-third Shiraz from Kalimna.

Penfolds Grange – the flagship wine of Australia's most prominent winery, Penfolds, and internationally, of the Australian wine industry.

phylloxera – a tiny yellow insect that feeds on the roots, and sometimes the leaves, of grapevines.

Picardan – a grape variety used in the Southern Rhône region of France.

premier cru – a term used in French wine classifications and referring to wines of superior quality.

Saamo – a Georgian sweet wine.

Salkhino – a Georgian sweet wine.

Sauternes – the district of Bordeaux that makes France's best sweet wines. Rich, luscious, exotic and hedonistic at their best.

Spotikach – a wine from the region of Spotikach in Russia.

tevzis buglama – Georgian salmon stew.

Tsinandali – a white Georgian wine fermented at cool temperatures that displays an aroma of quince, stone fruit and citrus.

Union des Grands Crus – a voluntary association of Bordeaux Châteaux (most of the very best) with the aim of developing promotional initiatives for their wines around the world. They conduct many brilliant and extensive tastings and dinners.

Vinotech/Vinoteque – climate-controlled cabinets and cellars designed to create the ideal storage conditions for wine.

vins blancs classés (white wines) – simply translated to 'white wine classes'. Sometimes used in Bordeaux, and elsewhere, for white wines of superior quality.

1990 Wendouree Shiraz – a tiny producer in the Clare Valley of South Australia. Highly sought-after wines of great ageing ability.

Wolfberger Altenberg de Bergheim – a Gewurztraminer wine from the Alsace region of France.

ACKNOWLEDGEMENTS

JOHN BAKER

I have many dear people to thank for this book's arrival. Having tried to write it myself, I realised how difficult it is to write a book when one is not a writer. Oh, I had written a lot of newsletters and articles, by having them just spin off my consciousness, but when I tried writing this story it faltered after not that many pages.

I was most fortunate to be recommended to a literary agency, Cameron Creswell, and on speculatively sending Jane Cameron an email of my adventure hoping she may be interested, it led to Jeanne Ryckmans taking me on as my agent. Jeanne introduced Nick Place to read my partial manuscript and massage it into the current book. I am indebted to Jeanne for her professional management of the process of publishing and for sympathetically working with me.

Nick has been marvellous, learning about the rarefied world of fine wine, our plunge into Tbilisi, Georgia, and in getting to know me. No mean feat! I thank Nick for making this story come to life, his understanding and his friendship.

Alison Urquhart at Penguin Random House Australia has been encouragingly supportive and enthusiastic about this book from the start, and Clive Hebard, our editor, has been enlightening and constructive in his careful editing. I love good wordsmiths like Nick and Clive.

Kevin Hopko, my accomplice in Georgia and friend of many years, has been very helpful in remembering details that I might have missed.

Finally, I wish to thank my good friend Peter Holder, who has been an invaluable confidant from the early days of 'how am I going to get this story written?' to the finished copies.

NICK PLACE
Stalin's Wine Cellar has been a remarkable project, giving me great joy, creativity, knowledge and some new friendships.

I'd like to sincerely thank Jeanne Ryckmans, my agent at The Cameron Creswell Agency, for being involved in the first place. Thank you, Jeanne, for your enthusiasm, belief and support, as well as for championing me as John's potential co-writer from the start. And thanks to everybody at Cameron's Management more broadly, including Jane, Sophie and Jo.

Big tigerish thanks also to Ali and Clive at Penguin Random House Australia for everything, as the project moved from a memorable, speculative coffee in Sydney to a finished manuscript. It's been brilliant, being welcomed into the family of the side-glancing Spheniscidae.

And of course, a heartfelt raise of the glass in the direction of John Baker, who fully embraced some Melbourne guy he'd never heard of being given charge of telling this wild, huge story that he'd lived. John's willingness to listen and accept my storytelling demands, to help make the yarn live and breathe, has been vital to the manuscript's success, and he has been not only endlessly gracious and accommodating, but has also become a mate along the way.

As for Kevin, Winnipeg's finest, well, you couldn't hope to invent a better character, let alone realise the actual person has done all the work for you by just existing. Thanks, Kevin and John, for allowing me to sketch the book versions of you. And for the breathtaking wine you've introduced me to along the way. Hopefully more of that to come!

Also, a shout-out to Victoria Heywood, who bobbed up with a perfect book, *Georgian Feast*, just when I needed it, giving me a sense of the food, culture and ambience of Tbilisi circa 1999. And to all the authors I've read and everybody I've spoken to along the way about Tbilisi, French wine, Stalin and the many crazy angles in this tale.

Away from the actual book, thank you to my wife, Chloé, for her support, love and so many days of selflessly giving me the time and headspace to write, especially with Colette la Punkette and Whirlwind Cassius rampaging through our lives at the same time. You know how I feel, Cloclo. Thanks, as ever, for the love and support of my big boys, Will and Mack, and the rest of my family and crew, in Australia and France, who have savoured this story from the very beginning. Big love also to my mum and sister, and I so wish my dad had been here to read this one. He would have adored it and asked a million questions. Unfortunately, he missed the first meeting I ever had with John by less than a week.

RIP, Papa Ronnie. This one's for you.

INDEX

Discover a
new favourite